From the Classroom

to the Boardroom:

Memoirs of a Student Leader

Michael D. Johnson

ISBN-13: 978-0-692-98783-4
Published by Michael D. Johnson
Distributed by IngramSpark

"Honest and direct, Johnson's story brings heart to the principles that guide good leaders to be great, and offers helpful tips to anyone seeking to discover the best in themselves."

-Gary Tuerack
Chief Visionary & Founder,
The National Society of Leadership & Success

"This 'coming of age tale' will touch the hearts of all who have made the challenging journey from adolescence to young adulthood. Michael Johnson writes with clarity, humor, and an honesty that invites us to revisit those wonderful years when we first began to understand and appreciate the person we were on our way to becoming. His many fine examples and chapter summaries help us to make his story our own."

-Seán Sammon, FMS, PhD
Scholar in Residence, Marist College, Poughkeepsie, NY

"Mike Johnson's *'Memoirs of a Student Leader'* provides a detailed and honest account of what can happen when we find our soul place, stretch our reach, and focus for the first time on the challenging act of coming into our own. It is the perfect description of the imperfect experience that characterizes the journey of young adults who are learning to lead in a college environment and beyond."

-Robin Diller Torres, MA, LMHC
Assistant Dean of Student Engagement & Leadership/
Adjunct Lecturer in Psychology & Communication, Marist College
Author and CEO, Crossroads Executive Coaching & Consulting

"

FRANCIS OF VERULAM
REASONED THUS WITH HIMSELF
and judged it to be for the interest of the present and future
generations that they should be made acquainted
with his thoughts
"

Added by the publisher beneath the title of NOVUM ORGANUM
at the request of its author,

SIR FRANCIS BACON

To my loving family and my home-away-from-home on the Hudson.

Go Red Foxes!

Photos courtesy of Giovanni Cosentino.

CONTENTS

FORWARD

Much has already been written on the subject of leadership, with myriad theories and "how to" remedies emerging in recent years. From corporate moguls to stars of the silver screen, everyone has a story to tell. When it comes to sharing stories of leadership at the collegiate level, however, there are very few pieces reflective of the current student leader perspective.

While tales of international political intrigue and professional stardom are captivating for their global impact and larger-than-life scale, the sagas of our modern times and the distant past draw their more lasting acclaim from the common fibers that resonate in every story, the echoes of human drama that permeate throughout the infinite narratives of a daily life. At least, that is what I told myself as I sat down to put this work to paper. The day-to-day decisions faced on a college campus may not hold high stakes for international stability, shed tantalizing details on celebrity gossip, drop earth-shattering behind-the-scenes revelations, or feature the epic clashes of heroic underdogs against the embodiment of all evils, but they are relatable. The challenges I faced and the scenarios I encountered are not entirely uncommon, and that is precisely the point.

As budding wallflower climbing through the social ladder of his new campus, I viewed my undergraduate journey through somewhat of a cinematic lens. It was an environment where you could feel like you were living out an episode of *Parks and Rec* in one moment and *House of Cards* the next. In tracing through the most impactful moments of my collegiate career, this work analyzes particular episodes from my past for the

i

fundamental gems of wisdom an experience that can be used more broadly to craft the principles of leadership into a roadmap for self-discovery. As I have looked back on my collegiate adventures, I took the time to record my memories of key events and the lessons they inspired in the hopes that they might contribute to the dialog on student leadership. In treating them like a saga of their own, I hope to convey the wonderful importance of taking ownership over your own personal narrative and its influence over those around you—the recognition that even the smallest of gestures or seemingly mundane experience can play a monumental part in forever shaping an individual life story.

Personified by the seemingly endless parade of perky admissions representatives and tour guides that could blindly traverse their campuses with the nimble grace of an overly caffeinated tight-rope walker, my introduction to the collegiate world would open the door to an entirely new chapter in my life. Though I would certainly hope to add to these stories as my career unfolds, the few that fill this space in time represent a significant part of the personal history that has shaped me into the person I am today. Extending from the college admissions process to the job search following graduation, I have decided to pen my memoirs as a student leader in the hopes that they will guide others in their own journeys of service and self-discovery.

For four years, understanding and serving the Marist community was my primary goal. I affectionately refer to the time I spent as a member of the Marist College Student Government Association ("S.G.A.") as a "mini-career", filled with a network of truly talented young individuals, the opportunities to create of some historic and deeply personal memories, and the imparting of my own mark on an already extraordinary campus. It equipped me with the knowledge and experience that I needed to find my way back, once thrown into the "real world", to the principles that I held most dear and carve out a new role in my hometown as a member of the Board of Education for the same district that molded me at the onset of this journey.

Today, I am fortunate enough to be able to share these stories with new generations of Red Foxes in an annual presentation for the College's Emerging Leaders Program. In these pages, I go beyond the core concepts shared in our hour-long presentation to further reflect on the highest and lowest moments of my career. These are the lessons that I have carried from the classroom to the boardroom.

Before we get started, I owe a tremendous deal of gratitude to a great many people who have played a part in shaping this narrative. Though there are far too many individuals to name in this brief passage, credit is owed to all of the students that I served alongside in the Student Government Association from 2009 to 2013. My personal thanks is also due to a number of club leaders, student delegates, campaign team members, faculty, administrators, and employees of the college—quite simply, my friends—who have supported me throughout each stage of this journey. They have forever impacted the course of this adventure.

Particular thanks is owed to Marist College's Director of First Year Programs and Founder of their Emerging Leader's Program, Robin Torres, who provided us with the opportunity to start the presentation that subsequently inspired me to finally organize these stories into a text—she even proposed the title that would eventually be shared with this book. I must also credit my co-presenter and S.G.A. peer, Daniel Torres, whose own experiences make up the sibling to this story.

     To Dr. David Gavin, my gratitude is owed for his detailed insights and sound advice in not taking the possibility of self-publication off the table too quickly. To Brother Seán Sammon, I extend my deepest thanks for his guidance and most enthusiastic support throughout the publication process. Likewise, my love and thanks goes to my family, particularly my Mother and Father for their years of support and, more recently, diligent reading of preliminary drafts.

     My surrogate family and closest friends, the residents of Lower Fulton 15D also deserve a special mention for the significant role they have come to play in the later chapters of this tale. Specifically, to Robby Kilian, Grace Camporeale, and Yeji Kim, I owe my deepest thanks for their many years of support and friendship.

     This work is also dedicated to my fellow students. To anyone who, like me, desired to seize upon an opportunity to start anew, I share these memories with you in mind. Whether life has steered you towards Marist, another institution of higher learning, or some other grand adventure, may they help you discover that trusted voice to faithfully guide you towards the future you deserve.

     Thank you for sharing this journey with me.

-Michael D. Johnson

1 - THE PROMISE

"In the middle of the journey of our life I found myself
within a dark woods where the straight way was lost."
- Dante Alighieri, Inferno

I was a persistent pessimist for most of my high school career. Often anxious, and rarely one to exude confidence, it was not in my nature to embrace risk or change. That is why I cannot fully explain what possessed me to apply to just *one* college. After completing the usual tour of prospective campuses, it did not take all that long for the idea of attending this one, particular school to nestle itself in my mind. In fact, the prospect quickly blossomed from a distinct possibility to a feeling of absolute certainty. Even so, in the time leading up to this realization, I had been uncharacteristically detached from the college selection process. My family toted me around from one campus to another in an effort to showcase the variety in communities and opportunities that each type of institution could afford, but nothing made a lasting impression. The looming reality of such a drastic lifestyle change left me petrified. I was unable to absorb the wave of places, faces, and informational traces that were rushing past me.

I felt as though I was lost at sea, directionless. I had an idea of where my life was headed but, more so than a degree or career, I simply longed for a place where I could fit in. Having spent most of my life up to that point in the same, quiet town that I grew up in, I did not know if I could get used to the idea of calling another place "home". That is, until my eventual choice set itself in my mind like a beacon. Something about this

1

campus stood out above the others, and I found myself wandering back to it in my thoughts. I could actually *picture myself* there.

Slowly, the storm clouds lifted as this fascination steadied my course like a vessel bound for the protective light of the coast. As I emerged from the haze, I placed my trust in some higher power to explain the source of these thoughts that compelled me to fill out the application for "early decision" admission and put down the pen, for good.

Indeed, in the years that followed, I could only describe that decision as a product of some form of divine intervention. Even now, just thinking about the prospect of consciously placing my future in the hands of a single application churns my stomach into a knotted mess. In the months immediately following my submission of that early decision application, however, I found myself caught up in an eerie sense of calm. It was not until a big, red envelope came in the mail that I was suddenly pulled back down into reality. The fog had cleared and the nature of my gambit momentarily overshadowed the reward hidden beneath this unintended risk. Even so, this sudden thrust of nausea quickly abated once the realization set in that I was going to be a college student. Just like that, I felt myself slipping back into the frenzy of the pre-college process, sprinting towards the finish line as an "accepted student".

◆

As I continued to count down the days to high school graduation, and the promise of warm summer sun began peeking just around the corner, my family and I headed back to my future campus to attend "Accepted

Students' Day". While our families were treated to presentations on financial aid and other, logistical matters, the other soon-to-be students and I found ourselves separated into yet another tour group. Rather than pace through the usual selling points, my second stroll across the grounds focused more on the day-to-day lives of the figures moving in the background. This time around, our guide talked less about the academic standing of the institution, or the history of the surrounding region, and instead began to shed light on what I was most deeply curious about, the spirit of the campus community itself.

I watched as a trio of upperclassmen brushed past our group. They weren't lugging the bulky backpacks that flooded our high school hallways. In fact, only one of them had so much as a single book slung beneath their arm. I watched, transfixed, as they floated down the walkway and plopped themselves at last on an open patch of grass. Sprawling out in the sunlight, they settled back in conversation, paying no further heed to our envious gazes. It was in that moment, as my eyes caught the light reflecting off the Hudson River, sitting just at the foot of the hill below us, that I began to picture myself among them. Slowly, steadily, I began to feel what had been missing—a sense of belonging.

After the typical procession of welcomes and the other, general presentations that followed the tour, we were led down to the site of the afternoon's main event. A long brick building nestled into the sloping hills beside the freshman quad, the McCann arena also served as one of the main guest parking areas on the campus. On a regular day, its interior buzzed with the same energy and excitement as the flurry of pedestrian and automobile traffic that paced through its lot. As we cleared the doorway, its

3

main hall thundered with the sound of the College's symphonic band, an electrified air guiding us deeper into its main foyer and the courts beyond. Once inside, I saw that our families had already been seated at tables sprawled out along one end of the open basketball court. As each tour group was lined up into the bleachers, a member of the Campus Ministry stepped forward to lead the room in a great, big cheer before passing the microphone off to various representatives from the College's administration. Chief among these dignitaries was their President.

Though he was only the third to hold this title in the College's history, he was the longest-serving leader with more than three decades spent at its helm. It was not sheer strength or stature that made the College President such a commanding figure, but a genteel warmth in the way he carried himself. As his bright teal eyes scanned the congregation of perspective "Red Foxes" and their families, he flashed a warm smile that reflected a sort of genuine excitement. Indeed, as his welcome message boomed over the arena's speakers, it was accompanied by an unexpected softness. His manner reflected a true love for the College and the people at its heart. His words carried a paternalistic pride from which similar attachments would blossom throughout the community, sprouting their roots from a common trust in his vision for their shared future.

More captivating to me than the College President's speech, however, was the appearance of a young man by his side. Seeming far too young to be a member of the administrative team, I was fixated on him almost immediately. Moments later, he would step up to the mic and introduce himself as the president of the student body.

4

That was the instant I decided I would join the Student Government Association. As I watched him effortlessly command the attention of a full auditorium, I felt a sudden tinge of envy creep through me. My ears perked up once again as the regal figure before the mic promised that "someone in this room" would, one day, take up his mantle as the chief representative of the student body. This, it seemed, was the only que my timid conscious needed to launch a bitter assault against my budding ambitions.

My heart sank. Throughout high school, I had never succeeded in running a successful campaign for student government. With each race, I found myself slipping into the background amid a sea of ambitious voices. My greatest weakness, time and time again, was my fear of public speaking. To make matters worse, my approach to public presentations was completely unpolished. With each attempted speech, I found that I could not help myself from stumbling back over my errors to stammer through each line haplessly. As a result, I lacked the confidence to assert myself as a candidate, and could not find a way to convince others that I was a worthy leader. Truthfully, I could hardly convince myself of the same. And yet, these past failures seemed to fade away in watching the inspiring figure before me, someone who could walk shoulder to shoulder with giants like the College President.

By the time the day's presentations had reached their end, my mind was swelling with lofty ambitions once again. Glancing back at the student body president as he was encircled by a fold of administrators and S.G.A. volunteers, I floated through the intertwining crowds in search of my parents. When I found them, they were not alone; they seemed to be enjoying a conversation with another, vaguely familiar couple. As I approached, my father made the quick re-introduction. The pair was also from our hometown but their son, another newly accepted student, was not among them. "He's over there," the mother reported proudly, gesturing to the center of the great mob.

As I peered through the haze of bodies, I noticed another, smaller crowd gathering at the center of the court. A group of students had surrounded a lone figure, the College President, who appeared to be nodding along politely as one of the congregants spoke. "You should go, too." the mother interjected, "Introduce yourself, and make sure he knows who you are!"

I felt the knot in my stomach tighten. "Know who *I* am? Why on Earth would he want to know *me*?" My mind produced this bile almost reflexively, the echoing words bleeding into an unpleasant chill at the pit of my stomach. "How could *I*," this inner voice coldly hissed, "ever stand shoulder to shoulder with people like *them*?"

Shaking my head silently, I quickly managed to mutter something about not feeling all that well before saying our good-byes. "How could I ever expect the College President to respect me," I wondered as we put the jubilant crowd behind us, "how could any of them respect me, if I didn't learn to respect myself?" Settling into the car for the ride home, I established the first goal of my undergraduate career. I promised myself that, by the time I graduated, the College President would want to shake *my* hand.

◆

I was not "Mr. Popular" in high school. I was a proud nerd, and I fit the stereotype rather well. I was a quiet, bespectacled, stocky little introvert who shied away from leadership positions—except for a two-year run as the president of a struggling chess club. I hated public speaking with a passion, and my fear of judgement scared me away from pursuing a number of opportunities throughout my high school career. By way of example, I had been an active member of the Kiwanis family of service organizations since I joined the Builders' Club in middle school. In fact, I rose to the rank of president in the 6th grade and held the position right up to my transition to high school. The move to a new environment, coupled with a faltering self-image, caused me to shy away from actively pursuing a new role in the Key Club, the next iteration of Kiwanis-youth involvement. It took me a couple of years to recognize just how debilitating these fears had become, as it was not until my senior year of high school that I finally felt compelled to do something to change my situation.

Indeed, this anxiety now threatened to steal away all that I had hoped to achieve at college. In breaking down the barriers that stood before me, I figured that my fear of public speaking formed the largest hurdle in my path to success. Struggling with a rather weak self-image, I constantly felt self-conscious in front of others. I dreamed of having the kind of confidence effortlessly exhibited by the student body president at Marist; the thought of being a part of that, particular team became so alluring precisely because it represented the very sense of belonging and respectability that I hoped to achieve in my own life. Joining the student government, of course, would involve a great deal of presentations and campaigning. The role I sought could not simply be earned; it had to be won. I knew then that, if I were to have any real shot at making a change in my life for the better, I would have to begin by overcoming this pervasive fear.

In seeking drastic results, I pursued a drastic course of action. For my senior schedule, I signed up for as many courses and programs that I could find with an oral presentation requirement. I even went so far as to finally push myself into joining the mock trial program at my school, as I figured I might as well put my resolve to one day enter the legal field to the test while I was at it.

It was in this setting that I first grappled with the depths of my phobia. Finding a way to shut out the negative voices rattling around in the back of my head in front of large groups was one issue, but facing down the focused stare of one-on-one exchanges proved to be a whole other beast. I suddenly found that I could not even bring myself to recite prepared statements in front of just one other person without breaking down. When it came time to rehearse our opening statements with my case partner or run through a practice round of witness examinations, I caught myself reverting to the same old defensive measures of retreating to my notes or cracking jokes. Our advisor at the time noticed my distress almost immediately. He pulled me out into the hallway one afternoon when I began circling back to my usual tricks. There, he told me to run through my opening remarks as best as I could.

After fumbling through the first few sentences without removing my eyes from the piece of paper clutched tightly in my hands, he let out a

8

sigh and motioned for me to stop. "I need you to imagine," he began. "Yea, yea... that the whole audience is in their underwear," I interrupted. "I've tried that one. No success." "Not quite," he continued, patiently, "I need you to picture the most dynamic speaker you can think of. Picture a President or a performer. Think Tony Stark."

To forget that I was even there, to let myself focus solely on the message that I wanted to convey and leave my concerns lingering somewhere in the distance, *that* was the greatest lesson he shared with me. Because in doing so, I finally cleared the air within my own mind long enough to focus on what I *did* do well. And in building upon these traits, I found a way out; I could focus my efforts to seize upon these skills as building blocks toward the success I hoped to foster. As a coach and mentor, this teacher helped me to recognize how the perceptions I created could influence my audience's reality, and ultimately my own. By stammering through statements and trying to cover up my missteps with humor, I had drawn their attention to the very faults that I hoped to bury. Embracing my wit and humor, using the theatrical to supplement my material, I could create a new image for my case, my client, and myself.

I took his words to heart, and began pushing the boundaries of my comfort zone with each new opportunity that presented itself. I would volunteer to read aloud in class more often, put a little more thought into my oral presentations in Spanish class, inadvertently becoming a more engaged member of our school community as a result of these efforts.

Even as I found myself getting used to simply moving through the paces, there were times when the process of speaking publicly still felt as excruciating as I remembered it to be from the offset. Nonetheless, I stepped out on the night of our mock trial with a profound sense of excitement.

◆

Dressed for the occasion in my suit and tie, I paced the floor of our high school rotunda in an attempt to channel my inner Atticus Finch. The foundation of my imaginary world was further fortified as we split into our respective carpools and made our way over to the venue for our competition, the chambers of our county courthouse. There, I staked out my little stage for our evening before the bench.

As the conversation among audience members lulled itself into a dull whisper, the students representing the prosecution in our case took to the floor to make their opening remarks. Bits and pieces of their presentation caught my ear here and there but I remained largely focused on my script, running through it repeatedly in the quietest corner of my mind. When the judges thanked our opponents for their piece and signaled for me to take their place, my response was precise and automatic.

As if acting on instinct, I rose to my feet and gave my first note-free speech without a moment of pause or hesitation. Speaking to the members of the jury as though we had been removed to a universe of our very own, I felt oddly at home weaving through the textures and tones of my monologue like a painter taking a fresh, new brush to an untouched canvas. In this moment, I broke beyond the barriers of fear and self-doubt to develop an appreciation for the art of public presentation. After delivering my remarks, I turned back to our table and placed a hand on our defendant's

10

shoulder. Though our case had only just begun, I felt as though my own battle had already been won.

Unfortunately, the fate of our mock client did not resolve as neatly. Our duo lost the case and was eliminated in the first round of the competition. Despite my partner's disappointment in losing the opportunity to advance, I could not help but beam with pride as we made our way out to the parking lot. I was even stopped along the way by a number of attendees who took a moment to compliment me on my opening remarks. For the first time in my life, someone told me that I had a knack for public speaking and, in another first, I was starting to believe that I did as well. Though Mock Trial represented a mere blink in the grand snapshot of my high school career, I count the experience as one of the most transformative moments of my life so far. This evening would even serve as the inspiration for my college admissions essay and, not long after, the foundation for my most ambitious personal transformation.

♦

My parents would look back and describe my college move-in day as a scene from a "land cruise". It was, after all, a seamless shuffle of human beings and their belongings across the scenic campus that was seemingly executed without flaw and, by all appearances, had become something of a true art form at the college. Only in the coming years would I learn of the minimal drama that surrounded the day, as any instances of roommate clashes and family quarrels were handled quickly and discretely, with all the precision and professionalism of a military strike team. As I waited among the other new additions to the community, we were guided skillfully through the grounds, cut from our parents with an almost surgical precision, and thrust into a variety of welcome activities that distracted us from the fact that the very foundation of our little worlds was shifting right beneath our feet.

Coming from a close-knit family, attending a live-away college apart from my home in New Jersey was a big move for me. I did not necessarily fear being on my own—I had traveled on my own and attended out of state conferences by myself. No problem—but I struggled with the concept of becoming a guest in my own house, a place that I had called "sanctuary" for most of my introverted life. It was a harrowing reality that had dogged me throughout the admissions process like a lingering shadow. Standing there now, with all of the budding courage that had welled after facing one of my biggest fears right at the outset of this new chapter, my worries abated.

As I saw it, I faced two options in that moment: I could either dwell upon the fact that everything was changing and resign myself to the notion that these events were beyond my control; or, I could once again focus on the positive thoughts that I had stocked under my belt and embrace the opportunity that had presented itself, perhaps even buying-in to the belief that I was there for a reason. Realizing that change would find me one way or another, and not wanting to miss out on the "Welcome Week" festivities, I opted for the latter. College would be my clean slate. Far from home and the same group of friends that I had followed from elementary through high school, I found the catalyst for the creation of a new me.

Lessons Learned

Action separates leaders from their followers. Often, it does not take strategic brilliance or unmatched ingenuity to rise up above the pack, but simply the courage to stand up and say, "Now is the time to set aside discussions and put our work into motion." More importantly, successful leaders recognize that the opportunities afforded by these calls to action do not appear alone; no great strides are made without stomaching some degree of risk. With any issue, you will likely find that there are a number of arguments that can be made both in favor of and against a particular course of action. As any student of philosophy will tell you, there is no one right way to approach such questions with absolute certainty. As human judgments are biased and imperfect, and our perceptions tend to capture merely a fraction of the "big picture", deliberations can run on endlessly without compromise and the drawing of a firm line. When persistent debate turns into a quagmire, leaders rise before their peers to guide the group in one direction or another.

It may be easy to forget that the need for such direction is not limited solely to the boardroom. Sometimes, we need to take command over our own well-being. Indeed, one of my greatest weaknesses throughout high school was persistent hesitation. Never willing to take a stand in one direction or the other, I allowed myself to instead be pushed about aimlessly by others. As I could not quite get the hang of saying "no", there were times when my kindness condemned me to taking on a heavier load than I was truly suited to bear.

As a result, I nearly resigned myself to continuing life as a wallflower. There was no one left in my corner to shake me out of my stupor and point to the opportunities just sitting at my feet. In the moment of clarity that struck me during that car ride back from Accepted Student's Day, I not only learned to prioritize my own goals above the perceived risks imposed by my fears, but to also take responsibility as the leader of my own destiny. It took me a long time to summon up the courage to silence the fierce assault that my own mind had waged against itself and thereby put my foot down before my harshest critic. Doing so, however, paved the way for the moments and memories that fill the subsequent pages of this text.

While many of us may look back and shudder at the thought of the hurdles and horrors that we have encountered throughout our journeys, we must never lose sight of one, critical fact: we have faced them and we have overcome them. These obstacles do not diminish or prolong our experiences; they enrich them. Just as no pleasure can be found in life without suffering a bit of pain, there is no triumph to be gained from a venture free of risk—even that of a total loss, for that matter. In selecting the quote to open this chapter and set us out on this journey, I felt that Dante's immortal introduction should also be accompanied by another classical view:

"The mind is its own place, and in itself
Can make a Heav'n of Hell, a Hell of Heav'n."
– John Milton, *Paradise Lost*

In life, there will always be challenges; there is always an opposing view. More often than not, however, the most vociferous objector is seated right in the back of our own mind. From this vantage point, it can twist and turn every lowly fear and doubt against us, raising minor issues into towering roadblocks. In their shadow, we lose sight of all that we still hold in our favor—the skills and opportunities that enable us to not only push forward, but to overcome such obstacles entirely.

The path to surmounting these fears is narrow and incremental. Little victories must be borne in time. Indeed, one of the most difficult milestones to cross is in mustering the courage to take that first step towards seizing your aim. Trust in your better judgment to know when the reward is worth pursuing, but do not let your fears remove the possibility altogether. Do not let hesitation lure you into limbo. Draw the line firmly between action and inaction, and stand by your decision.

Failing to act is not merely a bad habit borne in one's professional life; sometimes we have to take a deep breath and put our foot down when it comes to determining the *wants* and *needs* in our personal lives as well. Whether it is knowing when to stand up for something you want, or to pull back from taking on too much, aspiring leaders need to keep their own needs and limitations on their radars as well.

Self-reflection and personal awareness are, therefore, vital components to assembling a successful "Leadership Profile". Great leaders maintain a trained eye on their strengths, but also those areas in which they are in need of improvement. The greatest among them, however, will seek to actively overcome these weaknesses, rather than sweep them under the rug or overcompensate in other areas. Use your strengths as stepping stones to reach a vantage point whereby these obstacles appear more manageable, then face them head on to lock them in to your developing skill set.

15

Throughout this book, you will see that *balance* is a central theme in my approach to leadership. Whereas the leader who crafts their abilities to fit a given niche will find opportunity in times of need, based on the ebb and flow of their constituents' demands, those who maintain a broader array of skills will have the ability to create opportunities at any time. They are the ones nimble enough to set their own mark before themselves and leave it etched in time for generations to follow thereafter.

THE LEADERSHIP PROFILE: *Exercise One*

Throughout this book, we will take periodic breaks to not only reflect on the gems of wisdom buried in each of these personal stories, but also shape them into a framework for your own personal growth. This, dear reader, is the beginning of your "Leadership Profile."

To start, retrieve a fresh sheet of paper and keep it close at hand as you continue along this journey with me (I prefer to fold mine up like a book mark, so it is never too far out of sight). For this initial exercise, jot down three areas in which you believe you excel, and then list three areas in which you believe you could use some improvement—the three biggest hurdles that currently stand in your way. Even these perceived roadblocks will serve as the fundamental building blocks in your profile moving forward. As you seek to carve out your own niche on your campus, in your office, or simply in your own home, make sure that all six areas receive your attention and care. As the old saying goes, *"Jack of all trades, master of none, though oftimes better than master of one."*

2 – THE OPPORTUNITY

"Time is a violent torrent; no sooner is a thing brought
to sight than it is swept by and another takes its place,
and this too will be swept away."
– Marcus Aurelius

As hard as I tried to cast an aura of perpetual optimism throughout the transition, I would occasionally relapse into my old, pessimistic ways. In late August of 2009, after the move-in day dust had settled, I began to feel as though I was truly alone in charting out the next stage of my life. It is, after all, a natural part of the on-campus experience to grapple with one's separation from home. No matter how far (or near) your new residence may be, or how eagerly you have awaited the move, it is a monumental transition that we all must process in our own time. Having come from a relatively small town in Northern New Jersey, and growing up the product of a close family unit, this change hit me particularly hard.

Rather than stumble, I found a way to turn my fears into motivation. After all, I had a strong foundation for my transformation laid out in a very specific goal, the promise that I had made to myself on Accepted Students' Day. Entering my first year as a freshman student, I knew what I ultimately wanted to accomplish by the time my undergraduate career had ended—to become a leader worthy of even the College President's recognition.

Joining the Student Government Association seemed to be the best route toward attaining this goal. After all, community service was not merely a familiar concept, it was an area of personal interest that I had

18

exceled in during my middle school days with the Builder's Club and Kiwanis. In seeking to carve out a niche of my own in this new community, returning to something that I felt comfortable with seemed like a natural starting point.

♦

Before delving any deeper into the world of student politics, however, I believe that a quick overview of the organization could prove helpful. The Marist College Student Government Association ("S.G.A.") was established according to the example set by our national government: three branches equally sharing the responsibilities of the campus' governance, as outlined by our own Constitution and By-Laws. The most prominent of these three was our Executive Branch, comprised of the cabinet-level administrators that reported to the student body president (or "S.B.P."). The S.B.P. was, essentially, the CEO of the S.G.A.—a member of the student body elected by the entire campus population to serve a one-year term. The S.B.P. was assisted by an executive vice president (or "E.V.P."), who was tasked with managing the menagerie of vice presidents and directors appointed to oversee individual departments and boards that addressed ongoing campus issues, which ranged from club and academic affairs to coalitions on athletics and community outreach. These individuals were interviewed and selected by the incoming S.B.P. prior to the official transition between administrations that took place each year, and confirmed by the members of the outgoing Senate.

This second body, our Legislative Branch, consisted of five resident senators elected from amongst the members of the on-campus population, two senators chosen to represent the commuter population, and each of the four class presidents. These eleven individuals would vote amongst themselves to elect a Senate Speaker and Senate Speaker *Pro Tempore* to serve as their leaders. Whereas the S.B.P. and E.V.P. would manage the day-to-day administration of various campus organizations, as well as maintain relations with the faculty and other administrative offices that regularly liaised with the S.G.A., the Senate was meant to adopt a more long-term focus.

Its members would develop new policy measures, in the forms of bills and resolutions, to guide and codify administrative action. While the student body president had the power to form temporary ad-hoc committees, the Senate could vote to establish and renew more structured standing committees on a year-to-year basis. The Legislative Branch and its various committees were typically tasked with exploring emerging policy issues and concerns brought to the S.G.A. by its constituents. Over time, however, the committee system had largely grown into a network of planning boards for educational programs and related activities—as some had dubbed them, "party planners". As the role of a senator was rather vague, this blurring of responsibilities would lead to a number of discussions throughout the ensuing years as to the precise scope and intent of legislative authority under the S.G.A.'s governing documents.

The final branch of government, our Judicial Board, was also the most elusive during my tenure; its members typically played more of a "behind the scenes" role in the organization. As a result, it was the lesser known of the three branches within the S.G.A. The Judicial Board was comprised of five members: three resident justices, one commuter justice, and the Chief Justice. With authority akin to our highest court's power of constitutional review, the Judicial Board had the final say in any disputes related to parking tickets, club affairs, and all questions relating to the governing documents of the S.G.A. Another trait this board shared with the Supreme Court of the United States was the fact that these positions were considered "life terms" in the sense that they were held throughout the appointee's undergraduate career, following their confirmation by the Senate. Unlike their peers in the S.G.A.'s Legislative Branch, our student justices did not have the ability to elect their leader. Instead, the position of Chief Justice was yet another student body presidential appointment.

To further complicate things, Judicial Board members were discouraged from attending regular S.G.A. meetings for the sake of preserving their impartiality. After all, theirs was the body tasked with deciding all cases arising against, or from within, the S.G.A. As a result, a bit of a cultural divide had emerged between the Judicial Board and its siblings, which, unfortunately, led to their exclusion from the broader social circle of the S.G.A. During my time with the organization, some administrations would attempt to bring this branch back into the cultural fold of the S.G.A. by finding ways to include its members in a greater spirit of comradery, without compromising their impartiality.

After all, in looking back at the organization as a whole, each of these branches was intended to operate with some degree of autonomy. Over time, however, power ceded itself more and more to the Executive Branch. For the sake of shortening their weekly meetings and improving communication between their two branches, the Executive Board and the Senate would often hold their regular meetings in a joint session chaired by the S.B.P. Additionally, the long-term exclusion of the Judicial Board from social events had not only led to a rift in morale but its perpetual understaffing, as the needs of this branch slipped lower and lower on the list of immediate priorities. By the time I had arrived, each of these three bodies had formed their own reputations. The Executive Branch was the most popular, the Legislative Branch was the most underutilized, and the Judicial Branch was the most overlooked.

◆

The more I learned about the organization, the more I wanted to be a part of it. My confidence had hit an upswing following Accepted Student's day and held strong throughout the summer, with my ambitions following steadily in its wake. There were plenty of opportunities for growth and advancement in my new community, and I saw myself as an ideal candidate to get in and make some seriously needed changes.

Fortunately, the election cycle for freshman class officers was set to follow shortly after Welcome Week. While the upperclassmen held their annual elections in the spring semester, representatives for the incoming freshman class were held before the first full month of school came to a close. This would be my introduction to the campus' election process, as well as a chance to put my hard work in overcoming my fears of public presentations to the test.

Despite my lofty ambitions in the long-term, however, I set my immediate sights on the "Number 2" position as a candidate for vice president of the Class of 2013. Despite having some pretty grand ideas, I did not have much of a record to run on without prior S.G.A. experience of my own. So, I thought I would bide my time on a lower rung as I waited to ascend the ladder in the years that followed.

As it turned out, the overall race had attracted a number of like-minded individuals. While the competition for freshman class president consisted of approximately nine participants, our vice presidential race ended with somewhere around six or seven competitors. The remaining offices of Secretary, Treasurer, and Historian either saw a race between two contestants or otherwise went unopposed. Rather than be deterred by the swelling turnout, I elected to view our expanding contest as an opportunity to develop a larger presence on campus and, if I was fortunate enough to succeed, settle into a vantage point that would allow me to observe the inner-workings of the S.G.A. without committing myself to too much too soon.

I set to work preparing my first collegiate campaign with vigor. Blinded by my excitement, however, I did not notice another, potential hurdle rising in the foreground. My efforts to get involved in the greater community had superseded my efforts to make friends, leaving me to face this first challenge largely on my own. I was fortunate enough, nevertheless, to find some support between my two roommates. Although we did not exactly see eye to eye on many things in those days, we did share a common interest in student government. One of my roommates had even thrown his hat into the ring of aspiring candidates for the position of class president. Even if we were not singing "*Kumbaya*" each night before bed, at the very least we were able to confide in and vent to one another throughout the race.

As our speech night approached, I tried to put myself back into my old mock trial mentality. My plan was to hit the stage with a bold opening and power through my speech without any notes. Having just arrived on campus, I did not have any concrete positions to run on, so I sought to build a platform on my sincere devotion and work ethic. If nothing else, I hoped to simply leave a positive impression.

"I have a dream for 2013!"

I bellowed this slogan three times, pacing the stage enthusiastically before settling in behind the podium. When the night of my first campus performance had finally arrived, my plan kicked off just as I had envisioned. Hitting the ground with gusto had certainly captured their attention, but now it was time to switch gears and settle into the second phase of my speech.

Looking out over the crowd, I laid what few cards I had to play on the table. Believing that my future with the S.G.A. —along with any chance of fulfilling that initial goal that I had set for myself—was hanging in the balance, I left it all on that stage. I pleaded my case before a new jury of my peers, expressing my desire to listen to and serve them, admitting to my lack of formal experience, and outlining my vision for transparency and advocacy as one of their class officers. As I stepped down to a flutter of applause, my nerves melted away and were instead replaced by an odd feeling of satisfaction. I was confident that I had done my best to deliver my message and felt that I had succeeded in imparting my desired impression with commitment and confidence.

◆

Sadly, fate—or, at the very least, the electorate—had other plans. Shortly after the polls had closed, the current administration sent a notice to all candidates instructing us to report to the alcoves across from the S.G.A. office by 5:00pm that evening. As we eagerly awaited to see who would move on, and who would be resigned to go back to the drawing board in mapping out their campus careers, competitors chatted idly in the hall. All fell silent when the office's doors opened to reveal the current S.B.P. and E.V.P. After taking a moment to congratulate the participants on races well run, they acknowledged that only a select few would succeed in attaining the positions they so heartily desired. As for the rest, they expressed their hopes that they would find other ways to stay involved.

I knew before the list was posted that my name would not be among the elected. A familiar voice crept up in the back of my head to tell me so. Needing to see it for myself, though, I made my way through the huddle to view the results. As I passed the faces of my peers, some racing off with delight while others seemed to float aimlessly with a vacant and devastated stare, I recognized that I was not the only one who had staked the hopes of their undergraduate ambitions on this single gambit. Sure enough, I quickly confirmed that my name was not among those fortunate few who would serve the Class of 2013. But rather than dwell on my defeat, my attention suddenly turned to a second list hanging beside the election results.

It was an announcement for open positions within the "Junior Senate", encouraging students to seek an application within the office. I did not recall hearing about this board during the pre-election buzz, nor did I fully appreciate the opportunity it presented. In that moment, it was merely a shot at keeping my dream alive. Wasting no time at all, I dipped into the office to grab an application form.

◆

As a relatively new undertaking initiated by the current administration, the Junior Senate was the student government equivalent to an internship program. The student body president at that time realized that the best way to address dwindling levels of student involvement around campus was to expand the number of opportunities available to play a more visible part in our community, starting with the student government. He also recognized that freshman elections afforded a rather limited number of opportunities to a historically large pool of eager candidates. Rather than dismiss these potential public servants, or let their energy fade to apathy, his administration sought to create a program that would allow newcomers to shadow current officials and develop the experience they would need in seeking higher offices down the road.

As an ad-hoc program created under the Executive Branch, membership in the Junior Senate was not determined by the electorate, but through a direct appointment by the student body president himself. That is how I found myself sitting across from the young man who inspired me to join the S.G.A. in the first place. Handing over my résumé and application form, I battled a combination of nerves and admiration to maintain the calmest look of composure that I could muster. We talked about the S.G.A., my understanding of its mission and responsibilities, and the ideas that I had for the campus. Motioning to the corporate logo on my shirt, a souvenir from an old part-time job in high school, I expressed my desire to bring a customer-service oriented form of management to student governance. I also candidly expressed my hopes to build upon my current weaknesses to become a stronger leader, and to use the Junior Senate as platform toward becoming a more active member of the S.G.A.

I like to think that I made my first notch in carving out a campus legacy that day—I later learned that I had certainly left an impression on the student body president with my "Dream for 2013" speech. And yet, as the embodiment of the very aspirations that I hoped to attain, and in light of my recent defeat before the student body, I found myself wanting his approval more than anyone else's at that time. That is why I will always be grateful to him for giving me my first position in the S.G.A.

The student body president of the 2009-2010 Administration carried with him not only a tremendous air of dignity but the deep respect of his peers. He was a leader who cultivated his authority from connection to others, and would always make anyone who entered the office feel welcome and invited. More importantly, he served as a confidant and cheerleader for other student government officials, helping his administration to navigate the typical drama associated with student politics. I count myself very fortunate to have been able to look to him as a mentor and a friend. More than just an opportunity, he had given me back the hope of attaining my goal. At long last, it was time to get to work.

Lessons Learned

I learned early on in my career that one loss (let alone two or three) does not spell absolute defeat. *"Where there is a will, there is a way"* quickly became one of my favorite mantras. With a concrete goal set in your mind, there are usually a number of routes to take you from Point A to Point B. When the door closes on your preferred route, however, it may simply require a little more time and energy to chart an alternate course. It is rarely the end of the road altogether.

Admittedly, starting anew typically looks a lot cleaner on paper than it does in practice. Reaching a dead end can be jarring enough, and these moments do not often present themselves with additional luxuries like time and perspective. There will be occasions in which you are called upon to make quick calls, or perhaps will be tasked with casting a vote in an ultimatum that seems to include no favorable outcomes. To make matters all the more daunting, there really is no one, *right* way in which to prepare for these moments.

Instead, the old Boy Scout adage "always be prepared" carries the most beneficial nugget of wisdom for aspiring leaders. Just as it was foolish of me to believe that all of my aspirations relied on the outcome of single election, successful leaders recognize that they must never invest all of their hopes in a single strategy or course of action. Whereas all good leaders are responsive, great leaders must learn to make a capacity for *adaption* part of their very nature. It is o.k. to have faith in your Plan A (a little enthusiasm from the head of an organization can even have a tremendous impact on the overall morale of your team). But as the one responsible for picking up the pieces if and when the wheels fall off, you should also develop the foresight to recognize what other, lingering options still remain in play.

Fostering a strong sense of awareness for developments and emerging trends within your respective field or industry will assist you in recognizing what alternatives remain viable should a sudden change in course become necessary. From a student perspective, these practices ranged from keeping an up-to-date catalog of vendors (in case your go-to provider suddenly went out of business or was otherwise unavailable) to developing relationships with influential campus actors (generating quick access points to the fastest and most reliable sources of information for all of the latest activities and rumors swirling through the community).

To further complicate matters, sometimes the best course of action is not directly associated with your primary objective. By way of example, I later found myself sitting idly after my college graduation in a part-time job while looking to work my way into a full-time career. Rather than dwell on the pitfalls that I encountered along the way, I devoted my spare time to a hobby that provided me with a sense of fulfillment, community service. It was through these familiar activities that I discovered an avenue to opening new and previously unforeseen possibilities.

After joining the local Kiwanis Club, I was soon introduced to new individuals and opportunities that helped me to take on even more projects within my community. These connections would largely shape my future activities more than any other undertaking throughout my application process for a full-time position. Sometimes, it is worth taking our attention off a stalling Plan A to cultivate other opportunities. When we come to feel so lost in our own lives, following these secondary goals can potentially lead us right back to where we need to be.

More importantly, they will often open the door to new and unexpected possibilities. Those experiences which I now hold among my most memorable were very rarely the desired outcome of a primary pursuit. Instead, they resulted from the offshoots of various associations and friendly recommendations. Indeed, very little good came from my time as a wallflower. Despite its comforts, I did not start to make monumental leaps in my personal trajectory until I forced myself deeper into the unfamiliar territories awaiting beyond my usual routines. Leaders that maintain active connections to professional and civic associations, or remain dedicated to a personal hobby, expand the reach of their networks far beyond their peers who limit themselves to the familiar waters of their industry. In being careful not to dive too deeply into these opportunity pools, aspiring leaders should be prepared to wade out beyond the standard and familiar by regularly practicing old skills and interests, as well as developing new ones.

Additionally, the attitudes adopted by our leaders can have a tremendous impact on the spirit of the organization. I came to admire the student body president of the 2009-2010 Administration as a personal role model because of the professional and respectful manner in which he held his office. He would never let someone walk into the S.G.A. office without taking the time to personally greet them and, in his role as our C.E.O., he looked out for members of each of the three branches to ensure that no one felt disenfranchised or discouraged. He taught me early on that the energies cast off by the person sitting at the head of the organization have considerable influence over its operations at all levels. Having suffered my fair share of poor managers in the retail world, I found myself fighting even harder to be worthy of the praises that he extended to us. Sincere and unwavering encouragement fostered the successes of the 2009-2010 Administration, and would serve as the basis for the leadership style that I sought to employ as my work within the S.G.A. continued.

THE LEADERSHIP PROFILE: *Exercise Two*

The next step toward building our leadership profile is a theoretical exercise in turning the lemons of life into a fresh batch of leadership lemonade. Indeed, such tenacity appears to be a common ingredient in most guides to leadership. Yet, while some might advise you to plant your feet firmly in the face of rejection and make an even stronger case for your plans, time and experience have helped me to craft a subtler approach. Rejection, as I have come to know it, is rarely a dead-end; it is more of a re-direction.

"No" in business and in politics is often accompanied by some sort of logic, a differing perspective. It is rarely personal; it is just good business. While most people tend to shut down rather defensively in the face of rejection, overlooking these important little gems, it is my hope that you will train yourselves to pick up on them and act accordingly.

The best way to start is by playing "Devil's Advocate". Think of a project or idea that you have been pondering (and perhaps even wanting to share) at school, at work, or even at home. What is stopping you?

Putting yourself in the shoes of the harshest critic you know, what potential objections could they raise to your idea? Is it difficult to carry out? If so, jot down a few notes as to how you would recommend going about it. Is it costly? Include a point or two on how you might re-direct funds or cultivate new sources of revenue altogether. Start by identifying one or two, good reasons someone might object to your idea and take the time to think about how you could work towards addressing these items. Take a moment to turn the sour into something sweet and scrawl out your notes somewhere along the page.

Even if you do not come up with the perfect solution, you will start to develop a better sense of the opposing point of view. This will not only expand your own perspective (making it easier to identify flaws in the initial concept and devise solutions) but also help to humanize the folks sitting at the table across from you. After all, things tend to be a lot less frightening once we have a better understanding of what is lurking in the shadows. With a stronger familiarity of the opposing viewpoint, you might be surprised to find just how much easier it is to engage in that traditionally uncomfortable debate that comes with defending an idea against rejection.

Sometimes "No" *will* mark the end of the line for your idea or project—there is simply no need to go on haranguing someone who has made it clear that they want no part in what you are planning. In most cases, however, there are underlying political, fiscal, and logistical reasons that weigh upon your audience's response. Rather than give up, you may often find opportunities to tailor your approach in order to address these needs. This ability to adapt and grow helps leaders to see the hidden opportunities in difficult situations that others shy away from almost instinctively.

3 – THE VISION

"So many worlds, so much to do,
So little done, such things to be…"
-A. Lord Tennyson

Despite being overjoyed in formally joining the ranks of the S.G.A., I recognized that the real work had only just begun. Unlike many of my student government peers, who had held leadership positions on their high school class boards, I was a total rookie. My two bids for class presidency in high school had been complete flops. Now that I was actually in a position with some *real* influence over the lives and affairs of others on such a large scale, I feared that I might have leapt too far from the confines of my comfort zone. I had goals, true; ideas, of course; but I had no sense as to how I should go about implementing them.

"Gridlock" and "bureaucracy" were specters bemoaned by others well beyond my years. I could not yet appreciate just how prevalent they were in our humble little organization, befuddling well-intended student initiatives. Just as Newton once proposed that every action has an equal yet opposite reaction, it soon appeared clear to me that every attempt at policy creation spurred its own opposition. Arising almost instinctively, a dissenting opinion would often follow the introduction of a new measure; even the most moderate of proposals could not wind its way through the Senate without some, small debate.

While there were those within the organization who routinely took on the role of championing the minority opinion simply for the sake of fostering a discussion, I began to notice that many of our more heated disagreements stemmed from misinterpretations or miscommunications. Often the result of nothing more than an individual oversight or difference in perspectives, these little misconceptions could feed off the underlying ideologies of our members to spiral into larger issues if they went unnoticed and unchecked. In settling into my new seat beside the table, I came to appreciate just how diverse the opinions and outlooks comprising our governing body truly were, and how arduous a task it could be to bring these views together in agreement. More importantly, I began to realize that more battles could be won through mediating these differences in opinions and clarifying the underlying misconceptions, rather than waging an all-out war of wits.

I also recognized that I would not personally stand to accomplish anything if I let these inevitable, critical reactions deter me from presenting my ideas. I could not let the threat of opposition stall my efforts to make a mark of my own on our community. So, in starting small, I planned to host a series of board game nights in freshman residence halls throughout the campus. The underlying premise was simple enough: as a freshman student, I knew how difficult it could be to make friends from scratch.

As surely as I had anticipated, there were some initial objections raised. One senator assured me that residence area programming was job for Residence Life staff, and not a place for student government to interfere. Another questioned the necessity of such a program, as it was their impression as an upperclassman that there was already plenty to do around campus. Fortunately, I had already done my homework and was ready to expand upon each of their concerns.

In addition to my own first-hand experiences as a resident of the freshman community, I had a sizeable history of student feedback to work off of. Pouring through our records, I found a cache of data to support my position. Over the course of their prior election cycles, the student body had raised a lack of engaging weekend and late evening programming as a chief concern in an open questionnaire portion affixed to the ballot. I used these additional voices, past and present, to further draw my initial opponents closer to my own position. Even if I could not bring them fully onboard with helping to coordinate the program, I could at least get them to agree that it was worth pursuing. Thus, by starting with a fairly innocent project rooted in a widespread communal demand, I found a productive way to cement the foundation of my fledgling S.G.A. career.

Developing my plan proved to be the relatively simple part. Implementing it, on the other hand, was a whole other beast. First came the question of resources—a proper game night needs *board games*, after all, in addition to snacks and promotional materials. Fortunately, our campus offered a series of low-to-no cost options in securing supplies and other resources that made it rather easy to find alternatives well within my meager budget. Although color copies could be produced for a small fee through the campus copy center, black & white printing was free to students across campus. Games could always be purchased from the local mall and stored in the S.G.A. office, but our College Activities office also maintained a healthy collection of games that could be rented out to students upon presentation of a valid campus I.D.

Supplying snacks, however, is where things took a rather complicated turn. Although the S.G.A. had a large cabinet filled with enough sugary treats to energize a hungry horde of college students, its contents were the property of a separate division of the organization. Our Student Programming Council ("S.P.C.") maintained its own budget and supplies, operating *nearly* independently from the parent organization. These goods were strictly off limits. Moreover, purchasing my own provisions was an option wrapped tightly in red tape. The campus' food service organization maintained exclusive rights to providing food at campus-sponsored events, and was required to sign-off on and grant their blessing to any off-campus purchases.

Make no mistake, our campus' dining services certainly offered a fair bargain for their products, and regularly assembled assorted platters for larger meetings and other events. Anticipating a smaller crowd that would not necessarily require such portioning, and hoping to avoid the contracts and paperwork associated with the dining services route, I sought out a loophole. Resident assistants ("R.A.'s") would routinely order food for their area programs, and they appeared to be bound to this rule a bit more liberally. I had also come to learn that the door was open among many R.A.'s for collaboration in residence area programming, as a helping hand in meeting their monthly participation quotas afforded an opportunity for developing a *quid pro quo* relationship. Reaching out to my current R.A., I offered the S.G.A.'s help in promoting the event and securing board games in exchange for a menu.

As I continued to work my way through the event planning process, I quickly learned that there existed additional bureaucratic hurdles that would further chew at my timeline for coordination. In particular, the room reservation process for securing meeting spaces on our campus was yet another factor that drove me to seek an R.A. collaborator. Although there was a wide-array of common area spaces available to general students, campus organizations were required to submit formal requests through the Office of College Activities to secure a reservation. Prior to moving online later on during my undergraduate career, the room request process was initially comprised of hard copy forms. Requests had to be filled out and submitted to a mailbox just outside of their office in the student center. These submissions were then reviewed by a staff member and responses were returned to the mailboxes of the clubs or individuals listed on the request within a day or two—depending on how late in the day these requests were initially submitted. Teaming up with the housing staff to use a residential space for our event enabled me to once again work around the traditional campus programming process. Though in organizing future activities, I would need to budget this process and its turnaround time into my standard planning timeline.

Beyond its impact on the overall coordination of time, the room reservation process also presented a slight logistical hurdle for event publicity. In order to promote their events, students were also required to submit a draft of their notices and fliers to College Activities. Without their stamp of approval, materials could not be hung on campus bulletin boards. These drafts were supposed to include specific event details, including the date and location of the activity or program. Without this information, drafts would be returned to individual mailboxes for clarification and correction prior to being resubmitted for final approval. Thus, the process of event promotion could not be initiated before the reservation process had been completed.

With that said, I must pause to extend my praises for the hard work and dedication of the professionals in the Office of College Activities. Despite my own frustrations with the earlier incarnations of these processes, it has been my experience that the folks in this office were continually working toward developing the most concise (and painless) system humanly possible. If there was ever an issue with a form or flier, the staff and administrators involved would take the time to work one-on-one with students to help them navigate the necessary procedures. While the entire process was not a monumental burden, it could be a dizzying experience for the uninitiated. Having hit a few snags of my own along the way, the turnaround from submission to approval for my game night materials took a little longer than anticipated. As a result, my first ever S.G.A. event went off with only a few days' prior notice.

This was my first real introduction to the bureaucracy behind the process of governing, and a reminder as to the typical hurdles that can frustrate efforts at the campus and federal levels alike. Moreover, this experience served as a wake-up call. It reminded me of the importance in doing your homework before initiating a major project. In planning an event, regardless of its size, I should have familiarized myself with the related policies and procedures beforehand. Indeed, I would frequently recall the nerve-wracking experience of hosting that first game night, with so many pieces piling up in the last minute, in my later years with the S.G.A. In seeking to hold myself up as a leader among my peers, I had to be ready for *them* to turn to *me* when things started hanging precariously out of place, not the other way around. It also helped me to never lose sight of the importance of building in time to seek out a Plan B or C well ahead of my deadline—to always have an alternate route in mind.

In both the private and public sectors alike, such attention to detail is critical in delivering a quality product or experience. Indeed, practice soon helped me to perfect my craft. After repeating my game night program a couple of times in my own residence hall, I soon received invitations from other R.A.'s to bring it over to neighboring freshman areas.

◆

As I settled into a rather stable groove, time crept steadily past me. I was surprised to find myself facing yet another election period so suddenly. As the first half of my freshman year came to a close with our Winter Break, the time for choosing our future paths in student government was rapidly approaching. While a number of my peers in the Junior Senate had joined the boards of sitting vice presidents and directors in the hopes of taking over their appointed seats on the Executive Board, a few of us had set our sights on returning to the Senate in a more formal capacity. With only two upperclassmen returning to run for their resident senator seats, that would leave three positions in the Legislative Branch open for newcomers.

I decided that seeking out one of these seats would put me in the best position to expand upon the projects and initiatives that I had already taken on, as well as launch those ideas that had just started percolating in my mind. In addition to hosting my area game nights, I was becoming a more active member of the St. Jude fundraising committee that operated under the S.G.A. As a result of these activities, I was invited to join the campus' Emerging Leaders' Program and chapters of the National Residence Hall Honorary and the National Society of Leadership & Success. These experiences helped me to develop a broader perspective of our campus community and set aside my earlier thoughts of running again for an office on our class board. They clarified my vision for the future.

From a strategic standpoint, I also recognized that I might face better odds in a contest for a resident senator's seat over a position on the class board. After all, any attempt to steal away a class seat would mean squaring off against an incumbent. With the number of vacant seats in the Senate so greatly outnumbering our returning resident senators, it felt as though there were actually two, separate legislative races taking place—a rather tepid confirmation for the two returning sophomores and a heated battle that would pit any interested underclassmen in a tight contest for the three remaining seats. While I would certainly be facing an earnest fight to hold my own against my fellow junior senators in such a race, I also figured that my time and training in the program would grant me a competitive safeguard against any newcomers who might seek to challenge us from outside of the S.G.A.

The campaign process for campus-wide elections proved to be far more involved than the freshman elections we had braved earlier in the fall. Not only was there some additional excitement drawn in by those who were vying for the student body president's seat but the wider array of candidates spread across the four classes had attracted a greater deal of attention from the campus community than our earlier soiree.

The highlight of election week would once again be our speech night, held this time in the Cabaret—a communal hub in the heart of our campus. While S.G.A. speech nights had typically been held in one of the presentation rooms on the upper level of the student center, the current administration felt that the Cabaret's role as a central dining and social space would attract a more diverse crowd. Additionally, while the audience for our freshman race was mainly comprised of inquisitive underclassmen looking to learn more about their new community, the spring 2010 election cycle had attracted an audience comprised of more developed social circles and informal political factions. As members of a particularly close-nit community, the upperclassmen had considerable reasons for wanting to play a more active role in the campus' governance.

Even if you fancied yourself as more of an athlete or an artist, rather than a student political aficionado, every member of the campus community had some cause or program that mattered deeply to them. As such, individual interests in campus elections bridged far beyond social support for friends and acquaintances seeking office. In such a small community, everyone had a horse in the race. This, in turn, added additional layers of complexity to the experience that made it feel somewhat bittersweet when compared to the freshman contests. Although it was refreshing to see so many people take an interest in their campus community, the demand to prioritize certain causes and projects over others fostered the creation of fledgling partisan interests.

If it were merely perceived that a certain segment of the campus community was receiving greater attention or favor than another from their elected representatives, feelings of resentment and alienation could bubble forth into greater discord or foster detachment and apathy. Although there were no formal student political parties on our campus, candidates had to be wary of pandering to one faction over another, and ensure that their representation was balanced and neutral. Compared to our innocent little freshman introductions, this would be a true gladiator's match of political wills.

After the petitions for candidacy were collected and counted, there were six of us vying for the five open Senate seats, two incumbents and four members of the Junior Senate. This created a slight sense of tension in the race. As noted by a few S.G.A. insiders at the time, it was highly unlikely that either of the two incumbents would be beat out by the vying junior senators. Therefore, a race among six to fill five seats realistically dwindled to a battle between four freshmen for three open slots. What truly set this contest apart from your typical political race, and would further color my approach to future elections, was the reality that none of us really felt like *fighting* one another. Despite the fact that we all desperately hoped to win one of those open resident senator positions for ourselves, our ambitions had not yet spoiled our outlooks toward one another.

For the past year, we had all been similarly situated as outsiders trying to find our own ways into a well-established and closely connected community. As junior senators, we came to rely on one another for guidance and support in fleshing out our future S.G.A. aspirations. This made the prospect of winning somewhat poignant as, ultimately, one of us would be cast out of the rising Senate cohort. I would always carry this concern—that our process might be inadvertently excluding some truly dedicated talent—with me as I carried on through my undergraduate career.

Despite the heightened sense of scrutiny that we faced in this contest, I felt oddly at home in the larger race. When speech night rolled around, I knew that I stood to make my biggest impression of the race through my practiced approach to public presentation. Speaking once again without the aid of notes, I laid out all that I had learned in my attempts to build a stronger sense of campus community in the form of plans and promises for my fellow students. I shared my experiences and frustrations in shaping my fledgling game night programs, and reaffirmed my commitment to working through these hurdles so long as it made a difference to our community. I set forth my vision before the student body, and they responded with resounding approval. I was among the three returning members of the Junior Senate elected to serve a one-year term as a resident senator.

◆

As with starting a new job, or acclimating to a new school, it took some time to adjust to my expanding role within the student government. As I became more familiar with the system and its regular actors, I also developed a better sense of the goals that I wanted to accomplish—as well as the best approaches to take in setting out to achieve them. As I was still convinced that I wanted to become a lawyer one day, I began to view my new responsibilities in the Senate through a pre-law lens. Thinking back to my own confusion and lack of familiarity with the S.G.A. and related campus policies when I first started, I came to define my role as that of a "learned friend" for the student body.

As used in the legal field, this expression refers to one's ability to break down a process and its typical jargon into a relatable context for their clients. I felt that this outlook could easily be applied to my current situation, as well as used in fostering a more proactive approach to student governance. Rather than wait for people to come calling on me, I believed that a resident senator should seek out ways of actively communicating the role of the S.G.A. to the student body. After all, I had come to wonder how we could effectively serve our constituency if they had no clue as to *what* they could—or should—ask for, let alone *how* to go about asking for it. I was determined to learn the inner workings of student government, boil them down to the simplest of terms, and help others build the campus experiences that they desired.

In this role, striking a balance between impartiality and advocacy was crucial. I firmly believed that it was not my place to judge the merit of an individual's ideas. Whether I agreed with them or not, our students had a right to bring their views before their representatives and foster a discussion. I would use my office hours to meet with idealistic students, respond to email inquiries from club officers with questions about the system, or read up on our governing documents. Most of the time, I met with individuals who were interested in starting their own clubs. There were, naturally, the occasional walk-ins who simply needed to vent about a parking ticket or some other campus issue. In any given situation, I found that taking the time to offer others a seat at the table to voice their opinions could make all the difference. The simple act of lending an ear to their ideas and concerns meant the world to our students.

This, in turn, led to my working with a wide array of individuals, representing a myriad of opinions, backgrounds, and experiences. Some I agreed with, some I did not. Regardless of the individual, I gave each

46

attempt my best effort at carrying their ideas forward. There were, inevitably, a few fallouts; some personalities just did not mesh with my style of leadership. Though I have never found cause to *hate* anyone, I am not so naïve as to overlook the fact that, just as there are some folks out there who would recall my name with great esteem, there are surely those who would just as readily curse it. Though it is hard not to take these slight disagreements personally, I have come to accept that it is, indeed, a part of the job. Politics, whether it is at the campus, local, or national level, is a game of perceptions. When passions are tied to a particular outcome, it is difficult to separate the decision-maker from their vote.

Such an environment places additional pressures on political actors. Ours was, after all, a small, close-knit community; the closeness it fostered was one of its charms. Naturally, it was customary for S.G.A. officers to abstain from voting when matter pertaining to an organization with which they were formally affiliated came before them; but when the campus population is somewhere in the ballpark of 4,000 people, you occasionally come across a familiar name on the agenda with no formal relationship and a rather vague perception of conflicted interests. When this line becomes so terribly blurred, it is all too easy to inadvertently stumble across it.

In a place where everyone seemed to know everybody else, it was hard to draw a line in the sand and cry "impropriety!" Could some people use the student government to seek personal benefits from their work or corrupt their purpose in pursuit of greater power? The possibility is there, certainly. In practice, however, I have found corruption within student government to be a rare and often exaggerated occurrence. While I cannot speak for my peers as to how they grappled with such temptations, I feel

47

confident in saying that no soul has ever passed through our office that did not face the duties of their station with a profound sense of responsibility from the offset. I sincerely believe that the vast majority of individuals involved with student government signed up out of a genuine passion for service to others.

If anything, I would attribute those few examples of abused power to excessive pursuits of individual viewpoints that were grounded in noble, yet misguided ideals—not collegiate despotism. I will also take one step further by suggesting that these transgressions stemmed from a failure to distinguish between making a *change* and making a *difference*. Aside from our altruistic intent to serve our campus communities, I believe that each of us carries a small desire to leave our mark on this world. Like an artist ascribing a signature to their work, there is, undeniably, a small desire among public servants to leave their name on the pages of history. E.O. Wilson best described it as an innate human desire to prove that we are more than "animated dust". Though this spark varies in intensity from person to person, it can swell into an overpowering need to secure one's legacy, or risk fading away in the collective memory of one's community.

In seeking to make our mark, it is only natural to seek out an optimal route. Particularly in politics—where rigid, formal structures surrounded in unfamiliar and antiquated jargon often stand in the way of someone else and their desired goal— making a *change* presents a relatively clear course forward. Such frustrations provide the momentum for "reform candidates" to surge ahead of their peers. In seeking to serve my collegiate community, however, I did my best to avoid seizing upon such misguided charges. I recognized early on that behind each and every policy was a

48

person, their viewpoint, and a connected passion. I promised myself that I would not simply seek to change our established systems, but be a part in making little differences throughout their administration that better served our community.

Whereas many of my peers seemed motivated by challenging the *status quo*, I tended to shy away from such conflicts unless I felt it was absolutely necessary. In working with students to bring their visions to life, I found that I could make my mark without altering or overwriting someone else's. Political conflict and creative destruction certainly leave their scars on the pages of history, but the lasting impressions left on one individual at a time have always, at least in my opinion, etched out a more vibrant image. So I set out to make a difference, little by little, rather than initiating a sweeping change. That is the point that I believe so many of my peers in both student government and "real" government tend to overlook. There is more than one way to make an impression. Conflict is merely the simplest route to doing so.

This difference in approaches represents a fine line that I have regularly traversed throughout my S.G.A. career and beyond. Although my determination to provide a service for our students was sincere, there was always a part of me that wanted to prove to the world that I was capable of being someone other than that shy kid from a small town in New Jersey. Acting solely on that desire, however, would shut me out to the underlying needs of my peers, and ultimately leave me wallowing in the shallow pursuits of my own self-interests. Reconnecting to the true spirit of service helped me to identify the distinction between the two approaches that I could take.

◆

As my freshman year came to a close, there were still a few loose ends beyond my S.G.A. ambitions that had to be closed up. Despite their support throughout these endeavors, my roommates and I could not overcome our differences in personalities. When it came time to select our housing assignments for the following year, I was left all on my own.

While my more politically minded roommate—the one who had sought the class presidency—and I had begun to work well together throughout the election, behind closed doors we were a modern incarnation of a sitcom classic, *The Odd Couple*. Once my second roommate—the self-proclaimed "Switzerland" of our little tiffs—decided to join him in the split, I realized that I did not have any alternatives on deck. Despite keeping my S.G.A. purview open to external viewpoints and perspectives beyond my own aspirations, I had allowed other aspects of my life slip off the radar entirely. My grades remained strong, but my social ties to the campus were tenuous, at best. Though I found comfort in knowing that I would have another year to start anew with a solid position in the S.G.A., my narrow focus did not allow me to see just how closely I had come to circling the flames.

Lessons Learned

When I first moved into the corporate world from the retail world after graduation, I had to learn how to deal with the concept of downtime. To fill the gaps in my day, I began taking on new tasks around my office and eventually opened the door to new opportunities and responsibilities therein. Over time, I became a go-to for managing our internship program, as well as the first point of contact for many of the I.T. concerns in our office. I was not an expert in either field, but I had developed a reliable familiarity with our needs and capabilities by working in these areas routinely. In both the student government and corporate worlds, we all enjoy a certain degree of flexibility in defining our roles. Leaders are those who look beyond the standard job description to find new ways to further benefit their organization and the individuals they serve. Truly, your potential is limited only by your imagination.

An innovative approach to expanding your role requires a working familiarity with your field. You will surely find opportunities for growth if you take a moment to look closely at the mechanisms that spur an organization's functions. When it comes to implementing these visions for change, there are additional requirements for integration and collaboration. After all, a single person can rock the boat, but it takes a leader to get everyone rowing in the same direction. Whenever I took on a new project at work, I was sure to communicate my intentions with my supervisor and peers. A significant factor for consideration here was professional courtesy; no good can come from pulling strings behind another's back like a managerial Machiavelli. Secondly, I recognized that, as the newest member of the team, my overall view of the organization was rather limited. By keeping channels open for communication throughout the planning and initiating stages of my various projects, I was able to build off of their insights, expertise, and concerns to develop a more comprehensive proposal.

In becoming a voting member of the S.G.A. Senate, I learned that a common complaint among our newer representatives was that members of the Legislative Branch did not have clear job descriptions. Many knew that the weekly meetings were a requirement and that voting on proposed bills and clubs were standard expectations. Beyond that, though, they did not know where else to begin. In simply listening to the concerns of individual students, I knew that there were plenty of ideas for projects and programs floating throughout student body. In the absence of a formal directive, I developed my own job description based off of my perception of the community's needs, as well as those practical and professional concepts that were already familiar to me.

Furthermore, by framing my viewpoint according to a practiced understanding of the campus' policies and procedures, and leaving myself open to the comments and criticisms of the student body, I could pick out and join together these free-floating ideas to be strung together into a more coherent plan of action, eventually guiding others along the way. This approach to student leadership became a defining characteristic of my S.G.A. career. Years later, students would continue to describe me as someone who "genuinely cared" about their concerns.

Having the opportunity to voice their ideas and know that someone was sincerely listening on the other end meant the world to them. Built on the tenants of customer service that I had honed earlier in my professional career, this impression fostered a greater appreciation for their government among the students that I worked with, helping them to feel as though they had a direct impact on the course of campus events. In the end, these experiences were fundamentally shaped by the particular way that I approached my role as a resident senator. Setting out with a clear sense of direction from the onset—through my application of the "learned friend" outlook—helped me to not only stay on-task and on-target in meeting my goals, but empower others in meeting their own aims as well.

As the guiding force for our future endeavors, the development of a mission and vision are critical components of personal and professional development. Many organizations encounter issues stemming from "mission drift" by losing sight of those principles that define their very reason for operating. Those who lack these ideological anchors from the offset place themselves at a greater risk for distraction and self-defeat. In setting out to clearly define my approach to leadership early on, I charted a course that helped me to stay on track when things began to look their darkest.

As you look to find your place within a new position at work, in your community, or even at home, remember that the power to sculpt your role remains largely in your own hands. Have faith in your ideas, formalize them into a concrete mission or ethos, and trust in your supporting vision to guide you.

If there is yet another lesson to be gleaned at this stage, it is the importance of self-reflection. Though I had my mind set firmly on my personal mission, I was not paying a great deal of attention to other aspects

53

of my life at this point. No great voyage is ever complete by keeping your eye on the compass the entire time. The riggings must be trimmed according to the wind, the rudder must be steered in the proper direction, and a great deal of general maintenance is owed to ensure that the entire vessel continues to perform as needed. If one of these areas is left unchecked for too long, minor issues can unfurl into disasters of tragic proportions. Likewise, it is necessary for us to occasionally run a quick mental assessment, pausing a moment or two before the mirror to ask ourselves how we are holding up. Your body and spirit are your vessels; take the time to ensure they are treated with care.

THE LEADERSHIP PROFILE: *Exercise Three*

Now that we have had the opportunity to look closely at one project or objective, I would like you to think more broadly. Take a moment to think about what you want out of life, your current role, or a future career, and scrawl it somewhere prominently on the page. Let it sit proudly before all that you have written out thus far and all that is bound to follow. This is your personal mission statement.

As you return to look over your inventory of strengths and weaknesses that we outlined in Exercise One, read it over once or twice as well. Understanding where you ultimately hope to go will assist you in prioritizing the skills and tools you will need to develop along the way. As an aspiring lawyer, I knew that public speaking and presentation skills were going to be high on my list, but that may not necessarily be the case for you. Though they are tremendous skills to have, you may find that financial literacy, technical trade skills, an additional language, or even a fresh set of dance moves will be better suited to aid you in your journey. Without taking a moment to seriously ask ourselves where it is that we hope to be in five, ten, or even twenty years, however, we cannot begin to scale down that list, let alone separate our *wants* from our *needs*. These little internal discussions help us to not only assign priority, but also clarify our vision.

More importantly, we have set apart our mission here so distinctly because it is important to go back and read it over frequently as time winds on. With each reading, do not be afraid to ask yourself if this is still the path that you want to pursue. After all, if we could each see what the future held in store for us, there would be no need for undertaking such arduous trials and grand adventures. In reality, what awaits us is not so clear and concise. Roads diverge, interests change, and the occasional curve ball knocks us completely off course. As life changes around you, it is perfectly o.k. for you to adapt and grow as well. That is what makes this journey all the more exciting.

4 – The Ascent

"He who is unable to live in society,
or who has no need because he is sufficient for himself,
must either be a beast or a god."
–Aristotle

With our first summer break tucked away in my memory, I returned to campus and settled into a quiet residence area at its Northern end. The Gartland Commons consisted of little rows of white trimmed houses tacked onto the grounds during an earlier acquisition. Remnants of the College's own growing pains, these quant little dwellings were set distinctly apart from their peers in their appearance. But, what they lacked in aesthetic wonder of their own was readily accounted for in their formidable location. Sitting just along the border of the woodlands to our North, Gartland sat atop a steep hillside with a clear view overlooking the Hudson River.

As the student center was located closer to the campus' Southern end, and my classes were dotted somewhere in between, I would typically pack my bag for a full day's work each morning and return home late in the evening. This made the S.G.A. office my home away from home throughout my sophomore year, inadvertently pushing my personal life further out of balance.

My volunteer work began to consume the lion's share of my time, with whatever was left devoted to my academic responsibilities. As the school year began, there was already little time left to waste. My S.G.A. career was blossoming rapidly. I had been approached toward the end of the prior school year by the newly elected S.B.P. with a special assignment. As one of the few criminal justice majors in the S.G.A. at that time, he wanted me to take over the revitalization of the campus' Safety & Security committee.

Initially founded in the 1990's, the first iteration of the Safety & Security committee was more of a watchdog organization—early minutes and draft documents from their meetings described episodes of student patrols monitoring security's movements and critiquing their overall performance. In reviewing the existing records, I could not help but feel as though the tone of this preceding entity was largely antagonistic. I did not want to simply call out flaws; I wanted to play a part in forming solutions.

Adding to the list of potential hurdles, I faced yet another layer of opposition in garnering support for the project. This time, from more modern voices. When I told others that I was forming a "Safety & Security" committee, their reactions tended to split in one of two directions. The first group interpreted my mission as repetitive—"Why do we need *more* security?" To the second cohort, my project posed an even larger problem; they feared that my committee would be nothing more than a parrot for the Department.

After all, it had been our campus' Director of Safety & Security who first reached out to the S.G.A. with the idea of revitalizing the committee. Rather than simply channel his office's directives and alerts down yet another bureaucratic channel, his intent behind the project was far more altruistic. Building off of modern trends in community policing, he wanted to strengthen the relationship between the officers on our campus and the students they served. At a time when campus security and police officers across the nation were under scrutiny for the heavy-handed responses to student activism undertaken by some of their peers, the sitting Director wanted to create a more collaborative culture, founded upon an open dialog. To begin, however, he needed a student representative.

As a student in the criminal justice program, I sat in a prime position to serve as the link between these two worlds. Under my direction, the latest incarnation of the Safety & Security committee would focus on engaging the student body in policy discussions and develop informational campaigns to raise awareness on existing guidelines and practices. My goal was to foster a clear, two-way line of communication between their office and our student body. Setting my ideas to paper, I drew up my first bill for consideration before the Senate.

Upon its passage, and the formal establishment of the committee, I immediately reached out to the Office of Safety & Security to schedule a meeting with the Director. Particularly from the offset, I wanted to play a proactive part in defining the scope and duties of my new role. In further shaping our two-way communication stream, I would not only assist the office in publicizing its latest developments and initiatives, but also bring him current issues for comment or correction. From that point on, we would meet at least once each month during the school year to discuss student concerns, as well as develop potential programs and policies. I also made a point of having the committee host an annual "security appreciation day" in conjunction with the announcement of the "Security Officer of the Year"— the recipient of this award was selected by the student body during each election cycle via referendum. It was a collaborative relationship that not only helped to improve relations between the S.G.A. and the Office of

Safety & Security but also contributed to the development of our first campus-wide text alert system later on in my career.

In filling out the committee, I decided to incorporate a small leadership board to assist in organizing and administering its meetings and other events. Finding motivated candidates to jump on the Safety & Security bandwagon proved to be more of a challenge. In fact, when I first began accepting applications for open board positions from members of the student body, I only had one candidate. As a member of the junior class with a desire to enter the field of law enforcement, and an individual possessing a clear passion for this kind of work, I accepted him on the spot.

Incidentally, my new Deputy Chair and I came from two opposite ends of the political spectrum. On certain issues, we just could not see eye to eye. That, however, did not matter in the slightest to either of us. In managing the Safety & Security committee, all I needed was someone who was passionate about the subject matter and dedicated to the creation of a dialog on the topic. That is what I sought, and it is precisely what I got. Over the next two years, we formed a good working relationship off of our common interest in campus safety. Had we approached our professional relationship as an "all or nothing" stand-off, we never would have attained our mutual goals. If I had let these little disagreements cloud my perspective, and dismissed him outright, then I would have lost a truly valuable right hand.

As our to-do list continued to grow, I realized that our committee required more than just two, dedicated individuals. The Office of Safety & Security provided us with a healthy amount of material to bring back to the student body, far too much for our duo to handle on its own. Our current

Sheriff/Deputy approach simplified internal communications, but left us treading water as new requests continued to pour in. With each month, we had to not only prioritize our projects to make sure that we were not cramming too much information into a single meeting, but ensure that we were creating opportunities for students to share their insights and feedback as well. As we settled into a steady groove, we began to look past our basic tasks and focus on our broader organizational mission.

My motto became "dialogs, not directives." In the hopes of ensuring that our committee served as more than just a soapbox for the administration, we relied on monthly town hall meetings as our primary means of engagement. Through these forums, students would have the opportunity to question, expand upon, and digest the information and policies that we shared. In conducting the brunt of our footwork out in the open, our community could reach a consensus in a collaborative fashion, rather than leave the student body feeling as though new policies were simply being impressed upon them.

Responsiveness was a key component in building this relationship. Typically, our student meetings would take place toward the end of the month and my meetings with the Director would follow one week later. This way, I could collect new information to bring back to the students shortly after our initial town hall meeting, helping them to recognize that their comments and inquiries were being heard higher up the ladder. After all, they teach us early on in criminal justice that a key factor in determining the effectiveness of a punishment is the speed with which a response follows the deviant act; no one is going to take a penalty very seriously if it is carried out a year after the offense itself has taken place. So too does such timing impact the effectiveness of the carrots we extend over our sticks in leading others. In order to get the student body to buy-in to this new relationship with Safety & Security, I first had to establish trust, and that meant demonstrating a timely attentiveness to their concerns.

I also strove to keep our town hall meetings as open and attendee-driven as possible in order to attract a broader audience. The S.G.A. had already developed a reputation for furthering stagnation on campus, and I wanted to challenge that perception by engaging students in their governing process directly. In striking up a conversation that was likely to attract a large audience, I decided to dive right into one of our hottest topics: parking. After all, just about anyone who had received a parking ticket on our campus had an opinion as to how the system could be run differently. When students popped into the S.G.A. office to submit their appeal paperwork, they usually took a moment to share their two cents with whoever was present. As the organization in charge of monitoring and regulating parking policies on campus, the Office of Safety & Security had become the target of ire among a small but vocal portion of the campus community. Our new committee sat in a prime position to open the door to student feedback. If I could create a single channel for them to funnel their thoughts on the matter, I hoped to not only extract a few pearls of wisdom along the way, but ultimately tap into their frustrations as a catalyst for further engagement.

When it came to addressing issues with the ticketing appeals process itself, however, I could not only rely on my meetings with the Director of Safety & Security. While this office was responsible for issuing parking tickets and collecting fines, it was actually another team of S.G.A.

members who oversaw the appeals process. The Chief Justice also worked closely with the Director of Safety & Security and served as the chairperson for the monthly meetings of the Judicial Board, where members reviewed and decided outstanding appeals. These appeal packets typically consisted of a standard form developed by our office, a personal statement from the ticketed individual and any witnesses, and any photos or additional evidence that they wished to provide. The burden of proof fell upon our students in pleading their petitions to overturn the issuance of a ticket. While many of the emotional pleas the Judicial Board received did not meet the burden of proof required to waive the imposed fine, we found that some recent appeals were also being automatically rejected for other, "administrative" reasons at that time. For my first town hall meeting on the subject, I figured there was no one better to call upon to host a discussion on campus parking and the student perspective than our Chief Justice.

Unfortunately, convincing him to join me was easier said than done. Our Chief Justice at the time believed in maintaining a certain degree of anonymity, precisely to avoid drawing attention to the fact that he oversaw this contentious process. As tempers tended to flare when students found a "REJECTED" stamp emblazoned across their returned appeal form, he did not want to make himself a target. And yet, when it came to explaining the intricacies of the system, no one knew it better. If I was going to properly address the frustrations surrounding the ticketing process, I had to find a way to get the Chief Justice to join me.

For weeks, I continued to run the idea by him, appealing to our shared commitment to transparency and efficiency in student government. Despite his desire to distance himself from the process in order to maintain some degree of privacy, our Chief Justice was also a truly dedicated member of the S.G.A. who believed soundly in the role his board had to play in the campus community. A principled leader, his commitment to the student body and the function of the Judicial Board outweighed his own, personal concerns. In time, I won him over.

As the first guest of the Safety & Security Committee, he and I stood side-by-side in answering questions and taking heated criticism from the attending students as a team. After all, I did assure him that I would not be throwing him to the wolves, leaving him to suffer the wrath of our audience on his own. Instead, by engaging the Chief Justice in an open discussion, our dual experiences helped to provide our attendees with a clearer understanding of the ticketing and appeal processes. Our exchange shed new light on the little nuances that could doom an appeal from the start.

We faced the issue openly, and the audience responded in kind. Even the few, flaring tempers that stormed the mic that evening quelled once our attendees realized they were not being stonewalled by runaround responses and empty excuses; they were happy to receive an honest and sincere response, even if it was not the one they wanted to hear.

Though a few more people began to recognize our Chief Justice around campus as the "guy who handled parking tickets", our town hall meeting did not paint a target on his back. Instead, his calm, organized approach to answering student questions helped to reaffirm the effectiveness of student government in the eyes of our constituents. It was a proper first step in the right direction, a reintroduction to the role that the S.G.A. stood to play in our community.

An important part of maintaining this trust, I realized, was to deliver concrete action in response to their concerns. Bringing my list of notes from this initial meeting straight to the Director of Safety & Security, I was pleased to find that he was largely receptive to the students' feedback. Telling me quite candidly when one suggestion was not feasible, he would then follow up his comment with ideas for potential spin-offs and work arounds. More importantly, in those cases where students presented sufficient evidence to question the validity of a parking ticket or other charge, he was happy to review the situation and personally overturn an infraction that did not appear to be justly issued.

In fact, student feedback played a vital role in identifying a potential error in the ticketing system that had led to an improper fine. After a small number of parking ticket appeals had been submitted with the same, "miscellaneous" charge applied to each student, the Chief Justice suggested that I raise the budding pattern in my next meeting with the Director. The Judicial Board had already started immediately overturning the charge on any appeal that crossed their desks as a baseless fine, but feared that an improperly trained, or otherwise misguided, guard might be misapplying the charges. Instead, when the Director and I went to test one of the devices used to issue tickets ourselves, we identified a small glitch in the system that was tacking these miscellaneous fines onto other tickets. In working together and keeping an open door to student concerns, we were able to quickly catch a minor bug before it evolved into a larger issue.

Between the Senate, the Judicial Board, and the Office of Safety & Security, we formed a rather productive team. The Chief Justice would alert me to developing trends in ticketing appeals—allowing us to identify areas of potential confusion and plan informational campaigns accordingly—while the Director maintained an open and innovative approach toward addressing student concerns. The crux of our working relationship was responsiveness. I knew that I could turn to either of them with even the most outlandish of ideas and expect constructive, honest feedback in return. This was not an atypical set up for the S.G.A.; the collaborative atmosphere developed under the 2009-2010 S.G.A. Administration continued to thrive under our 2010-2011 leadership.

While this warm and inviting atmosphere created the perfect climate for engaging others in our work, it also lulled me deeper into an overwhelming sense of calm that distracted me from the other, crumbling pillars of my own personal well-being.

Lessons Learned

In setting off on an adventure, one of the most crucial tasks that you will face is forming a team to support you. After all, very few heroes complete their quests alone. Indeed, as they say, the people make the journey. Surrounding yourself with a broader cohort of individuals will not only provide you with richer company along the way, but also expand your own viewpoint according to the collective wisdom of your new advisers. Including individuals who had different, even competing, viewpoints on my own board proved to be an invaluable component in the Safety & Security committee's recipe for early success.

If there is one thing that I know to be true after all of my years in public/student service, it is that I do not have all of the answers. The best way to fill in the gaps of personal knowledge and experience is to surround yourself with people who cannot only supplement your opinions but also challenge them to adapt and grow. I never let partisan politics get in the way of personnel appointments or committee assignments, because I recognized how tremendously impactful these civil exchanges between clashing opinions can be in guiding the work of an organization. Like striking a flint to spark an invigorating pyre, the exchanges fostered by these differences in perspective hold the potential to power a furnace of innovation and growth.

Just as a warming fire tends to draw others in toward its glow, a broad and diverse community within an organization yields a greater potential to attract others in pursuit of collaboration, as well as promote individual achievement. Though I may not have worded it quite so eloquently at the time, this principle rested at the heart of my efforts with the Safety & Security committee. Nationally, a notable divide had formed between college students and campus safety officers. These current events only spurred the perception that campus police were heavy-handed enforcers tasked with shutting down student activities that ran counter to the will of their respective administrations. Having grown up in a family of police officers, I knew that this perception was not a fair representation of all campus officers, particularly those in our community. Chief among my personal objectives for the committee was the desire to challenge this perspective by actively engaging students in the dialog on campus safety.

In time, this outlook even helped me to bridge the division that had formed within the S.G.A. itself. Although the Chief Justice may not have initially been too keen on facing an angry crowd to talk about parking tickets, I eventually won him over through our shared commitment to student governance, as well as a mutual desire to clear up misunderstandings about the appeals system in the hopes of making it as efficient and helpful as possible. Developing a clear and concise message not only helped me to communicate my viewpoint to others but draw connections between their goals and my own. These commonalities formed the foundation for professional partnerships that would not only help the committee to grow, but expand the scope of its responsibilities as time went on.

When stoking the flames, however, one always runs the risk of being burned. Civility and respect are critical components in this equation, acting like a dowsing pale in ensuring that tempers do not flare too widely beyond control. Sometimes it is difficult to disentangle our emotions from the causes we so passionately defend. To this end, leaders must monitor the emotional well-being of their peers, and can benefit from fostering organizational cultures that promote group activities beyond their typical labors. In breaking bread after our S.G.A. meetings in weekly lunches, the leaders of the Executive and Legislative branches hoped to teach their members to leave business at the meeting table and see that these disagreements did not affect our spirit of comradery around the dining table. I could have twisted the arm of our Chief Justice to call him into our meeting by touting his attendance as an apparent duty of his office. Instead, I elected to employ a more respectful approach, convincing him to join us willingly. Why? I did not just want him there in his official capacity; I wanted him to become a partner in our efforts.

In working with so many talented leaders over the years, I have come to envision teamwork as more of a sprawling network than a condensed cohort. That is, the team itself stands to gain more as its individual members branch out in pursuit of their own missions and goals, rather than being penned into a singular mission or framework under the direction of *one* leader. By loosely coordinating individuals under a shared vision, while allowing them to also go on and develop additional pursuits and teams of their own, the original unit is supplemented by the worldly experiences collected and brought back by each member.

As individuals continue to build upon their experiences, their expanding worldviews may even frame the initial, shared mission in a new light. Such a transition might even diminish its attainability or desirability among your original members, prompting evolution. Thus, communication and adaptation are vital components in developing and maintaining a healthy organizational culture as it continues to evolve. In adjusting to the pressures of these growing pains, civility and respect play crucial parts in ensuring that frustrations sparked from our differences in perspective do not swell into all-consuming infernos. As time would quickly illustrate, there is a valued wisdom in maintaining the patience to disagree without being utterly disagreeable.

THE LEADERSHIP PROFILE: *Exercise Four*

What had initially opened the Director of Safety & Security to the idea of collaborating with the student government was his understanding that no facet of our campus community could thrive—let alone function—apart from our overall spirit of community. On a national level, campus safety organizations were being broadly painted as distant, para-militaristic arms of their respective administrations that seemed wholly unnatural when affixed to the greater body of academic institutions. From the distant echoes of Kent State University to the seemingly callous application of pepper spray in one, timely example, law enforcement and higher education were two concepts that did not seem to come together quite so neatly.

And yet, our Safety & Security committee thrived. This project succeeded because it tapped into what was, perhaps, the greatest resource available to us at the time, our spirit of community and the common interests that it held. No leader, no team, no organization can thrive without first understanding the role it plays in a much larger arena. Just as there will always be a bigger fish in the pond, there is always another level of competition or collaboration that hurries ahead of us as we continue to ascend through the various levels of our individual networks.

For this exercise, take a moment to picture yourself or your organization in the context of your local community. Whether it is a single club on a college campus, a business in the heart of a small municipality, or an agency waiting in the wings of the federal government, we all have a unique space to fill. We are never out there floating on our own. At any

71

given time, we are surrounded by myriad actors drifting through narratives of their own, filling spaces on the same, grand stage.

While some of these actors may, indeed, be viewed as competition, branding them with this singular label risks closing the door to additional opportunities. As members of a shared environment, they are also potential partners and collaborators. Take a moment to identify two or three individuals or organizations that fill a role within your community that is similar to yours. How are you alike? How are you different?

In understanding these subtle distinctions in the ways that you each go about your business, you can begin to identify opportunities for collaboration. After all, a common thread can be found at just about any level of operation, no matter how small. A local hair salon and automotive repair shop may not share much in the way of business goals or even target audiences—at first—but they do share a common attachment to the same community. At the broadest level, they both reach out to the same group of people and regularly serve the same, familiar faces. While one may not be able to directly contribute to the business of the other, they can team up to make an impact on this fundamental segment of their shared universe. In time, these efforts may open doors that neither would have previously sought out or even considered on their own.

Write these two or three potential partners somewhere in the margins of your leadership profile, as their roles will be more loosely tied to your broader outlook. Nonetheless, as we continue to develop our profiles throughout this text, it is worth taking a moment or two to consider how the skills or tasks that we are outlining might be utilized in concert with these individuals. Is there any way that they might help you in completing one of the exercises outlined herein? Or, perhaps, would they see value in having you come in to guide them through the Leadership Profile process? You might identify opportunities for little exchanges that not only help to improve the quality of life within your shared community, but open the door to new and unforeseen opportunities for you both.

5 – THE DARK

"I dream'd there would be Spring no more,
That Nature's ancient power was lost:
The streets were black with
smoke and frost,
They chatter'd trifles at the door…
…Till all at once beyond the will
I hear a wizard music roll,
And thro' a lattice on the soul
Looks thy fair face and makes it still."
-A. Lord Tennyson

I continued my work throughout the fall of 2010 at a break-neck pace. Although I remained dutifully attentive to my studies, my routine coordination of town hall meetings and involvement in other S.G.A. projects left little time for much else. Adding to an already overflowing plate, a potentially game-changing rumor began circulating through our ranks as the winter break closed in. Word had begun buzzing throughout the student body that our current Senate Speaker was contemplating spending the coming semester in Egypt. If that proved to be the case, then a top spot in the administration would be opening up, as S.G.A. members were prohibited by internal policy from holding their offices while studying abroad.

Such a prospect sent our collective fantasies into a frenzy. After all, the Senate Speaker was third in the line of succession for our S.G.A., the highest office one could aspire to in the Legislative Branch. Additionally, like many internally selected positions, it was easily held by incumbents; there were not many who would openly challenge a sitting upperclassman who held the gavel. If these rumors held true, then it would create a career-defining opportunity for one of us in the Senate.

As time passed and these rumors persisted, I began to compile a mental list of the most likely candidates to vie for the seat. In looking at our sitting senators, there was a mere handful of upperclassmen. Among our resident senators, there was only the departing Speaker and another representative from the junior class. Turning to the four Class Presidents, the head of the senior class had only one semester left with the organization and delegates from the sophomore and freshman classes had about as much experience or political pull within the organization as the rest of us newcomers. In my mind that meant there were just two likely candidates: The resident senator from the junior class and his peer, the president of the Class of 2012.

Admittedly, I had a tough time choosing between the two. The resident senator was an ambitious go-getter with a fair collection of noteworthy projects already stored under his belt. The president of their class, on the other hand, held a strong record on a number of campus issues, along with enough charisma and charm to make Ben Stein swoon. As the outgoing Senate Speaker was also one of the Class of 2012 presidents' closest friends, and thus likely to give him her endorsement prior to departing, the scales seemed to be tipping steadily in his favor. And yet, even the most astute political analyst could not predict what would happen next.

Shortly after these rumors proved true, and just before the matter of selecting her successor came before the Senate for a vote, I happened to run into the resident senator from the junior class at a campus performance. We

75

chatted briefly about ongoing projects and, when the conversation turned to the soon-to-be vacant Speaker's seat, I expected to hear his plea for support. Instead, he wanted to talk about *my* recent projects, and complimented my earlier focus on developing a series of game nights in the freshman residence halls. We talked about the growing Safety & Security committee, and he shared stories from his own experiences as the chair of a large campus committee. Admittedly, rather than feel flattered, I had to fight off a slight sense of suspicion. I was speechless when he asked me if I would consider taking the position of Senate Speaker.

Only a few weeks later, he followed up on his inquiry with bold action. When the prior Speaker's resignation was formally accepted and the Senate opened its discussions on her replacement, he nominated me for the position. With his endorsement and the support of my fellow underclassmen, the motion was carried through to victory. By a narrow margin, I beat out another nomination for the Class of 2012 president to become the head of the Legislative Branch.

The prevailing opinion within the Senate at that time was that a younger member of the student government would be able to affect the sort of long-term change that the Legislative Branch needed. Rather than appoint another upperclassman to briefly hold the position, a rising sophomore had plenty of time to grow into the role.

After falling into the routine of holding meetings in joint session with the Executive Branch, the boundaries between the two bodies had begun to blur. Losing sight of their policy-oriented role within the organization, many of the senators and their committees had turned to program and event planning instead. My record for toughing it out when faced with the usual bureaucratic entanglements and overcoming opposition in a collaborative fashion to get the job done had garnered the attention and respect of my peers; my attempts to stay somewhat below the radar had actually propelled me further into the fray of student governance. Having barely reached the mid-way point of my sophomore year, I was now sitting in one of the highest offices in the S.G.A.

Though I had begun to take on a more active role within our campus community through my various S.G.A. projects, it was not until I stepped into the role of Senate Speaker that I began to truly appreciate the challenge of being an effective leader. As I was charged with directing students that were both my juniors and seniors alike, I had to develop a style of management that would foster collaboration and spur productivity without being too pushy or overbearing. In recognizing that the role of a legislator in the S.G.A. was best fulfilled when expectations were left open and flexible, I crafted my approach to once again act as a resource for those who I hoped to lead, spurring their success from behind. Within the first few weeks of attaining my new title, I took the time to re-acquaint myself with the sections of our Constitution and By-Laws pertaining to the Legislative Branch. I developed strategies for following up on mandated procedures, like the weekly collection of reports from each of my senators, and drafted informational blurbs and materials to guide them in selecting their committees. My role, as I came to see it, was simply to guide them in adopting that core project or issue that would largely define their year. From there on out, the rest was up to them.

I also took on more of a passive role in leading our weekly meetings. In my view, we—as representatives—stood to gain more from

77

being active listeners than active mouthpieces. As the Chair of these sessions, I thought it was more important to provide opportunities for our individual Senators to report back on their meetings with committees and constituents and let the discussions and goals develop organically, rather than lock us in to a more rigid agenda based on my own observations and priorities. The jurist in me sought to administer these proceedings in a calm, level-handed manner. I was not necessarily looking to foster a debate, but a discussion.

Naturally, conflict could not be avoided entirely. As noted in *The Circle*, our campus paper, my Legislative Branch soon came to "clash" against the will of the student body president himself.

As the successor to my freshman year idol, the student body president for the 2010-2011 Administration proved to be both eager and capable in filling the shoes of his predecessor. An S.G.A. veteran, and somewhat of a diehard fan, this S.B.P. drove the agenda of his team with charisma. A true people-person, he carried on many of the traditions and mannerisms of our former leader, particularly when it came to greeting and engaging the constituents that came in to our office. He and I worked well together as I stepped into my new role, striking up quite a rapport between my more reserved and occasionally stoic responses and his boisterous, youthful character. Nonetheless, one reason we worked so well together as the heads of our respective branches was the fact that neither of us held any compunction in putting our foot down when we believed the other had crossed a line.

This particular episode arose from a proposal to amend the requirements of our petitioning process for S.G.A. elections and was drafted by my former roommate, who had been appointed to the 2010-2011 Administration as our Elections Commissioner. Having already established an impressive résumé in the political arena as a member of his local school board—in addition to maintaining an active level of involvement in a number of local political organizations—he brought a worldly expertise to the role that went beyond the typical rubber-stamping of established guidelines. Instead, he focused on making sure the process was as fair, equitable, and efficient as possible.

Through his review of the S.G.A. Constitution and By-Laws, the Commissioner had uncovered inconsistencies regarding the required minimum number of signatures for individuals to establish their candidacy. The documents were, in fact, utterly contradictory. One section called for a flat, static number of signatures while another stated that the required minimum was to be based off of a percentage of the population comprising the constituency for the position in question (i.e. the minimum number of signatures required to run for class president would be based on the total class size, while resident senators would have to collect a number of signatures based off of the size of our total on-campus population). As overall class sizes continued to grow at a somewhat steady pace, the Elections Commissioner proposed a bill that would increase required signatures for campus-wide officials (the student body president and resident senators) to reflect recent changes in the student population. The requirements for class officers would remain the same, as this recommendation would also remove any language referring to elections requirements based on percentages in our governing documents.

I joined the Commissioner as co-sponsor for the bill and assisted in drafting the document that would ultimately be brought before the Senate. What we saw as a simple housekeeping matter quickly exploded into one of the greatest controversies of the 2010-2011 Administration, according to the campus press.

After passing through the Senate, the bill was immediately vetoed by the student body president. As a result, the next issue of *The Circle* bore the headline "[Student body president] clashes with S.G.A. Senate regarding signature increase for potential candidates" on the front page. Despite the media buzz, attitudes within the administration were rather tepid. While I supported the Commissioner's notion that the signature requirement should be reflective of the target constituency, justifying a slight increase, the S.B.P. felt that the S.G.A. should refrain from creating unnecessary barriers to student involvement. He feared that even a slight increase in required signatures might discourage more timid individuals from throwing their hats in the ring. Despite these differences in ideologies, neither side harbored any animosity. At the end of the day, the change sought was deemed to have been too minimal to warrant any larger conflict, and the president's veto was not overturned. Instead, we came together to adopt a minor fix which conformed the language in our guiding documents, without changing current requirements.

This episode unfurled during a particularly poignant time in history, as partisan gridlock at the national level brought about the threat of a potential shutdown of the federal government around this same time. While agreements over a minor amendment to voting procedures on a college campus may pale in comparison to the more daunting task of passing a federal budget, the episode reaffirmed the abilities of our members to disagree without being disagreeable. Make no mistake, tempers have flared and passions swelled throughout the course of our S.G.A. history but the blessed bearing provided by our small community has helped us to maintain a greater perspective in the course of our work.

The 2010-2011 Administration operated under the banner of "actions speak louder than words" and, despite any ideological differences that may have lingered beneath the surface, our shared identity as members of a greater community superseded any individual interests or motives. Perhaps our national leaders could learn something from the microcosms of governance that operate across the country on a daily basis. The political animosity that plagues our system may not solely be the fault of individual ego, but a loss of this valuable perspective. Above all else, we are servants of a larger, shared community.

"Clashing" with the student body president in my first year as Senate Speaker also provided me with the opportunity for a little self-reflection. My ascension through the ranks of S.G.A. had been a rapid one. It appeared that I had a knack for politics, something I had never really considered until some folks began asking me whether or not it was a path that I wanted to pursue as a career. While I had certainly come to enjoy the role that I played on our campus, I had no other budding political ambitions. I simply resolved to continue to serve my community so long as I had a purpose to fulfill. The day I ran out of ideas, or could no longer be of any service, was the day I retired.

Still, despite all that I had accomplished, I continued to fear that I might relapse under pressure into old habits and veer off course from the mission that I had set before myself—to become a leader worthy of the College President's recognition. More so than corruption, I was concerned about the potential for a slow and steady drift in purpose that might ultimately steal away my focus and leave me wondering aimlessly in a cycle that had chewed up and spit out aspiring politicians—far more daring and cunning than me—throughout the ages. My purpose in joining the S.G.A., after all, had been to rebuild a sense of identity. If I allowed myself to be pulled apart under the weight of other, external interests, then I risked losing everything that I had fought to attain.

In my attempts to safeguard against such distractions, however, I failed to recognize the personal issues that posed an imminent threat to my future goals. As the end of the semester closed in upon us, I should have felt as though I was on top of the world. Instead, I was consumed by a persistent feeling of loneliness. In reaching out for the highest branch I could find, I did not hear the ones snapping just beneath my feet.

◆

I soon found myself eagerly counting down the days on my desk calendar until I could return home again; my trips to and from New Jersey had now become a weekly occurrence. Despite my success in overcoming my fear of public speaking, I never fully addressed a deeper social anxiety that prevented me from developing interpersonal relationships with those around me. Though I participated in S.G.A. outings and greatly enjoyed the company of my peers in various circles around campus, I could not bring myself to open up to them beyond our professional roles.

I could certainly put on a good act at playing "Mr. Personable" when campaign time rolled around, but I felt incredibly awkward in regular social settings and began to avoid them entirely. This led me to spend most my time on campus alone, barricaded away in the Gartland Commons. During those few weekends that I did not return home, due to some other engagement or S.G.A. event, I would spend my time wandering around campus, stowed away in the S.G.A. office, or in the deep sullen sanctuary that I had carved out in my room.

On most nights, I would venture away from my doorstep and over to the stone retaining wall that sat atop the hill overlooking the river. I would climb up on the wall and dangle my feet over the ledge, just a few feet from the grassy slope that rolled down into the valley below. In the darkness, I would watch the lights as they twinkled on the Mid-Hudson Bridge and listen to the wind as it kicked up along the river. As they danced in the distance, I would pretend their steady glow was that of flickering Christmas lights as my heart ached to return to my loved ones and the comfort of the same, old traditions that would play out back home.

These were the nights when I felt most alone, so far from every anchor and foundation that had supported me thus far. Without these stabilizing forces, and their memory drifting further in my mind as my sights lingered on the flickering lights in the distance, my mind drifted with the waters to some rather dark places. My fears seized me once again and in the theater of my mind they constructed scenarios of a Marist without me. I wondered how long my projects would last without me there to run about tending to them. How quickly would my mark fade if I was no longer around? How long would it be until it was as though I was never even there?

It was always in thinking of my family that I managed to pull out of this stupor and trudge ahead to face one more day. Had it not been for the intervention of some rather tenacious individuals, however, I am not sure that I would have been able to overcome this prolonged loneliness on my own. I was pulled from my comfort zone and shaken from my self-pity by a persistent and incredibly loyal group of peers that would soon become my closest friends. One of my former roommates, Mr. Switzerland; an upperclassman girl from the band that took to looking after us; and her friend in the education department began filling the time that I would otherwise spend on my own. They came knocking on my door to pull me from my silence. Although our personalities did not always align, they helped me to challenge, and eventually overcome, the weighty expectations that I had piled on top of myself.

I found that I could confide in them all of my hopes and ambitions for the S.G.A. and receive their honest and sincere feedback in return. They even took on active roles as officers in the Safety & Security committee and continued to look out for me as I began to wade deeper into the realm of campus politics, playing the part of my closest advisers. It was a pleasant change to come out of a late meeting and have trusted voices to bounce ideas off, or simply eat a meal without sitting alone. They also helped me to appreciate how narrowly I had focused on my S.G.A. related ambitions, catching just how far I had drifted into a world all my own. They provided me with honest criticism when I stepped out of line or tried to take on too much, and encouraged me when I began dreaming of that higher office.

They anchored me back into reality and helped me to reclaim a much needed sense of perspective.

Even so, I managed to leave a bit of my own mark on them as well. Years later, as we watched another generation of students launch their campaigns for the presidency, I brought the three of them along with me to a "Meet the Candidates" event. One by one they proceeded to question each of the three student body presidential candidates, and I enjoyed listening to their detailed assessment of each contender on our way out the door. Their knowledge of student politics had grown to rival my own. Indeed, one of the candidates later approached me to say that the questions presented by my trio of inquisitors were among the most rigorous interviews they had faced since seeking office. If they could win their votes, they told me, they knew their campaign had a sturdy leg to stand on.

Together, we were the "Core Four", the foundation of my social network. These close friends not only provided me with an escape from S.G.A. life, but also helped me to find the feeling of acceptance that had eluded me to this point in my undergraduate career. Though I could work and get along with others, I never allowed myself to feel as though the people around me truly enjoyed my company. It was not until this motely crew worked their way past these instinctive defenses that I began to let my guard down further.

Through their own connections and the comfort they fostered, my social circle began to grow. An upperclassman from the I.T. program, a friend of Mr. Switzerland, joined our Safety & Security board as a regular fixture. The upper-class girls' housemates adopted my old roommate and me as wards under their care, taking an active role in looking out for us as we grew into our own. As they each began to play a more reoccurring part in my narrative, I began spending less time sitting out by the river.

Facing the fears that led me to that point was far from easy, and recognizing that something was wrong in the first place proved to be an even greater challenge. It is only with the benefit of hindsight that I have come to appreciate just how truly indebted I am to these individuals. In focusing so narrowly on a single goal, I had overlooked the other, crucial needs for personal and emotional fulfillment that played a part in shaping my overall well-being. Sophomore year would prove to be the lowest point in my collegiate career, and perhaps the darkest period of my life to date. I emerged from this episode with a newfound appreciation for self-reflection and the need for balance in one's life. I realized that it was o.k. to set aside time for myself and my interests, occasionally putting the S.G.A. on the backburner. From that point on, I began to lighten up a bit more, worrying less about looming deadlines and stopping to appreciate the beauty in a bigger picture. It was not necessarily the presidency that I was after, but a legacy as a leader that others could respect and look up to.

Only in being true to myself could I hope to attain it.

Lessons Learned

As the consequences of ignoring my own emotional well-being reached their boiling point, I was forced to reassess not only my place within the student government, but our campus community. I count myself very fortunate to have come across such a supportive group of friends at a time when I needed them most, recognizing that I would have been in serious trouble if I was left to grapple with the weight of these demons on my own. As I said before, those little issues we encounter in our lives risk growing into greater specters if left unchecked.

I learned early in my career that leaders recognize it is not simply a matter of *if* you will be faced with making a tough call but *when*. A decision is made no less difficult by kicking it down the road. Whether you are the manager of a large office or a resident senator on a small campus, we are inevitably tasked with making painful choices. In these moments, we come to realize that sitting at the top of the chain of command carries its disadvantages as well. In many cases, there is no one else to turn to in making these calls. Thus, great leaders learn to balance the need for deliberation against the demand for action.

Indeed, sitting on an issue for too long can spawn additional, unintended consequences. Therefore, great leaders develop a strong sense of timing to feel for the right moment to render their judgment. It is a delicate balance that sets aside enough time to review the underlying details of a matter considerably, if not thoroughly, and devise a final plan with enough time left over to initiate, implement, and review. This process is not restricted to navigating professional ultimatums; each point in the decision-making process represents a valuable step in assessing life goals and choices that can help to keep us on track and in tune with our personal needs.

Be it something as small as choosing a fresh salad over a juicy hamburger or sitting out a campus event to catch up on some much needed sleep, part of becoming a responsible adult involves taking over the reigns as the keeper of your well-being. From time to time, that means making a difficult call between a desirable reward and an undesirable necessity. In these situations, it is just as important to take the time to weigh your options and reflect on the outcomes to ensure your house is in order.

By way of example, my rising status within the S.G.A. caused me to feel that I had to keep up regular appearances at as many campus functions as possible. While I initially pushed myself to attend more of these events as a way to overcome my fear of large social functions, the mounting pressures that I piled on top of myself eventually led to a sort of reprogramming. My expectations evolved into a mental mandate, making me feel as though I was in the wrong when I occasionally had to sit out of the action. In time, I became so used to attending these events that I would feel slightly sick or guilty whenever I was forced to stay home. It began to feel like I was playing hooky every time I decided to say "no" and dedicate some time to myself. Only after approaching the brink of a mental breakdown did I realize that it was o.k. for me to pass up the occasional S.G.A. event to have dinner with my friends or simply enjoy some much needed quiet time on my own.

Regardless of your level of involvement, it is imperative that you take an occasional "mental health break" by setting aside some time to get yourself back on an even keel. Growing up, my parents afforded my brother and me the opportunity to take one or two "mental health days" throughout the school year. We learned early on to tune in to our sense of well-being and sound the alarm when we felt like things were reaching their boiling points. Although it took some fine-tuning to get myself back in touch with this fundamental sense of awareness, appreciating the need for the right amount of "me time" became a valuable component in my approach to student leadership. As the years rolled on, and my schedule continued to swell, I learned to block off an entire day here and there for social activities with my friends, or set aside some personal time to catch up on individual hobbies and projects. These little retreats into the quiet of my own mind helped me to prioritize my lingering tasks and form concrete plans of action.

Having already pulled myself out of an isolation spiral with the intervention of the other members of the Core Four, however, I also recognized the slippery slope that presented itself in this approach. Although there were certainly times when I simply felt that I had to shut myself away in my room and retreat to the quiet of my own mind, these more solemn retreats were far less frequent than they had been. Instead, most of my new escapes from my professional routines involved the Core Four or our other friends around campus. They were no longer sought as a means to escape the stress of life around me, but as an opportunity to recharge my mental batteries and prepare for the next round. There is a big difference between taking a break and retreating altogether.

As you continue on your leadership journey, self-reflection will continue to be one of your most crucial tools. While you should listen to yourself above all others when it comes to determining when and how to act, you must also remain open to the insights of those closest to you. Try to be cognoscente of your own needs and limitations, but never shut out the opportunity of an intervening voice to shine a light on an alternate perspective. As you strive to carve out personal time to mend your spirit and strengthen your resolve, do not delve too deeply into the safety of individual retreats. Always seek balance between the comfort of isolation and the invigorating stimulus of social engagement, even if it is by simply reaching out to just one other person. After all, the person you touch might need it more than you can ever know.

THE LEADERSHIP PROFILE: *Exercise Five*

To remind ourselves of the importance in carving out little swatches of time for *us* along this journey, I would like you to take a moment and draw a little box somewhere on your leadership profile. In this space, write a list of activities that you enjoy doing which have *nothing* to do with your goals or current responsibilities. Instead, this space should be solely for your interests & hobbies, a retreat from the stresses of the self-refinement process that acts as a personal sanctuary. These are opportunities for you to step away from your public/professional persona and simply be *you*.

As you move forward, make sure that at least one of these activities is scheduled in your monthly planner. Should you find yourself stressed or anxious, work more of these items into the mix as frequently as possible. Just as even the most skilled divers must inevitably surface for air, no leader can bear the weight of their position for a full term, let alone their entire lives. We must all take a moment to set down that load, gather our strength as well as our wits, and soothe the soul before undertaking the next, great leg of our journey.

Mark or color this box so that it always stands out to you, and never forget that even these guilty little pleasures have a very important part to play in crafting a balanced profile.

6 – The Fall

"Fiat justitia, ruat coelum
[Let justice come, though the Heavens fall].
My toast would be, may our country be always
successful, but whether successful or otherwise,
always right."
– John Quincy Adams

As my sophomore year neared its home stretch, yet another generation of S.G.A. leaders braced themselves for that career-defining race. Veterans of the S.G.A. proved to be rather adept at picking out who was scurrying to forge the necessary alliances and garner support in an impending bid for the student body presidency. It was a skill hardened by participating in the general election process a number of times themselves. More importantly, one could develop keen eyes for spotting those young leaders who demonstrated the drive and potential to thrive within student government; the upperclassmen would track their progress with great interest as they grew from wide-eyed newcomers into more established leaders.

It was a process that began with each new academic year, as the sitting administration was greeted with a crop of talented freshmen who were driven to serve their campus community. In watching enough of these contests unfold, one began to notice certain patterns, detecting the traits that could help an individual attain success or steer their campaigns towards jeopardy. We thought we had seen everything.

The election of 2011 challenged that perception, and proved to be one of the most controversial cycles in our campus' history. Still the subject of discussion at S.G.A. reunions, its lingering scars have influenced every race that has followed. But in the calm that preceded this storm, life at Marist marched on with the tranquil pace of the river that ran beside its grounds. While most students were enjoying their winter breaks, members of the student government were finalizing their re-election strategies and preparing for their return to the campus. February brought us more than Valentine's cards and the hopes of warmer weather; the start of the spring semester meant that election season would soon be upon us.

Campus-wide elections for S.G.A. officers were part of a regimented process that unfolded according to a specific timetable outlined in our By-Laws. In those days, they afforded very little wiggle room. The administration's Elections Commissioner was tasked with coordinating these mandated events according to a series of deadlines that left no room for error. Although there was no official start date listed among the detailed requirements in our By-Laws, the process would typically kick off in early February in order to adequately address each required step, as well as afford additional time to the elected for training prior to the traditional transition between administrations in April. This included just a little more than a weeklong period for individual campaigning, broader community outreach events by the S.G.A. as a whole, candidate speeches, debates, and the voting period itself. Missing just one requirement in the series could mean immediate disqualification from the race.

To formally kick-off their campaigns, aspiring candidates would have to attend one of three information sessions hosted by the Elections

Commissioner. At the end of these sessions, attendees were asked to sign a document specifying their intended office in order to receive a petition for candidacy. With this document in hand, they would then have to go out and obtain signatures from their constituency to validate their candidacy. To be officially counted, however, completed petitions had to be submitted to the Elections Commissioner's mailbox in our office no later than 5:00pm on the Friday night before the designated campaign week.

The subsequent Saturday would offer a nerve-wracking respite before all campaigns were officially given the green light to begin actively lobbying on Sunday evening. Then, for a period of seven full days, election frenzy would sweep into high gear as posters, t-shirts, and promises for a better future littered the campus. At 11:59PM the following Sunday, all campaigns were required to come to an abrupt halt; active campaigning was strictly prohibited as voting commenced for the next three-day period.

As we entered the 2011 campaign season, it seemed safe to say that at least two candidates would be competing for that top seat: My predecessor, our former Senate Speaker, and the resident senator from the junior class that had nominated me to replace her. Once again, I was faced with a very tough choice between two strong incumbents, as they had both gone off to create detailed, yet unique, campus records through the course of their collegiate careers. Prior to traveling abroad, the former Senate Speaker was a leading voice on our campus for sustainability initiatives and environmental programs. The resident senator from the junior class, on the other hand, had served as the chair of the campus Dining Hall committee and even founded the student Booster Club that rallied behind our various athletic teams. Although neither side had officially declared their candidacy, members of the student government community began to anticipate a close race—but nothing particularly surprising.

Like the flicker of an ice cap on a dark horizon, a relatively minor blip intruded upon the commencement of the election cycle. Once the last information session had closed and petitions were in circulation, there appeared to be a slight change to the expected line-up. While the resident senator had formally declared his intent to run for the office of student body president, the Senate Speaker had not. Instead, she would be running as a part of a ticket. Her close friend, the president of the Class of 2012, had recruited her as a prospective E.V.P. in his own bid for the office. With a well-known and highly respected R.A. pegged as the resident senator's running mate, excitement for the coming race was nearing its tipping point.

All four names expected to appear on the ballot for the top seats in the S.G.A. that year were well known around campus for their extensive involvement. While some within the organization made their allegiances clear by openly endorsing one team or the other, many of us opted to sit back and look on with quiet anticipation. As the sitting Senate Speaker, I felt it best to avoid throwing out an endorsement too readily, understanding that the race would be close enough and that no additional fuel would be required to stoke the fire that was building beneath our community. This decision to sit back was also prompted, in part, by my connection to both sides, feeling deeply torn between openly discarding one in favor of the other. So, like many of my peers, I remained quiet.

That is, however, until things once again took a rather sudden and unexpected turn. While everyone was so intently focused on the looming race, none of us picked up on one, lingering thread that threatened to

95

unravel the whole contest. As the deadline for the submission of campaign petitions approached, it did not seem to register with anyone that only one team had submitted their paperwork. No one had been attentively looking out at the looming shadow on the horizon.

Though unusual, it did not raise any immediate red flags. As all campaigning was prohibited until the official kick-off on Sunday evening, the timeline for completing this final requirement was left largely to the preference of the individual candidates. While some preferred to get it out of the way as quickly as possible, others would request multiple petition forms to safely surpass the mandatory minimum signature count. So long as they were submitted before the deadline, it did not matter either way.

It was not until Friday evening, moments after that deadline had passed, that a minor bureaucratic hurdle opened one of the most chaotic chapters in our S.G.A. history. In that moment, as the Elections Commissioner waited in the S.G.A. office for any last-minute submissions under the watchful eyes of a small crowd of curious onlookers, the 2011 race for student body president came to a close. The iceberg had pierced our side.

The Class of 2012 president/Senate Speaker team had not submitted their petitions. Their representative arrived at the S.G.A. office with one complete set of signatures—just meeting the minimum requirement— roughly ten minutes *after* the deadline had officially passed. Despite only narrowly missing the deadline, the verdict from the Elections Commissioner was quick and absolute; the By-Laws simply did not afford any wiggle room. At that time, the elections process was so rigidly outlined in our governing documents that the role of the Elections Commissioner was truly one-part timekeeper and one-part referee. Petitions were required of all candidates prior to the established deadline. There would be no exceptions.

Adding to the swelling drama, nearly all of the witnesses present in the S.G.A. office at that time were key members or supporters of the opposing campaign's team, further backing the Commissioner into a tight corner. Unable to acquiesce to their requests for an appeal or further reconsideration, the Elections Commissioner disqualified the Class of 2012 president/Senate Speaker team on the spot. The remaining team would continue their race uncontested.

It did not take long for an appeal to the Judicial Board to follow. With a formal challenge submitted to the Chief Justice and his team, the elections were temporarily suspended and members of the campus community found themselves faced with ample time to debate the merits of re-opening the race. While many accepted that it was the one team's responsibility to ensure that their documents were completed and submitted on time, the idea of an uncontested race for the most important position in the S.G.A. did not sit well with many members of the campus community.

Those who most vehemently protested the disqualification did not appreciate the fact that their representation could hinge so gravely upon a technicality or, depending on the outcome of the appeal, an administrative decision. These debates sparked the first, real discussion on campaign reform for our campus. Not wanting to be locked into any future uncontested races, the student body began demanding that mechanisms be put into place that would allow for a more discretionary review—and even total reconsideration in these types of cases—or the creation of additional avenues for candidates to enter the race when there was no contest. While these were valid proposals, they were only loosely tied to the matter at hand. Even if the S.G.A. were to consider and expeditiously act upon such policy amendments, the fate of the present race would have to depend on *current* policies and procedures.

As the issue presently set before them first arose from the procedures outlined in the governing documents of the S.G.A., the Judicial Board held jurisdiction over the dispute. In such cases, this board was tasked with leading a series of investigations, reviewing case documents, and examining witness testimony in order to compile enough evidence to render a decision. Accordingly, the process took time. It was not only exhaustive, but depended upon the combined availability of the individual Justices who, less we forget, were still full-time students.

Once all of these individuals were brought together, and the necessary information was collected, the scope of their deliberations was still strictly limited to that of a procedural review. As in any court of law, their deliberations could not be subjective; their determinations had to be linked to campus common law arising from past determinations or remain otherwise defendable by the existing doctrines of the organization. That is, much like the appellate courts in our U.S. legal system, the decision of the Judicial Board would have to be based upon a technical error, omission, or oversite. It was a matter of determining *what was* and not asking *what if.*

In that respect, the board had to isolate its thoughts from the mere prospect of an uncontested race; determining whether or not the student body would be better served by reopening the race was not the question that had been placed before them. A decision warranting judicial intervention would have to stem from a gross dereliction of duty or deviation from student government policy. There was no way to sift the water out of our bow once the iceberg had done its work.

Nonetheless, the seriousness of these claims did not only weigh heavily upon those students who had now been handed the responsibility of levying judgment against the actions of their peers and deciding the fate of the race. As the case progressed, it became harder and harder for many of our S.G.A. members to maintain their neutrality, to stay silent. Since the dispute involved at least three, active members of the administration, everyone in our office had been personally impacted by the matter in some way. Battle lines were being drawn within our little world, boundaries that would soon divide our entire campus. Those who understood the unfolding process raced to one camp or the other to offer their counsel. As some members of the Judicial Board also found themselves personally linked to candidates involved in the dispute, they hurried to sequester themselves so as to preserve what remained of their impartiality.

As the episode continued to balloon, members of the College Administration entered the fray as advisers to the Judicial Board and other top-tier S.G.A. officers battling the public relations backlash. They hoped to ensure that our existing policies were being adhered to, as well as provide additional support and resources in navigating a deeply emotional—and increasingly public—event. Their intervention, however, was not received warmly by all members of the campus community. As reported by *The Circle* in a March 1, 2011 article, the intervention of the College Administration had already been cited as a cause of action in the aggrieved team's complaint. Critics asserted that their involvement in the S.G.A.'s decision to uphold the initial pronouncement of the Elections Commissioner was a desecration of the organization's autonomy, and that the matter should have immediately proceeded to the Judicial Board without such interference.

As the Judicial Board began their deliberations, the eyes of the community fell upon our current S.G.A. leadership. Internal divisions had begun to spread throughout the campus, as students following the case steadily gravitated toward one side or the other. *The Circle* reported on the rising tensions, with several members of the S.G.A. openly condemning the Commissioner's decision to close the race. As reported in their article from March 3, 2011, "SGA recognizes its faults", several members of the sitting administration expressed their disdain for the call to allow the election to proceed uncontested.

In reality, there was little that could have been done differently. There was no emergency measure to enact or executive order to pass down; nothing short of an amendment to our governing documents could create an alternate route to candidacy. Even then, the passage of such a measure—which would undoubtedly take considerable time to draft, review and execute—could not be applied retroactively. Furthermore, in adopting a hypothetical perspective that assumes that such drastic measures were an option, the execution of such endeavors would require us to restart the entire elections process over from square one. No matter how unfavorable the prospect of an uncontested race seemed, there was simply no looking past the truth. The current election cycle was lost. The ship was going down.

The apparent hopelessness of the situation did not do much to help diminish other, lingering frustrations toward the S.G.A. Many of our fellow students still saw us as an exclusive organization, a glorified clique on campus. Aghast at the number of vacancies in other areas of the ballot, many asked why the S.G.A. had not taken proactive measures to recruit contestants. In truth, we had made extensive recruitment attempts throughout the year, including "dorm storming", the coordination of targeted, town hall meetings in freshman residence areas. None of it, however, had much of an impact on our community's historically minimal participatory interest in student governance. In this respect, we were not entirely alone; our apathetic approach to S.G.A. elections was consistent with typical trends demonstrated by student communities on college campuses throughout the country.

To make matters worse, the same stringent deadlines that had contributed to this debacle also made it impossible to know for sure whether or not a race was contested until campaigning was slated to begin. As candidacies could be confirmed right up to the last minute, and the doors closed firmly once campaigning had begun, there was no way to collect a proper headcount until we were well underway.

As emotions became so inextricably tied to the arguments surrounding the case, it became all the more difficult for individuals to look past the simple cases of human error that had led us so deeply into this maze in the first place. It took a simple mistake for us to realize how horribly entangled and unmoving our own policies had become.

We were being strung along through a Rube Goldberg machine of policies and procedures, watching helplessly as the case proceeded from one stage to the next in accordance with the stark and unyielding text of our Constitution and By-Laws. Interviews of witnesses and named parties were

101

conducted by a panel of administrators and Judicial Board members, chaired by the Chief Justice. As these sessions proceeded, additional evidence was being collected from around campus as supporters of the Class of 2012 president's campaign began collecting statements and submissions of their own. With the Judicial Board proceedings well underway, these groups sought to disqualify the remaining team for alleged infractions committed during the hiatus, in the hopes of clearing the slate and forcing the committee's hand in calling for a complete do-over.

Such was the intense desire to upend the present process; if one candidate would not be restored, then both would tumble. In the end, however, there was not enough evidence to warrant the disqualification of another team, and the facts as they stood could not save the other's campaign. The Chief Justice upheld the decision of the Commissioner; the race was officially closed by March of 2011.

Thus, the remaining races for open positions were given the green light to pick up where they had left off, and the campus transitioned into campaign week at last. Nevertheless, for those who opposed the disqualification from the beginning, the battle was not yet over. Students organized protests in the hopes of spurring an administrative override, changing their Facebook profile pictures to a stock yearbook photo of an individual with their eyes and mouth scribbled out behind the bolded text: "No Choice, No Voice". As major campaign events approached, these hardened idealists prepared to follow the examples of John Stewart and Stephen Colbert at the national level by holding rallies "to restore sanity" in the shadow of an election that they so vehemently opposed.

Despite the noble intent of the orchestraters and many of their participants, these protests quickly took a nasty turn. As tempers flared, personal attacks were levied against the incoming student body president, executive vice president, and the Elections Commissioner. Deeply personal ties had prevented some people from separating their anger against the outcome of the appeal from their feelings toward these individuals. Rumors and misunderstandings surrounding the election process caused many to believe that the disqualification and subsequent closure of the race were part of a personal political attack, rather than a mandated action.

Accusations of political conspiracy began to spread as the friendship between the Commissioner and the incoming student body president was used to propagate allegations of internal collusion—an S.G.A. coup. In further crossing the boundaries of civil discourse, some attacked the Commissioner for his personal relation to a member of the campus faculty. They alleged that this connection was the reason that his decision was so readily upheld by the College Administration and no additional course of action was pursued. These were, of course, utterly false assumptions. The emotional force behind the race had stirred the campus' imaginations into a frenzy.

It became difficult to maintain a positive outlook during this time. None of us were truly innocent in allowing the S.G.A. to reach this point. We all shared in the responsibility of monitoring our governing documents to catch and correct issues like this before they grew into larger debacles. We all shared in the responsibility of steering our campus and keeping a trained eye on the horizon for the potential obstacles that laid ahead.

Moreover, whether you agreed with them or not, you could not help but feel for both teams of candidates.

Despite the rigors of the race, the student body presidential contest was seen as the capstone to a dedicated S.G.A. career. The unfolding turmoil would not only blemish that memory for the four of them, but loiter in the collective conscience of our organization for generations to come. As the individual stuck at the center of it all, I sympathized with our Elections Commissioner above most.

Having performed his duties according to his interpretation of the By-Laws, abiding by those harsh rules which left little room for his own discretion, he stood resolutely behind his decision with the utmost confidence and an honorable sense of conviction. Despite facing considerable pressure to recant, of which there was plenty from both inside and outside of our organization, he did not waver.

The disdain for his decision, however, was palpable. The campus community found it difficult to separate the individual from the call, resulting in a series of personal attacks that made this election so infamously ugly. In the end, the lingering bad blood that had pooled throughout the race proved too deep to wade through. The Commissioner would not be invited back to serve in the coming administration, and instead chose to retire from the S.G.A. altogether at the end of the year.

Though this marked a rather turbulent ending for one chapter in his life, he did not let it define his story. He would go on to pursue a number of opportunities outside of the S.G.A. as an active member of the campus community, eventually expanding upon his own passion for politics to found the campus' Young Democrats Club. Additionally, outside of student governance, his local projects and service initiatives continued to flourish. As I began to think about how I wanted my own S.G.A. story to unfold in its final chapters, I always considered our Commissioner's firm stand throughout the 2011 election to be a truly inspirational example to follow.

This episode would also mark the final chapter in the S.G.A. careers of the president of the Class of 2012 and our former Senate Speaker. Like many of the candidates to miss their shot at this top office, they spent their senior years in pursuit of other opportunities around campus. Each of them a devoted leader in their own right, they would continue to impact our community through clubs and organizations beyond the confines of the S.G.A. Indeed, this had become somewhat of a pattern. I cannot speak for these two, particular candidates when it comes to speculating about the underlying motivations that drive so many to walk away from the organization after losing the presidential race. In observing a number of candidates come and go, however, I believe that the strain of the race itself plays a considerable part. The ambition to serve the student body as the head of the S.G.A. becomes a deeply personal goal, a testament to one's devotion throughout years of hard work and volunteerism. As such, the race can be a relentless endurance test set against a battery of individual scrutiny and heated accusations that not only strains the mind, but the spirit as well. After bearing the weight of such an onslaught, one could certainly understand the appeal of a quiet retirement.

While history proved to be far kinder to the remaining candidates, the success of the coming 2011-2012 Administration is due in no small part to their dedicated efforts toward addressing the lingering concerns that had bubbled forth from the election process.

As the student body president and executive vice president-elect, they chose to face the controversy head on. Taking ownership of a bad situation, they worked to develop a proactive approach toward addressing student concerns. On what would have been their speech night—and despite not having to speak at all due to their lack of formal opposition—they opened the floor to questions and comments from the audience. Students were given the chance to voice their anger and concern over the faulty process, and the duo was able to demonstrate their commitment to building a better system during their administration. Through this discussion, they acknowledged that the process could be better and devoted themselves to addressing the changes that our community had demanded during the race. In setting the tone for his coming administration, the student body president-elect proved that he was not going to shy away from the harsh realities that had surfaced. The S.G.A.'s place within our community was now in jeopardy; it would take a dedicated effort to restore the faith of our constituents.

If he was looking for a strong example to follow, he certainly had one in his predecessor. With the end of his term marred by the election controversy, the student body president of the 2010-2011 Administration faced the situation with the utmost dignity and poise. Having been asked early on to recuse himself from the turmoil and let the Judicial Board take the reigns, it would have been all too easy for the S.B.P. to relegate himself to the sidelines for the remainder of his term. Though he had made a point of maintaining his neutrality in the unfolding dispute, having worked closely with both teams throughout his years of service, he would not back down from defending the S.G.A. Instead, he inspired an outpouring of support for the organization as a whole, championing the core principles of student governance. Indeed, after rising steadily through the ranks of the organization since his freshman year, the outgoing student body president had developed an unquestionable loyalty to, and deep love for, the Student Government Association. Rather than sit aside helplessly while the fate of the election was passed into the hands of another board or committee, he focused his efforts on addressing the underlying issue of communal morale by trying to share his love of the organization with his community.

Our student body president for the 2010-2011 Administration recognized that the S.G.A. was not without its faults, but also understood that any lasting changes would have to come from within the organization itself. Leading by example, he inspired his fellow officers to take responsibility for their influence over the organization and to work together in devising solutions that would lead to lasting reform. He was our shepherd, a devoted leader who wanted nothing more than to see those following in his stead to flourish in their own ways. This passionate, reassuring spirit would not only help to pull the S.G.A. back from the brink in facing the backlash of the 2011 election, but also serve as the foundation for his greatest legacy on our campus, the Civility Campaign.

Lessons Learned

Between my earlier soul-searching, the intervention of the Core Four, and the political turmoil that rounded out the year, I can certainly say that my sophomore term was the most transformative period of my undergraduate career. Though the 2009-2010 Administration had braced against its share of ominous winds—the "readership" program initiated by the S.G.A. to provide free copies of nationally syndicated papers to students left the 2010-2011 Administration with a staggering bill, for tens of thousands of dollars, which subsequently prompted its cancellation in the following term—the collapse of the 2011 elections swelled upon us like a maelstrom. The experience our organization had garnered in coordinating charitable responses to national and international tragedies provided us with some bearing in coordinating a response to such a large-scale, communal event. Yet, nothing could prepare us for shaking off a blow that had landed so close to home. We were not accustomed to working under the kind of intense focus that was suddenly thrust upon us when our members began turning on one another in the midst of such a divisive incident.

Civil discourse had been obscured by the deeply emotional responses that stemmed from the heart of this controversy. Students reacting to the notion of an uncontested race fought back against the perceived threats of corruption and cronyism. Student leaders, hating to see close friends so quickly denied a chance at their dream, fervently sought any opportunity to change the game. And as all of this unfolded, our organization was tasked with deciding what was right & just. Would *justice* be found in discarding these emotional pleas and simply playing by the book, or would the *right* call be to discard the established protocol and yield to the sudden demands of the vocal majority? It was not an easy choice.

In the end, I do believe that the Elections Commissioner made the correct call; the rules as they were laid out at that time simply did not afford an alternative. While there should have been a mechanism in place to ensure that our races did not pass uncontested so easily, turning the rules on their head in order to immediately affect our desired change would have been a terrible way to go about doing things. In the ensuing years, we would continue to throw around ideas such as maintaining a "write-in" line on the ballot or developing a written protocol for assessing and reopening elections prior to starting the campaign week. We never lost sight of the students' demands for change or our responsibility to follow up on them. In the following year, the student body president would bring forth a plan for comprehensive election reform that was readily seized upon by our administration.

Unfortunately, maintaining the ties of civility that bound our organization together proved to be a more difficult puzzle, as flaring tempers had led some to cast aside logical arguments in favor of making personal attacks. Writing this in the midst of a national election cycle that has grown all the more infamous for its vitriolic rhetoric and childish attacks makes me think that this is not solely a lesson suited for our student leaders.

Indeed, it can be difficult to ignore the naturally defensive impulse that creeps up when someone disagrees with us. It is nothing personal; differences in opinion are as natural as differences in eye color. This act of self-control becomes all the more arduous when the weight of emotional ties continually pulls against our composure. Many of us open ourselves to the scrutiny of an election process in seeking a public office because we care a great deal about the work that we hope to accomplish. We are willing to face direct attacks and personal gibes because this momentary pain is outweighed by the sense of accomplishment that can only be found through public work. This sense of pride also breeds investment, which makes it even harder to distinguish professional disagreements from personal ones.

There is no miraculous strategy for overcoming the temptation to give in to these basic impulses. Instead, I will share some advice from my childhood that has proven particularly helpful in navigating my own career in local politics. Having always been taught to take the high road in a disagreement and to value my dignity over the fleeting joy of a momentary victory, I knew that there were simply some fights that were not worth starting—let alone dragging out to a bloody finish. As my grandfather would always ask my brother and me when we broke into some petty quarrel, "who's going to be the bigger man?" His prodding evoked a simple realization, that there was more honor to be won in swallowing our pride and letting one slide than stooping right down to the other's level to launch a counterattack.

With this lesson in mind, I approached the process of drafting and defending my public image as though I was developing a professional brand. I took the time early on in my career to set out the types of characteristics that I wanted to be known for, and let these goals frame my moral compass in approaching my professional decisions. Most importantly, when the occasional shot was fired across my bow, I always paused to remember my grandfather's words. I would not throw away all that I had built for the simple satisfaction of revenge.

This prioritization has helped me to assess which routes were most in line with my principles and which were not. These regular reality checks have also helped me to safeguard against individual mission drift and losing sight of the broader values that have played such an important role in guiding me to this point in my career. Above all else, I have committed myself to conducting my offices with patience, transparency, and humility—the pillars of true servant leadership. When one's convictions are so clear, and dearly held, they cannot be diminished by defeat or failure, only further refined. They are the tethers by which we learn to pull ourselves up when we fall.

THE LEADERSHIP PROFILE: *Exercise Six*

Think about a time when you have failed at something in your life. Trust me; we have all got at least one moment that fits the bill. In my experience, the line between success and failure is rarely a distinct one. In nearly every instance that I can recall, there comes a moment where the glass shatters, the pieces slip off the board, and you just *know* that things are headed south. Oddly enough, these telltale signs also appear just prior to our moments of triumph. We just tend not to dwell on them for too long when everything works out in the end.

This crucial juncture, when all the wheels begin to come off, is a defining moment in times of success and failure alike. If we resign ourselves to the futility of the moment, then we have ultimately accepted our loss. Only in pushing through with the struggle, carrying on in the face of the growing shadow of defeat, can we hope to salvage redemption from an otherwise hopeless situation.

What often proves to be more difficult than holding tightly to our faith in these moments, however, is staying true to our convictions. When all appears to be lost, easy escapes may often present themselves at the cost of your original goal or guiding principles. As your moral compass may have very well steered you into this mess in the first place, it can also be very tempting to abandon ship and swim for a new shoreline altogether.

In looking back on your example of a past loss or failure, how did you approach the situation? Did you throw your hands up and accept defeat? Did you switch sides and abandon your guiding principle? If so, how did that make you feel? Take a moment to look back and ask yourself, *"What the heck happened?"*

Our darkest moments are often our most impactful. Just as the 2011 election would influence the policies and practices of our organization for years to come, these little moments present new seeds wisdom that linger and take root in our minds throughout our careers. What did you learn from your mistakes? How do these lessons relate to the strengths and weaknesses that you outlined in Exercise One? Looking back at your goals and mission, were there any lessons that you learned through the experience that might better guide you in achieving these aims?

Mark a special place for mistakes and failures somewhere on your profile. For all the pain they may bring initially, these scars become an important part of who we are and all that we hope to be.

7 – THE ANSWER

"We cannot live only for ourselves.
A thousand fibers connect us with our fellow man."
–Henry Melville

A defining characteristic of our campus was its incredible spirit of community. As a fellow member of the S.G.A. once noted, "We may not know what this campus will look like in ten or fifteen years, but we will always know what it will feel like," the feeling of coming home. That sense of warmth and belonging beneath the banner of "Red Fox" pride was the secret ingredient that helped our student body to come together and share in some truly stellar triumphs, as well as weather some particularly devastating blows. Like all communities, after all, ours was prone to negativity and acts of cowardice that threatened to dull the shimmering luster of our collegiate family.

From the moment social media sites first sprung into being, the luxury of quick and open communication has been paired with the added risk for anonymous scrutiny. Just as it became easier to share good news, so too could individuals effortlessly launch reputation-shattering attacks from the safety of their digital perches. Before my arrival, the College had already squared off successfully against similar attacks. The student body had rallied against anonymous comments and personal jabs posted to a digital message board just a year or two prior. The forum allowed users to brazenly admonish their peers behind the secrecy of a keyboard. Storming the digital dais, a handful of users launched a virulent assault against the College and its students without hesitation.

114

As individuals were singled out, and some turned to their laptops to launch their own counter-attacks against perceived perpetrators, the S.G.A. found itself at the center of a growing feud that threatened to shatter their shared spirit of community. Borrowing from the wisdom of Dr. Martin Luther King, Jr., the administration at that time was determined to drive out hate with love and developed a series of programs that would allow students to re-establish that spirit of cohesion by countering the negative comments with ones of thanks, acceptance, and admiration. Though they did not know it at the time, the student leaders that organized the first response to widespread cyber bullying on our campus were also laying out the foundation for one of our most impactful S.G.A. legacies.

Sadly, it did not take long for the digital beast to rear its ugly head once more. Following quickly in the footsteps of its predecessor, a new website nestled itself into the popular culture of our community just a few years later during my sophomore term. Having watched this scenario unfold once before as an underclassman, our student body president for the 2010-2011 Administration was prepared to meet the rising challenge when it first revealed itself early on in his term. Having seen how rapidly these negative attitudes regrouped in the face of the S.G.A.'s past efforts, he concluded that a single series of activities simply would not be enough to stifle such a relentless foe. Instead, he came to the Senate and the College Administration with the idea of forming a "Civility Campaign" to establish an ongoing partnership between the students and the faculty in an effort to continually safeguard our spirit of community.

Though the idea initially received unanimous support in the Senate, debates quickly arose as to how the Campaign should be coordinated and led. Some felt that it should be run primarily through the S.G.A. as a subcommittee, spurring a sense of ownership and responsibility for the maintenance of the program from the student body. Others believed that it should be run as an administrative project or assigned to a member of the faculty, in order to ensure its long-term sustainability. Those directly involved with the creation of the program settled on striking a balance between these two viewpoints.

The first Civility Campaign committee brought together members of the faculty, administration, student body, and campus ministry under the co-direction of the student body president and an Assistant Dean of Student Affairs. As the Senate Speaker, I accompanied the S.B.P. and our Director of Public Relations as the first representatives from the S.G.A. In addition to student government representation, delegates from clubs and other organizations with a direct impact on the campus climate and culture—such as Greek life and athletics—joined us at the table. With each segment of the campus community well represented, we sought to create a firm foundation for openness, collaboration, and support in enacting our shared vision. As we settled in to our relatively new and undefined roles, however, a sudden tragedy hitting rather close to home would further guide our efforts in defining the mission of the Campaign.

A freshman student at Rutgers University, located in my native state of New Jersey, committed suicide after being publicly outed as a gay man by his roommate and a web camera. The incident sent shockwaves across college campuses throughout the nation. Many of us were fighting our own battles against anonymous animosity, but the public loss of this nearby peer reminded us all just how gravely these attacks could wound a community. Our campus' Lesbian Gay Straight Alliance ("L.G.S.A") wanted to commemorate the occasion with a vigil in his memory, and it was through working together to make their vision a reality that the Civility Campaign truly found its footing.

The S.G.A. afforded the L.G.S.A. access to a whole new network of resources by elevating their program to the highest levels of administrative attention. In working together, we secured the Rotunda, a focal point of the campus' layout, as our venue. Congregants lit candles and sang along with an ensemble of student singers as a member of the campus ministry led us in a collective prayer for peace, kindness, and understanding. Representatives from the L.G.S.A. and other collaborating organizations took to the podium to share their remarks. Among them, the student body president voiced his hope for a community united against these types of cowardly attacks, and the resolve to stand firmly against any such pettiness and vileness that sought to drive our campus apart. He was joined by the president of the Class of 2012 in reminding students that "we have the power to create the atmosphere we want here. This is our home, let's make it that way for everybody." (*The Circle*, "SGA kicks off civility campaign with candlelight vigil", November 11, 2010).

This demonstration of communal unity would also mark the end of the current anonymous message board struggle, as the shaken nerve of the student body solidified into a firm resolve to defend its shared sense of identity. And yet, despite the tremendous strengthening of student spirit, the Civility Campaign began to falter soon thereafter. The committee could not agree on a clear purpose or mission. Without a specific issue to address, conversations began to stall. Instead of continuing with our communal structure, leadership over the Campaign transitioned primarily to the student government and was backed closely by administrative support.

To salvage what little momentum remained, we began hosting monthly programs under the banner of the Civility Campaign, drawing attention to a different issue or charitable organization with each event. While responsibility for the Civility Campaign was initially shared by all three branches of the S.G.A., it eventually found a more lasting home under the Legislative Branch. As Senate Speaker, I was responsible for ensuring that each senator had a committee or project to work on during their term. While this had traditionally involved chairing a committee of their own creation, we expanded the expectations for active involvement to include the responsibility of leading at least one Civility Campaign event during your term as a senator or class president.

The program limped on in this manner throughout the transition phase that took place between the installation of the 2011-2012 Administration and the departure of the 2010-2011 Administration. As the new Executive Board sought to hit the ground running in the aftermath of the election's controversial end, we knew that the Civility Campaign would have an important role to play in addressing those doubts that still lingered in its wake.

In the face of division, we needed to inspire unity and cohesion; the campaign became our focal point in these efforts to reach the student body on a more personal level. Once again, the Campaign would showcase a more collaborative side of the S.G.A., highlighting its ability to work alongside the other segments of our student community. Although now, in recruiting club officers to join us, we would have to go beyond our traditional approach of simply garnering physical attendance at events. Our members had to enact a more personal plea in restoring weakened bonds of trust by engaging them as partners in the process. We were no longer just fighting to ensure the longevity of the campaign, we now found ourselves caught up in a battle to save the credibility of the S.G.A. itself.

The elections debacle had shone a light on the darker side of student ambition, where individual hopes, dreams, and fears can turn a bureaucratic process into a hurricane of emotional drama. This is how the greatest threat to the stability of the S.G.A. struck us not from beyond our borders, but from within the very heart of the organization itself. The resulting emotional rift furthered the ideological division between our members and soured a number of relationships within the sitting administration, causing many of our members to leave after their terms had expired. As a result, the 2011-2012 Administration was tasked with not only training new leadership but also rebuilding a spirit of comradery that would allow us to face our disagreements in a professional manner and prevent these simple differences from driving us further apart.

The incoming administration responded quickly, making tremendous strides toward restoring the S.G.A.'s credibility and internal morale when the student body president for the 2011-2012 Administration fulfilled his promise to reform the election process. At the onset of his term, the Senate approved an amendment to our By-Laws that would remove many of the set deadlines and allow the process to progress in a more fluid fashion, according to the initiative of the individual candidates. That is, rather than set aside one week for petitioning and another for campaigning, petitions would be accepted on a rolling basis, right up to the scheduled speech night. This would give latecomers the opportunity to jump into the race if they felt that a certain office was close to running unopposed or was otherwise underrepresented.

The student body president's plan also allowed candidates to begin campaigning as soon as their petitions were received by the Elections Commissioner, providing them with an added incentive for getting the paperwork out of the way as quickly as possible. When both of these pieces were brought together, the newly proposed elections process would allow us to form a more representative candidate pool by continuing—and even targeting—our recruiting efforts while the campaign period was still underway. Indeed, the transition to a rolling enrollment process afforded the administration more options in addressing the competitiveness of the races by assessing participation rates prior to speech night. This created a potential route for bringing late entries into the race and heading off the specter of potentially uncontested elections. Though our S.G.A. elections have not been entirely without flaws or hiccups since the 2011 incident, they have certainly come a long way from that old, rigid process.

These significant policy revisions were not the only changes brought forth through their reform efforts. After facing significant political pressures following the 2011 election cycle, our former Elections Commissioner was not brought back to the table for reappointment. Rather than simply replace him, however, the new administration considered an entirely new arrangement.

In looking back on the drama of the past year, it was decided that the weight of the burden thrust upon our Commissioner throughout the debacle should not have been borne by one person alone. In response, the new student body president proposed splitting the role into a 3-person "Elections Commission", chaired by an individual who would retain the title of "Elections Commissioner".

In recruiting entirely new talent to manage the elections process, the responsibility of chairing this new division under the S.G.A. was entrusted to a rising sophomore. As the manager of the elections process, she brought a newfound energy and vigor that would help to restore the legitimacy of the races as a true contest. She also motivated the organization to set its sights on a rather lofty goal. Historically, and even nationally, it was unusual for student government races to see a voter turnout above an average of 15% (of the total student population). Seeking to make a profound mark in her first year and overturn the stigma of the preceding races, our new Commissioner pushed the administration to aim for a record-breaking voter turnout of 35% in the upcoming 2012 elections.

We all found ourselves striving to do better, to be better, following the embarrassment brought on by the prior year. The dizzying spectacle had reminded us of our greater purpose in dutifully reviewing the documents and policies with which we were entrusted. We could not assume that all was well simply because the *status quo* appeared to be working. The S.G.A. as a whole needed to adopt a more proactive approach in assessing potential pitfalls and identifying outdated directives before such minor issues could balloon into more drastic episodes.

Furthermore, our new Elections Commissioner recognized the symbolic importance behind ensuring a successful election process for the 2012 cycle. Attaining her goal of a historic participation rate could potentially garner genuine communal excitement in a process that had otherwise been rather disenchanting in the prior term. More importantly, reaching this goal would require the S.G.A. to engage students to not only follow but also participate in the campaign cycle; it served as an additional impetus to step up our public relations initiatives tied to the elections. Attaining this benchmark would do much more than simply spur our collective morale; in bringing the student body together to overcome the wounds of the past, we could all move forward together.

The incident had not only left a lingering mark on the S.G.A., its imprint was felt throughout the campus community. Nonetheless, through coordinated efforts under the banner of the Civility Campaign, we believed that this haunting scar could be substantially diminished. While the student body president's amendments and reorganization efforts helped to direct our focus, the Campaign would channel a communal push from outside of the organization to affect lasting reform. This, of course, would require that some slight adjustments be made to the Campaign itself. While earlier programs had focused more generally on messages directed at broader audiences, the breakdown of civility within the S.G.A. had drawn attention to the need for a more introspective focus as well. Rather than continue to parrot distant, national causes, our new lens retrained our attention closer to home. We adjusted the priorities of the Campaign accordingly to ensure that its programs not only provided basic information to the student body but also offered education and training for our campus leaders.

In addressing the issue of internal division, we recognized that there was a present need for investment in team building initiatives and the promotion of open communication policies in the hopes of building a stronger foundation for collaboration and civil discourse. Ultimately, we had to re-learn what it meant to be student leaders and develop the disciplined awareness required to set aside one's own interests to act on behalf of the students that we were elected or appointed to serve.

For those envisioning a political career filled with ticker tape and red, white and blue balloons, I strongly recommend that you take this point to heart. A standard job requirement for political actors is balancing competing perspectives within a community or organization to devise solutions and plans that offer a "best course of action". Unfortunately, the criteria used in determining what constitutes the "best" option available is left to largely subjective standards and individual interpretation. In navigating these varying interests, people cannot always be brought over to your point of view and, all too often, unyielding perspectives will clash with the proposals that you have set forth.

As illustrated by the present divisiveness in the U.S. political arena, the natural response to these scenarios is to bunker down and draw out battle lines. These are basic reflexes, the alternative to which is set upon a far more difficult path—one that requires us to face our opposition with an open palm. One need not be combative or obtuse when standing firm in their convictions; it is o.k. to be resolute in your beliefs and hold the door open to collaboration and compromise at the same time. Though your opponents may not always seize upon the opportunities that you present to them, we fault ourselves as well by immediately retracting them in spite. In our political, professional, and even personal pursuits, nothing is lost in trying to be the bigger man or woman except, perhaps, a bit of pride. Even then, it is only a minor sacrifice.

Our student body president and executive vice president for the 2011-2012 Administration set a similar tone throughout their term. Adopting the Bon Jovi lyrics, "we weren't born to follow" as the tagline for their administration, they were a team that not only led with principled distinction but actively sought opportunities for collaboration with other student organizations. In following up on the demands for greater transparency from our constituents, they organized regular press junkets that not only allowed them to share details on developing projects but take questions from an audience of representatives from our campus media outlets. The new student body president had been somewhat inspired by Franklin D. Roosevelt's fireside chats, and he attempted to distinguish the role of the S.B.P. as an individual—rather than just an office—through these direct exchanges. More importantly, the coordination between the S.G.A., *The Circle*, and our other campus media outlets created yet another avenue for sharing news and information between our subsets of the student body and the greater campus community.

In order to break away from the cliquish and bureaucratic image that continued to trail us, the 2011-2012 Administration sought a more creative route in broadening the perception of the S.G.A.'s role on campus. Increasing our public presence by directly engaging the student body beyond routine media junkets also became a core component in our strategy to rebuild the S.G.A. brand. As the founder of the College's Booster Club, our newly elected student body president had already developed a strong reputation for channeling his love of sports in fostering student engagement. As a former resident assistant, he had also coordinated a number of communal programs around major sporting events, recognizing the immense draw they had in pulling together segments of the on-campus community. He combined the two into a solution to mend our current woes and restore Red Fox pride.

Through practice, he came to appreciate how important the feelings of comradery spurred in watching these competitions as a part of a larger audience could be in fostering a sense of familiarity and belonging among his residents. In carving out a communal space to share in the excitement of the event, he was able to appeal to students who would otherwise have settled into the solitude of their rooms. As student body president, he would turn his passion for communal celebrations into yet another one of the S.G.A.'s lasting legacies, one known best for its ability to reach marginalized students.

Its success stemmed from its ability to tap directly into a lingering concern among our student community. Indeed, a growing refrain among the various requests received by the S.G.A. in its annual surveys, which were affixed to the general election ballot, was a demand for more social activities beyond the typical offerings of the local bar scene. While the Office of College Activities and our Student Programming Council did wonderful jobs of coordinating programs and activities for the student body, it was impossible for one or two organizations to fill every hour of the day on their own. There were, inevitably, lulls between programs where students were left to their own devices in making the most of these remaining hours.

While there were a great number of clubs and organizations that added to the campus' offerings, and resident assistants coordinated regular activities in the hopes of spurring communal connections, it was difficult for students who had not yet found their niche within our community to find alternative opportunities for socialization and expand their private networking circles. This rift had a particularly strong impact on our freshmen and commuter students—the former finding themselves in the process of reshaping their social identities in a new environment while the latter were seeking to breach the communal bubble of established social networks. In both cases, it was not uncommon for some students to feel as though they were outsiders on their own campus.

Building upon his experiences as both a resident assistant and the founder of the student Booster Club, the student body president for the 2011-2012 Administration devised a program that would not only add to the list of things to do around campus but offer students the chance to mix, mingle, and learn more about other established groups and activities. The first "Red Fox Den" was hosted in our own S.G.A. office, an attempt at further breaking down the perceived barriers between the administration and the student body. As the program evolved, collaboration would also become a key component in managing the Red Fox Den, as the S.G.A. recruited other organizations—like the campus' gaming clubs and musical ensembles—to take the lead in coordinating future activities.

Like the Civility Campaign, the Red Fox Den became a mechanism for student leaders to come together and link their organizations to their campus peers in an effort to meet a common goal. As an all-encompassing theme across our campus, each club and organization served as a spoke in propping up the larger wheel of community that enveloped us all. At the center of this mechanism was the S.G.A., the nucleus through which each individual spoke came together and branched out to play its part in supporting this broader aim. It was our duty to not only maintain this fundamental unity across our various campus sub-cultures and student groups but to also ensure that the whole unit continued spinning in harmony.

Moreover, at the heart of this initiative was our desire to create a sanctuary for our students, an escape from the rigors and stresses of their academic and extracurricular activities to simply take in a movie, sporting event, or other activity as members of a shared community. After all, in balancing these various, established sub-groups, it was all too easy to lose sight of those students who did not easily fall into one category or another, let alone identify with any existing group at all. The Red Fox Den became a communal safety net of sorts, one through which our organization could cast out a helping hand to those who felt lost within their own community. Although it was not a panacea for the deeper issues that lingered around campus—there was still a feeling of disenfranchisement among many commuters and transfer students that would take more than just a few programs to pierce—the Red Fox Den added a deeper sense of purpose to the programs sponsored by the S.G.A.

Lessons Learned

Humans are social creatures. Although just about every college classroom will elicit a notable groan when asked to split up into working groups, there is no denying that—deep down—we need one another. What truly stands out among my other memories associated with the college experience are my recollections of the people that I worked with, the people that I lived with, and the other assorted characters that filled the various supporting roles in the development of my life story. The impressions left by their presence continues to linger long after the other details of our interactions have faded into memory.

Did we always see eye-to-eye? Certainly not. Were there people on campus that I was not entirely close to? Of course. Despite our small and close-knit communal feel, I was still struggling to overcome some of my old "shy kid" habits. And yet, we all found a way to come together over one commonality. Although they may not have shared my vision for, or even been a part of, *my* particular journey, we nonetheless shared an identity as students and alumni of the same college. We were all part of a much bigger element.

When tragedy struck or triumph arose, we could count on one another to be there, no matter how tenuous the connection. It was that particular spirit that led so many of us to refer to our peers within the community as members of a common "family". Like the fundamental social unit that guides us into the world, our campus had come to fill a certain evolutionary role in bringing together individuals for security, stability, and advancement. For many young minds, much like my earlier self, it was an anchor upon which one's efforts to establish a more lasting identity were steadied.

Even so, it is not uncommon for some rogue player to occasionally sweep through the scene and fire a shot across our common bow. Facing down a threat to our social safety net can be startling enough, but it becomes all the more jarring when we trace the threatening shot back to the confines of our own backyard. While we still puzzle over the motives that drive some to act as lone wolves and break from the pack in such a violent manner, one possible answer may lead us back to the very formula that provides us with that warm, fuzzy "*Kumbaya*" feeling in the first place.

Noted sociologist Travis Hirschi once proposed that social bonds and individual attachments play a crucial part in shaping individual behaviors. As we grow to feel more connected to an individual or group, we become all the more motivated to modify our behaviors in order to please them. Conformity is our evolutionary ticket to maintaining our place within the safe confines of a social order.

Power and stability alone, however, are not enough to spur conformity. Instead, Hirschi believed that the influence of attachment, the very bond formed between individuals and those around them, might lead some to defy the security of the *status quo* and even break from the herd entirely.

Think back, for example, to your earlier school years. A common trend among juveniles is that they grow from attentively trailing the first adults in their lives (their parents/guardians/teachers) to eventually follow the whims of their peers. This trend typically emerges around those harrowing stages of the infamous teenage years, wrought with rebellion and social exploration. In addition to the raging hormones and a broader societal awareness that accompany this period, our degrees of attachments to individual groups may also hold a stronger grip on the steering wheel when it comes to determining whether we are going to stick with the pack or rebel with the renegades.

In particular, views on authority and the depth of our attachments to figures such as teachers, administrators, and our peers may play a particularly large part in this calculus. As youngsters, we tend to cling to the hips of the oldest folks in the room. There may even be a strong evolutionary reason behind our compulsion to look up to and model the older, more experienced members of our social groups. As we age, however, these attachments are weekend by a myriad of factors that flood our worldview and are subsequently replaced by bonds forged within our own peer groups. These pressures supplant the traditional messages of restraint espoused by our elders and may yield to more rambunctious, exploratory, destructive (pick your poison) behaviors exhibited by those who we deem to be on our level.

Such were the musings of this humble criminal justice major as my peers in the S.G.A. and I tried to make heads or tails of the pages of nasty, degrading messages that our fellow Red Foxes fired off against one another without compunction. How could we go from cheering together on the sidelines of the football field to stabbing one another in the back with the stroke of a key board? The longer we puzzled over the unfolding digital mess, it appeared all the more apparent that such deteriorating attachments might be to blame for our faltering spirit of community.

In the wake of the 2011 election, we saw the immense pull of such fundamental loyalties firsthand. Like animals startled by an encroaching storm, an air of conflict had sent us scurrying into self-imposed corners. When our shared identity as members of the S.G.A. faltered in the wake of a perceived injustice or the alleged overreaction and betrayal of our peers, this top layer attachment yielded to the connections that had branched out and grown just beneath it over the years. Our shared identity was superseded by more personal attachments, a source of stability when everything else seemed to be falling apart at the seams. As we worked to mend these wounds in our own house, the 2011-2012 Administration certainly came to appreciate how a weakened spirit of community could open the door to such troubles.

In watching so many of our peers splinter off to engage in the digital mayhem that accompanied these anonymous social sites—not just once but twice in the span of a few, short years—we recognized that our best efforts in effectively curbing the trend would have to target these connections from a communal standpoint, rather than narrowly focus on singular incidents and individual sub-groups. Yet how, precisely, does one go about repairing these individualized bonds on such a large scale? Our determination was to start at the top and work our way down, by creating an umbrella of opportunities that afforded our students the chance to identify with our concept of communal values and embrace a role within the social fold from its center.

The Civility Campaign and, later on, the Red Fox Den represented two prongs in this broader communal approach. In first bringing together various voices from within the campus community, the Civility Campaign sought to identify these common values early on and refine them into a more concise message that could be repeated and shared across our various social channels. Following up on these fundamental concepts, the Campaign sought to engage students through programming and further empower them in taking ownership over the process—with no shortage of trial and error, clearly.

Only after stumbling through the learning curve ourselves could we come to appreciate what worked and what missed the desired mark in crafting such an ambitious effort. In time, however, our attention to assembling a platform constructed upon principles that struck closer to home helped us to sprout some truly engaging and innovative programs that resonated with our student body. Whereas our earlier efforts had lost their stamina in treading the waters of our communal conscious on their own, each program that we conducted under the new model bolstered the next by branching off from the same, shared soil.

Indeed, every community needs a nucleus, a common denominator that individual members can cling to in forming identities of their own. When properly identified, it can be utilized as a societal rallying point that evokes pride and ownership, drawing others into the fold. Identifying the common denominator within your own community, however, is not enough to simply declare it a nucleus. As a fundamental seed around which a shared identity is woven, accessibility is a critical component. In order for these common threads to properly bind individuals to this central component, they must be able to get a firm hold on the line.

In our case, the College was built upon a sturdy ethos passed down to us by the Marist Brothers and had cultivated a notable brand of its own throughout the years. Stemming from these traditions was an array of clubs and organizations that had fostered their own, individual sub-cultures throughout the campus. Perceptions of dissonance stemming from a lack of activities and opportunities for certain social groups on our campus had developed a sense of cultural drift, allowing other peer bonds and attachments to supplant the communal bond. Disenfranchisement had blossomed into contention before collapsing into outright rebellion.

In order to re-establish these fundamental connections and ensure that every student could take pride in adopting these shared values into their own identity, we had to ensure that opportunities for engaging as active members of our community, our "Red Fox family", were expanded and preserved. The Civility Campaign became the missing link through which we could finally begin binding these floating fragments to our established nucleus and re-secure our shared campus identity.

THE LEADERSHIP PROFILE: *Exercise Seven*

It is time to find your nucleus. Although it may not seem utterly apparent at first, there is undoubtedly a common theme that connects you to certain social groups in your life. While we may share a number of interests and traits with those around us, a true nucleus rises above typical commonalities to become a part of our very identity. These fundamental pieces in defining our sense of self can be cultural, geographical, and ideological. Each of these three elements transcends the other, and weighs upon our lives in varying degrees of importance.

The first step, therefore, is to sit back and consider which among these is most important to you. In glancing back at some of the items you have recorded so far, how would you best describe yourself? Have your answers been linked to a regional identity—your hometown, your state, your country? Have they stemmed more so from a cultural identity or the values that surrounded you therein? Or, perhaps, you have come to adopt another ideological code outside of your cultural parameters to live by some other dogma entirely? By tracing back the roots of our individual thoughts, we can better identify the soils in which the trunk of our branching identities has laid its roots.

Take a moment to think over your response. Again, it is possible that all three of these pieces have played a part in shaping your thoughts so far. Which *one* stands out the most? Take a moment to reflect on the influence that this key pillar has had in supporting your current social networks. How has it influenced your associations with your friends, family, and co-workers? Take a moment to consider your closest friends and peers. Do they share a connection to this common theme?

Taking the time to identify the influential sources of your own lines of thought can also be immensely useful in expanding meaningful social and personal networks. Like many things in life, these pieces are jumping points from which we can initiate more meaningful exchanges. They are the gateways through which initial connections are formed and more lasting attachments are eventually established. If you can soundly point to one of these three as a potential nucleus, set a space aside for it on your profile as a constant reminder of the underlying wellspring that feeds your spirit and connects you to a bigger world.

8 – THE CALLING

"If a man will begin with certainties, he shall end with
doubts; but if he will be content to begin with doubts,
he shall end in certainties."
-Sir Francis Bacon

It was his down-to-earth approach to working with our constituents
that made the student body president of the 2011-2012 Administration a
great resident assistant and, in the time following his graduation, a great
teacher. While the S.G.A. had hosted other social events in the past, the Red
Fox Den stood out because of its focus on creating a safe haven for students
who felt marginalized on campus. It also proved effective in tapping into an
organic process through which new relationships could be cultivated. In
working closely with him as the Senate Speaker throughout his term, I
detected a common thread between the student body president's
achievements and his future vocation. More than just a leader, he was a
protector. As the chief voice of our student body, he took a proactive
approach toward identifying and solving campus issues. Much like his work
with the Booster Club, he started his own "fireside chats" out of a desire to
reach new pockets of the campus community, ones that may not have
necessarily known the resources and opportunities open to them through our
organization.

His zeal for student service was further propelled by the resilient
support of a dedicated executive vice president. Having worked with her for
a number of years on the housing department staff as a fellow resident
assistant, he asked her to join his ticket in order to bring an outsider's
perspective to the organization. Though she had served on the St. Jude

Fundraising committee in the past, rising up to lead the effort as its chair later in her career, she had never formally been associated with the S.G.A. in any other capacity. While some applauded the decision to appoint an outsider to a top position within the student government, others found in his choice cause for concern. Such controversy did not stem from her record in student service but her shared role as a member of the residential staff.

Our new E.V.P. was not the only resident assistant recruited to serve in the 2011-2012 Administration. A number of the student body president's appointments, as well as the newly elected Class of 2012 president, served on the housing staff. Branching off of the heated opposition that had greeted their inauguration, some accused the incoming administration of deepening the cliquish allegiances that colored the S.G.A.'s more notorious reputations. Although each and every appointee selected in that year went above and beyond the scope of their duties in serving the student body, we once again waded into the fog arising from the impact of *perceptions versus reality* in public organizations.

Having found their niche on our campus under the Office of Housing and Residential Life, the leaders of the 2011-2012 Administration had surrounded themselves with a team of dedicated peers that shared their commitment to—and view of— public service. Just as I had relied on my close friends to help me in filling the ranks of the Safety & Security committee, our new S.B.P. and E.V.P. found a similar comfort in turning to trusted sources to guide their administration through these tempestuous times. While the perception of collusion may not have helped them to win any favor under the intense scrutiny already fixed upon them, their appointments proved to be valuable additions to the S.G.A. team nonetheless.

Indeed, the 2011-2012 Administration brought a number of welcome additions to the campus community. Beyond the development of the Red Fox Den and the passage of his election reform plan, the student body president tapped into this familiar network to spearheaded the consolidation of residence area governing boards and councils into a single entity: the Student Life Association ("S.L.A.").

Outside of the S.G.A., each residence area had its own local board that acted as a form of municipal governance. Elected to serve their respective communities on campus, these individual councils could organize programs and voice their concerns to the S.G.A. on behalf of their constituents. Though they collaborated routinely, no formal connection existed between these various representative bodies and the S.G.A. at that time. This would occasionally lead to confusion, as some viewed their residence area boards as the "House of Representatives" that balanced out the S.G.A. Senate. In reality, the chasm between these two organizations was much wider than most students realized. The former had no policymaking power whatsoever.

Having been directly involved with the coordination of certain residence area boards during his time as a resident assistant, the student body president sought to give them a greater role in the campus dialogue by formalizing their organization under the auspices of the S.G.A. Rather than restructure the Legislative Branch entirely, he sought a more creative route. Working with his board, the S.B.P. modeled his proposal after an example that he had seen in a conference for the North East Affiliate of College and University Residence Halls ("N.E.A.C.U.R.H.").

The plan would reorganize the presidents of the various residence areas into a new representative body under the banner of the Student Life Association ("S.L.A."), which would report to a newly created position on the Executive Board, the "Vice President of Student Life". This consolidation offered these local boards a clear and concise channel for voicing the desires and concerns of their constituents directly to the student government. The Vice President of Student Life would organize monthly meetings for these representatives and submit a report on their findings and activities to the student body president and the rest of the executive board during their regular meetings.

I became particularly familiar with this body later on in my collegiate career as the president of our campus chapter of the National Residence Hall Honorary ("N.R.H.H."). As an honorary board devoted to recognizing leadership in fostering culture and community within college residence areas, the N.R.H.H. selected its members carefully from a pool of campus community activists whose programs had constructively impacted residence life in some way. Due to its close affiliation to student life initiatives, its president also served as one of the delegates on the S.L.A. Having been inducted as a member of the N.R.H.H. toward the end of my freshman year for my game night programs, I was later elected by my peers within the organization to serve as its leader.

From this vantage point, I witnessed firsthand the wealth of insight brought forth by student delegates who, in turn, felt a sense of empowerment in their newly expanded roles as the voices for their subcommunities within the greater tapestry of our campus's government. While some students may not have felt the desire to engage themselves so deeply in student politics as to run for a campus-wide position like resident senator or student body president, there was still a desire among many of our peers to serve in a more limited capacity. In reorganizing these scattered boards and their programs into a more formal network under the banner of the Student Life Association, the 2011-2012 Administration created an alternate route to representation that afforded students the opportunity to seek involvement in the greater campus dialog through this happy medium.

As the leader of the Legislative Branch, I must also pause to praise the establishment of the S.L.A. as a major step towards expanding the inclusivity of the S.G.A. Having visited other campuses whose student senates consisted of a much broader body of volunteers, our meager collection of eleven representatives did not appear fully capable of effectively encapsulating the wide array of views, opinions, and experiences that shaped our community. On our campus, roughly 4,000 undergraduate resident students were represented by only five resident senators. The commuter population, whose members tended to suffer the greatest feelings of dissonance from the broader campus community, was only represented by two senators on this board. Graduate students, themselves a fractional portion of our community, were omitted from the equation entirely. The legislative body was further rounded out by four class presidents, each representing their peers within their graduation cohort. Despite the appearance of such shortcomings in representativeness, discussions on potentially reorganizing and expanding the Senate always stalled in the face of two significant challenges.

The first stemmed from that classic argument of quality versus quantity. Proponents of maintaining a smaller Legislative Branch argued that a collection of a few, dedicated individuals was more productive than a boisterous hodge-podge of volunteers. This argument was further supported by the second issue: it was already hard enough to find individuals willing to run for the few seats that we had.

While freshman races always produced a healthy slew of ambitious candidates, this energy waned significantly by the time campus-wide elections rolled around in the sprint. In recent cycles, the seats for resident and commuter senators had typically gone unopposed and sometimes unfilled. Therefore, expanding the number of available seats without first addressing the underlying issue of involvement would not improve the representative nature of the S.G.A. At worst, we risked opening the door to more uncontested races, the opportunity for corruption, and the presumed inevitability of bureaucratic impasse. Thus, it is no wonder as to why we so often found ourselves talking in circles. There was no single, perfect response; every turn brought additional consequences that, if left unchecked, merely threatened to compound upon the initial problem.

That is how its simplicity helped to define the S.L.A.'s formation as a wonderfully impactful and brilliant change to our S.G.A. roster. Rather than re-invent the wheel, the S.L.A. reform merely crafted a new channel for a pre-existing network to play a more direct role in campus governance. Although they did not have a say in legislative matters, the chorus of new voices and ideas brought forth by our residence area representatives helped to shed light on new perspectives and issues that could easily be taken under the wing of a senator or class president looking for a new project. As I had hoped, it did not take long for this new bud on the branches of our S.G.A. tree to become a valuable addition to the body as a whole.

◆

As the S.G.A. continued its efforts to promote a positive presence on our campus, I was personally looking to broaden my own outlook in life. Rather than continue to devote all of my free time to the S.G.A., I began to seek out opportunities to join other clubs and organizations. In working closely with a former S.G.A. colleague and friend, I was eventually drawn into our campus' chapter of Toastmasters International. As one of the most outgoing and bubbly individuals you will ever meet, she simply had a knack for engaging others and recruiting them into new projects. It did not take her long to find her calling among the Toastmasters, as she wasted no time in teaming up with their executive board to save the struggling club from dwindling attendance. As the Vice President of Club Affairs under the 2010-2011 Administration, my friend brought a wealth of experience in (student) organizational management to the table. Effectively translating her ideas into concrete results, however, required overcoming one, slight hurdle: Toastmasters was not an officially recognized club.

On our campus, administrators utilized a priority point system in ranking individuals and groups for the selection of housing assignments each year. Students would accumulate points based on their involvement on campus, their academic standing, and their abilities to stay out of trouble. Their annual totals (capped at 36 points per student) would then be averaged together within their self-selected peer groups to determine their order in staking out housing preferences for the coming year. Only clubs that were formally registered with the Office of College Activities, and approved by the S.G.A. Senate, could issue priority points for participation. This made it tough for the Toastmasters to compete with other clubs in recruiting regular members.

Fortunately, Toastmasters did have a small budget that was generously provided by the School of Management, as well as a great deal of pluck. Working with the other officers, my friend developed a marketing campaign that would help Toastmasters promote their club by not only walking the walk but talking the talk. They were able to get a number of professors to agree to let them have five minutes at the start of their class period to pitch the club to their students. Focusing on Toastmasters' ability to prepare individuals for group and solo presentations, they were able to further garner support and favorability from the academic side of campus. Eventually, some professors even agreed to offer extra credit as a reward to those students who attended a certain number of Toastmasters meetings throughout the semester—with the added hopes of curtailing some their pupil's more monotone end of year PowerPoint presentations.

The Toastmasters' campaign proved so successful that I not only found myself drawn into their weekly meetings with a handful of other students, but inevitably joined my friend as a member of their executive board as well. I served in a number of roles on this board over the next few years, including positions that oversaw its practices relating to membership and education/training. I also found in Toastmasters the opportunity to flex my public presentation muscles. Aside from the annual S.G.A. campaign season, there were not many occasions at that time in which I would find myself in front of a crowd. Not wanting to let old habits slip back into place, I signed up to give a number of speeches throughout the year. I hoped that actively staying one step ahead of my fears would help me to shine if I was ever called upon to take center stage, like the S.B.P. I watched eagerly on Accepted Student's Day. As it turns out, such a calling came much sooner than expected.

In my freshman year, my involvement with the Student Government Association had also earned me an invitation to join the campus' Emerging Leaders Program ("E.L.P.") and chapter of the National Society of Leadership and Success ("N.S.L.S."). As a national organization founded to empower students in identifying and acting upon dreams of their own, the N.S.L.S. had grown into an impressive network that united student leaders and administrators from coast to coast. Our Emerging Leaders Program was a campus-based leadership training program developed to work in concert with the society's mission, grooming potential inductees while affording all participating students the opportunities to develop a sense of direction and hone their own skills.

After attending a number of the workshops coordinated by the E.L.P. and continuing to distinguish my résumé through my own S.G.A. projects, I was not only inducted into the N.S.L.S. but invited to serve on our campus' student executive board. I held a general board member position for the last two years of my undergraduate career, working with its officers to develop programs, coordinate workshops, and even introduce guest speakers. I was particularly strong when it came to doing the latter. My speeches in Toastmasters had earned me some notoriety on campus for public speaking, and I helped the E.L.P.-N.S.L.S. board to refine their scripts for introducing guest presenters at regular workshops and telecasts. Routine practice had not only prepared me to be more comfortable in facing audiences on my own, it also helped me to develop a confidence and style in guiding others through the process.

Indeed, facing my fears early in my career had proven to be an immeasurably rewarding decision. Throughout my time as an undergraduate, my efforts in public speaking afforded me a number of opportunities that I would have otherwise shunned out of fear and self-doubt. In time, my work with the E.L.P.-N.S.L.S. board extended the chance for yet another, career-defining moment. As my first year with the E.L.P. Board drew to a close, the program's Director asked me if I would like to introduce the keynote speaker for our annual induction ceremony. Our guest that year was renowned philanthropist Ray Lamontagne, perhaps best known for his dedicated leadership as chairman of the "Hole in the Wall Gang" camps for children fighting life-threatening illnesses—founded by his good friend, famed actor and philanthropist, Paul Newman.

In the days leading up to the presentation, I would meet regularly with our Director to go over drafts of my introduction. Despite growing to a point where I could effortlessly waltz through a presentation before my fellow Toastmasters or rouse a crowd to action during the S.G.A. elections, I began to feel the familiar flutter of butterflies as I prepared for this next, great step forward. At that point, I was faced with yet another ultimatum. I could either decline the speaking opportunity and leave it to the Director to do—as she had in years prior—or I could focus on the exciting prospects that this moment not only extended to me but to future students involved with the program as well.

If I was successful, then we would carve out a new tradition of student speakers that would, in turn, afford similarly career-defining opportunities to generations of future participants in taking on a new degree of ownership over this incredible program. The promise of this exciting legacy became my motivation for swallowing those fluttering butterflies and pushing ahead with the presentation. No matter how proficient I became in public speaking, I always recognized that my original fears would constantly shadow me as I progressed through life. Though ever-present, they could only form a barrier to my success if I afforded them such power.

That is why I was so thrilled by the warm response that I received following the presentation. In fact, I later learned that keynote speaker was kind enough to write a letter to our Director after the ceremony with high praises for my introduction. Far more than an ego boost, the occasion served as personal benchmark in my growth as a public presenter. I was finally able to see my work in the same positive light shone upon it by my peers.

As I had hoped, this successful introduction also marked the beginning of a wonderful new tradition. I was even called upon once more by the E.L.P.-N.S.L.S. team to introduce the speaker for our 2013 induction ceremony, the College's Executive Vice President. Afterwards, the task would cede to future generations of board members following my graduation.

It is a legacy that I have had the pleasure of witnessing firsthand. My involvement with the Emerging Leaders Program and the N.S.L.S. has continued well beyond my undergraduate term. In addition to returning annually as an alumnus to run a workshop with my former roommate and S.G.A. peer—our Elections Commissioner for the 2010-2011 Administration—I was deeply honored to return as the keynote speaker for their 2015 induction ceremony. This time, it was my turn to stand beside the podium while one of the student leaders, whom I had worked with through both the program and our Toastmasters Club, stepped up to the mic. It was a moment that shall always stand out chiefly amongst the other memories from my time with the program.

Beyond the sense of emotional fulfilment that it provided, this episode served as an affirmation of a most important lesson. As with most of my experiences with battling fear, the opportunities masked by the shadow of doubt tend to greatly outweigh the dire prospects enlarged by our gloom. Looking back, I can most assuredly say that the tradition we crafted under the E.L.P.-N.S.L.S. board certainly outweighs any potential embarrassment that might have been brought about by a slight *faux pas* on stage. As my greatest hesitation arose from a fear of making mistakes in front of large audiences, this opportunity also served as a stepping-stone in my journey to further explore the art of public presentation in overcoming such doubts. The aim of a strong public presenter, after all, is not to avoid making mistakes, but to overcome them with grace.

Like a single player in an orchestra, no one will know when you have skipped a note unless you draw attention to it by attempting to stumble back and do things over. Whether you have a performance at Carnegie Hall, a speech at a campaign stop, a group presentation on cross-cultural strategies in training police canines, or a PowerPoint on how your dog came to be named *"Captain* Snowball", your audience's reality is shaped by the perceptions that you create. Through our use of tone, inflection, visual aids, and even the smallest details in posture and appearance, we craft a collective image that has a profound impact over the messages we transmit. With this in mind, overcoming the most basic jitters associated with public presentation can have a tremendous impact on your overall performance, as well as the reception you garner.

Having filled the shoes of both the interviewer and the interviewee throughout my subsequent professional career, I can honestly tell you that the nerves associated with these types of presentations are inescapable. We catch them on both sides of the table. Everyone feels vulnerable to a certain extent when we put ourselves out in front of audience, be it just one other person or a room full of strangers. The trick, if there is one, is to separate yourself from your audience and train that little voice in your head to act as your biggest cheerleader, rather than your biggest critic.

Trust me; I know it is far easier said than done. Nonetheless, you will be surprised by just how far a bit of self-confidence can take you. In fact, the process is practically cyclical. The more comfortable you become in standing before an audience, the more readily your message will be accepted. This impression on your audience is returned to you through positive feedback and constructive criticisms that, in turn, will propel you even further in your next presentation and make your message even more impactful. Support and encouragement have a tremendous, cumulative effect.

So, as you go about chasing down your own personal and professional pursuits, I would not only hope that you receive similar praises but that you take the opportunity to pass the positive karma along by recognizing others for their efforts. As the student body president of the 2011-2012 Administration liked to remind us through the *Star Fish Story*, what appears to be a relatively small act on our part can completely change someone else's world.

♦

This can be both a blessing and a curse. For leaders, ensuring that the impressions we impart produce positive outcomes involves understanding the difference between *leading* and *managing*. This distinction requires us to recognize that just because we can command an audience does not mean that we must always run the show. Sometimes, a leader has to step back to let others take the stage, or affect their desired outcomes subtly from behind the scenes. Great leaders forego the spotlight because they recognize it is not only unnecessary but occasionally detrimental. In playing with the perceptions of others, one misstep can lead an actor to misread gentle encouragement as scathing judgment and compound a simple mistake into a spectacle. Sadly, it is a reality that I came to appreciate through experience.

By my junior year, we had truly assembled a stellar team of aspiring young leaders on the E.L.P.-N.S.L.S. board. As the organization continued to grow, our leadership team expanded to represent a wider array of the various sub-cultures and individual networks that made up our campus community. A good friend of mine from the paralegal program had even taken on the role of president for the board, and this new title meant that she would also serve as the Master of Ceremonies for the organization's annual inductions.

With a warm personality, she easily carried an air of comfort and support that energized our members with her infectious enthusiasm for the program. She excelled in one-on-one encounters. As her leadership style embodied the principles of leading from the heart, she supported each and every one of our members by taking on the role of their "number one fan". Like me, however, she battled a fear of public speaking, a shared specter that we would often joke about in our classes together. As my role with the board had grown to encompass training and coaching in public presentation, I hoped to help lessen these fears as best as I could.

At our next board meeting following her first induction ceremony, I shared my observations in what I thought was a constructive manner. Instead, another member of our board seized upon my aside as an opportunity to list off his own criticisms of the event. In the heat of the moment, it came off as more of an ambush than a helping hand, easily leaving our president with the impression of a divided board. After we had adjourned, I sought out our president to clarify my intentions and extend my apologies. I learned the hard way that there is indeed a proper time and place for these types of discussions, and sometimes the worst of mistakes can be made with the best of intentions.

I, of all people, should have recognized that the issue deserved to be handled in a more delicate manner; this was a topic far better suited for a one-on-one conversation, rather than a full board discussion. I had let our sense of informality and comradery cloud my judgment, and a friend was hurt in the process. Although I felt that I had already attained a great deal of experience by this point in my undergraduate career, I came to fully appreciate that there was still much more left to be learned. Indeed, just as the process of facing our fears is one that never truly ends, we never cease being students in this school of life.

Lessons Learned

By the time I entered the second stage of my collegiate career as an "upperclassman", I had already witnessed a number of changes unfold around campus. Not only was the College physically expanding—with the opening of a new, high-tech business center in the spring of 2011—but the dynamics of our community had begun to shift as well.

Of the small contingent that first sought to be a part of the S.G.A. in our earliest days as freshmen, only a few of us remained actively involved in student government. Many of my friends, like our future Toastmasters president, found more suitable avenues for their passions outside of the S.G.A. Others still, came to find that their priorities had shifted entirely, taking them out of the "public eye" of our campus community to settle into more private activities within their own social networks. Thus, I came to appreciate how hindsight can be beneficial in setting realistic, long-term goals. Taking a moment to stand still and look back at where you first started and appreciate how far you have come can help you realize how often we tend to veer from our original course, or how these occasional diversions can sometimes prove to be more beneficial than the track we originally set out on. While it is good to develop a five-year plan, it is also important to avoid locking yourself into a particular goal or outcome.

Being open to new possibilities does not necessarily mean that you are bound to make a complete 180-degree turn in the course of your professional pursuits; it simply keeps you open to the possibilities presented by unexpected opportunities. When it came to managing the Safety & Security committee, for example, I feared it could slowly become a living "suggestion box" for student concerns on our campus, playing no more than a responsive role to individual complaints. As I proactively worked to incorporate a community policing focus into the committee's duties, someone outside of our ranks took notice. With a surprise nomination from one of our former student body presidents, a new chapter in my safe & secure story would be written. In the fall of 2011, my initial fears for the legacy of the committee were put to rest when I was selected to serve as a student representative for the American Student Government Association at a national summit on campus safety hosted by Johns Hopkins University and the Bureau of Justice Assistance. In this role, I provided the sole student voice in a discussion that included campus security chiefs from across the country, respected researchers, and members of the national law enforcement community.

Far from being something that I had in mind when I first laid out my plans for the committee, our inclusion in the national summit was a significant milestone for Safety & Security matters on our campus. More importantly, it helped me to realize a hidden potential within the organization that I had not seen before. As a growing issue of national importance, developing a mechanism for students to join the emerging dialog could significantly influence major policy discussions.

From this point on, I was always sure to include a bit of "wiggle room" in my personal planning process, recognizing the possibility for greater, unforeseen opportunities to come along and steer my projects in entirely new directions. It is this openness to innovation and willingness to adapt to new parameters that sets our leaders apart from mere managers. Whereas the latter are content in simply following an outlined plan, leaders keep a trained eye on the lookout for new opportunities that build upon the existing potential of their organizations.

Doing so, however, requires more than just a healthy sense of imagination and a tolerance for risk; maintaining an open mind requires us to acknowledge that we do not already possess all of the right answers. This can be a particularly difficult reality for some established leaders to embrace, as pride often fosters a powerful sense of ego that makes it difficult to avert our gaze from the path that has already led us to such a prosperous point. Seizing upon these new opportunities is, in large part, a leap of faith.

Leaders must assess these opportunities in a responsible manner to determine whether the potential for reward (for their entire organization, constituency, or client) is greater than the risk of failure. All the more crucial still is the leader's willingness to abandon the course that they had initially outlined for a new path, the potential of which remains largely unproven. True leaders must be willing to set personal pride aside to recognize that other avenues to success exist, while continually placing the well-being of their organizations and beneficiaries ahead of their own interests.

Such an approach had certainly helped the 2011-2012 Administration in overcoming the controversies surrounding the preceding election. By recognizing the faults of the organization and actively addressing student concerns, the S.G.A. allowed itself to be guided by the needs of its constituents. While the student body president certainly brought his own vision to the organization at that time, accomplishing a great deal within a short period, he also recognized that the culture and climate on our campus required a more open approach to governance.

To that end, the 2011-2012 Administration prioritized communication and transparency chiefly among its core values. In addition to their regular press junkets, this administration worked with the Office of Safety & Security to bring the first text-alert system to our campus. Rather than maintain a firm grasp on the wheel, the leaders of the 2011-2012 Administration demonstrated their willingness to share the helm with the student body, actively engaging our constituency in major policy decisions.

Indeed, most leaders recognize the tremendous value in maintaining an open door policy. Though individuals may not always see their ideas come to fruition, I have found that a great many will find solace in simply knowing that their voices have been heard. Watching the ball begin to roll as pieces fall into place and others start to take a sincere interest in the task's completion helps to establish a sense of inevitability. It is, once again, an example of the role played by trust in cultivating a healthy relationship between an organization and the constituency it serves. As the mere perception of transparency can make or break morale within a group, leaders should make seeking out the views of their peers, employees, and clients as to the management of the organization an absolute priority.

Particularly on a college campus, where our overall time together is short, no great effort could be expected to reach completion in so a narrow window. Only in working together, openly and honestly with all expectations and concerns laid flatly on the table, could we reach that point where all sides felt comfortable in believing that our ends could be achieved through the continued efforts of our peers, including those of generations yet to come.

At the end of the day, we remain leaders of *people*. As such, there is an additional, unknown variable that works its way into the necessary equation. One that, taken alone, could serve as the subject of a wide collection of leadership texts. The human heart is far from predictable or quantifiable, yet it holds tremendous sway over how we perceive and, in turn, are received by others. More importantly, it shapes the overall image colored by these various interactions to add its own hue to the shade of reality that we each interpret as our own. What seemed right to me was not always the best, or even a desired, course of action sought by others. Constantly encountering such barriers, it became harder for me to stick to my guns and shut out the mounting chorus of opposing voices that seemed to grow as my career progressed. So, I opened myself to this broader audience of followers and critics alike. I extended an avenue to further interaction, instead of seeking to close them out. I heeded their call. Like the tide that smooths the stone, these influences helped to round out my overall leadership style through adaptation, which also allowed me to effectively navigate these differences in opinion to reach a point of compromise and action.

After all, leading from the heart compels us to not only manage others but to collaborate with our peers through an open exchange of ideas. As my time in student government continued, I never went into a meeting with a decision firmly set in my mind. By keeping myself open to the possibility of change throughout a discussion, I was prepared to more readily digest new information that could change my viewpoint entirely. In fact, my views on a particular issue have occasionally flipped between the moment I walked into a meeting and the moment I walked out; such is the consequence of an engaging, informative debate.

By the midpoint of my undergraduate career, I started actively looking for opportunities to expose myself to new segments of our community outside of the S.G.A. These new activities gave me plenty of room to experiment and stumble in my continual efforts to master the art of public speaking, as well as take in new perspectives from around campus. They prompted an incredible epiphany. I stopped worrying about making mistakes when I accepted the fact that I would never have all the answers in life and, moreover, that no one really expected me to. Without such fears holding me back, I discovered new room to grow into my own. I became a better public speaker and a better leader when I got out of my own head.

My time as an undergraduate helped me to realize that pride can be a powerfully corrosive vice in leadership. Instead, humility and empathy are the cornerstones required in building sturdy foundations in professional relationships that help us to weather even the most tumultuous of clashes. By keeping ourselves open to new possibilities and expanding similar opportunities to others, we invite the rewards of unforeseen opportunities.

I was finally ready to face my greatest challenge yet.

THE LEADERSHIP PROFILE: *Exercise Eight*

It is time to draw yet another box on your profile. Unlike the other spaces that we have already carved out, however, I would like you to leave this one blank. Rather than identify skills or perspectives that have already been established, this space is reserved for the new ideas and opportunities that you are bound to encounter along your journey. Let it be an open door to alternative (and even opposing) viewpoints as you wend your way along the path that you have set out on. There is no more to do in this exercise; the real work will come later on.

9 – THE PROPOSAL

"No passion so effectively robs the mind of all its
powers of acting and reasoning as fear."
-Edmund Burke

As the winter of 2011 faded into the spring of 2012, I became increasingly listless. An internal countdown clock that had been ticking away since I first arrived on campus was steadily nearing its end. The moment that I had been waiting for, the event to which all of my efforts had been leading since that fateful Accepted Students' Day, was about to arrive. The 2012 election was almost upon us.

As my excitement continued to build, I found myself poised with excellent footing for the looming competition. Following a rather bumpy ride through my sophomore year, my term as a junior was off to a much brighter start. My social circle had grown considerably, with the Core Four still serving as my emotional bedrock. I had grown to surround myself with a group of dedicated people who shared in my hopes for the coming student body presidential race, dubbing themselves "Team Johnson".

The new semester would also bring a significant change in scenery. Through my role in the Senate, I had become increasingly involved in matters relating to the concerns of our transfer student population. Due to a bit of a housing crunch on campus in the wake of rising acceptance rates, newly transferred students were placed in a hotel just a few miles down the highway. The College had a special arrangement with the hotel, providing a residence director ("R.D."), two resident assistants, and a campus mentor on site to coordinate programs and build a sense of community for the students that populated this little satellite campus. Depending upon the number of credits carried over by our incoming transfer students, however, some quickly found that they were not able to move between their new residence area and the main grounds as freely as others. There were many students situated in the hotel that did not qualify to have a car on campus (you had to have completed enough credits to be counted as a "sophomore" before you could apply for a parking permit at that time). This had left a significant portion of them dependent on developing their own carpool systems or hiring private transportation in order to travel to and from their daily classes. As a result, it was far more difficult for these students to feel like they were active members of our greater community.

When housing selection for our junior year rolled around, I was joined by my old freshman roommate, Mr. Switzerland, in selecting the hotel as our housing assignment. As the first to join me in forming the Core Four, he has been my closest friend throughout my collegiate career and beyond, my right-hand man. Upon reaching the end of a tumultuous sophomore year that rallied us back together in the same corner, we agreed to take on a new adventure together, along with another member of our core group. In coordinating with members of the housing staff, I laid out my plan to be an S.G.A. representative onsite and report back on the conditions and needs of the hotel's students. Based on an earlier recommendation by the S.G.A., the hotel would also begin running a shuttle to conduct regular loops along the highway and back. In keeping an eye on this developing service, as well as any other issues that might arise, I hoped to affect a change in communal climate directly from the front lines.

On a personal note, life at the hotel also proved to be utterly luxurious for an established student. My friend and I settled into a four-person suite with just one other new roommate, occupying a space that consisted of a small kitchen—complete with a dishwasher and a stove—and a living room that was flanked on each side by one, two-person bedroom. These bedrooms had been emptied over the summer and restocked with standard on-campus furniture, so that each student had a bed, a dresser, and a desk, in addition to the standard hotel end tables and closet space. To add to our delight, each bedroom also featured its own bathroom—no more communal set ups!

In addition to the relatively spacious layout, each room kept their standard hotel television sets (complete with a full listing of satellite channels). This proved to be just one, small feature on the long list of amenities available through the hotel. Students also had unfettered access to each of the site's common areas, which included a pool and hot tub, a television room, a small fitness center, outdoor patio spaces, and a basketball court. Residents also enjoyed a daily hot breakfast buffet in addition to three buffet style dinners throughout the week. If students did not like the hotel's culinary offerings, there were two strip malls within walking distance. Better yet, most of these shops and restaurants accepted the main campus' debit currency system. We took to our new residence area immediately.

Unfortunately, for many of our friends, their upperclassman term would not have such a relaxing start. The onset of this new school year had been met by Hurricane Irene on move-in day, leaving many to wade through the downpour and seek shelter once they had reached the campus. It did not take long for waves of tweets and Facebook postings reflecting widespread damage—including exaggerated rumors of the collapse of one of our academic buildings—to prompt the College's public relations officer to step in and wage a fervent counter offensive against the unchecked imaginations of our student body. All the while, just a few miles down the road, we were spectators in a state of bliss, surveying the digital chatter as we lounged beside the pool. This was our first, real taste of life outside of our campus' communal bubble. Enjoying our dinner with friends after a trip to the pool, we discussed these developments as tourists might comment on the quaintness of their host communities from the comfort of a luxury resort.

And yet, it did not take all that long for the lustrous sheen of hotel life to fade. Despite the short drive to campus, commuting back and forth quickly became tiring. As we struggled to make the most of our time on the main grounds, the resulting cultural rift became utterly apparent. On most days, my roommate and I would pack our bags as though we were commuting for work and planned to stay on campus until we were finished with the last of our classes or activities before returning home to catch whatever was on the *Food Network*, pack our bags, and do it all over again. We were now the folks with bedtimes in our social circles, as we always had to be mindful of the waning hour in order to avoid traffic and make it home in time to prepare for the next day's trip. Even social media and cellular communications could not help us make up for the sudden strain on interpersonal connections. We were vanishing from the campus as we continued arriving later to, and ducking out earlier from, our social and extracurricular events.

Thus, hotel life grew to represent a separate and distinct entity from the larger community. Though my roommate and I were fortunate enough to have a small collection of close friends around us in the hotel, we nonetheless began to feel as though something was missing from our experience. While the rest of our friends on campus frolicked together on snow days or raced off to evening activities hosted by their residence area boards, we were barricaded into our remote little paradise down the road. Its charms quickly paled once we began to feel as though this distance had removed us from their college stories. Heck, even Adam got bored of Eden when he did not have someone to share it with.

As we began to miss the rest of our peers on campus, my friends at the hotel and I started to truly appreciate just how desolate the experience could seem to a new face. We could now understand just how disappointing it could be for someone to gain admission to a school they loved only to feel as though they were watching its story unfold from behind a distant window. All the free breakfast and hot tub soaks in the world could not make up for this missing link. And yet, the newly implemented shuttle was already making a notable impact on morale in the hotel. For the first time in their history, students without parking permits of their own could now move between the campus and the hotel at no personal cost. As we were still in the early days of its implementation, though, the shuttle schedule was in need of some fine-tuning. By way of example, the very first schedule devised had the shuttle leaving campus on the hour. As our class schedules tended to let out either fifteen minutes after the hour or at a quarter to, many folks would just miss the mark and find themselves waiting around for an hour or so to catch the next shuttle.

Nonetheless, and despite such relatively minor growing pains, we were making significant strides towards closing the cultural gap between hotel students and their on-campus peers. In addition to the programs held by the resident assistants onsite, my role as an S.G.A. liaison to the hotel allowed me to extend additional resources toward their programming and community building efforts. With the S.L.A. now fully operational, I also worked with the Residence Life team to ensure that their area board was well staffed and ready to join the student governance dialog and represent the hotel perspective.

Together, we worked with the newly elected officers of the hotel community to set out their own roles and responsibilities in coordinating and sustaining local meetings and activities. Not only did this ignite a small spirit of communal pride among the residents of the hotel, but the regular participation of their board president in monthly S.L.A. meetings helped us to further narrow the divide that separated them from the broader college community. This relationship proved to be extremely valuable in moving forward, as it not only afforded students at the hotel a direct line of communication to the S.G.A., but also enabled their president to bring back information on events and programs that were being offered on campus.

As I could also direct funds from the S.G.A. account toward outreach projects at the hotel, we were able to work beyond the standard Residence Life budget for community events and programs. Keeping it simple, I returned to a rather familiar starting point: area game nights. Renting a few crowd favorites from the College Activities office, we would order some food and host a couple of game nights in the main lobby for residents of the hotel to mingle with one another on their way back from class. Reconnecting with my S.G.A. roots to restore these communal bonds was a real treat. I was even surprised to find that a number of people recognized one another from their classes but had no idea that they were actually neighbors back at the hotel.

By creating opportunities for residents to come together and develop a shared identity of their own, we hoped to first build a small, localized unit that could grow to one day stand independently as a distinct segment of the larger community. From there, we would be able to position the hotel and its residents as their own municipal body, creating a lasting bridge to the greater campus community through a dedicated exchange of two-way communication and programming under the broader network of the S.G.A. In acknowledging their existing communal frustrations and using them as the catalysts to both drive and direct our efforts, we had rooted our strategy for community building in the very same approach that my team had utilized in establishing the Safety & Security committee. In returning to these deeply familiar strategies, we set out to build our communal bridge from the ground up.

♦

In addition to its comparably lavish amenities, living at the hotel also provided me with a solid base of operations in forming my student body presidential campaign for the coming spring. With three of my friends from Team Johnson now living onsite with me, we could work around the clock to gather materials and talk strategy without having to worry about who might be listening in. Stowed away safely from the buzz of campus politics, our little sanctuary along the highway served as the central meeting place for all of Team Johnson's discussions. As the fall months trailed along into the winter season, my comrades began huddling frequently with me around the warm hearth of the fireplace in the main lobby to share their counsel.

Although the official campaign period itself would last for a little more than two weeks, there was still a great deal of work to be done in the time leading up to the race. A former student body president had once told me that a successful campaign team should aim to have all of their materials prepared by the end of November, or else they would risk running into crippling delays during the race. After all, posters and other promotional materials required approval from the Office of College Activities before they could be distributed to the student body. Having witnessed early on in my career how this chain of deadlines and turnarounds could drag out a timetable, I heeded their warning and worked with my team to compile our wish list well in advance. This included not only posters, table-toppers, and pamphlets but also T-shirts, which had become a customary favor distributed to eager onlookers in S.G.A. campaigns. To avoid delays and make an early impact, aspiring candidates had to factor in the processing and delivery times associated with these large orders, as well as count on the additional, standard approval times required by both College Activities and the Elections Commission.

Although coordinating campaign supplies required dedicated attention to both time and detail, it also proved to be the relatively easy part in forming a student government campaign. In addition to these standard fan-favorite trinkets, there was still one, monumental factor that aspiring student body presidential candidates had to lock away long before petitions began circulating. I needed to recruit a partner.

Much like our national races, it had become customary for candidates seeking the office of the student body president to campaign with a running mate. Over the past few years, those who sought the position had become rather creative in building a collective brand around themselves and their teammates in forming a ticket. Our community had now come to expect these battles between S.B.P.-E.V.P. teams when they headed to the polls each spring. Naturally, as a "make or break" component of our S.G.A. election calculus, this process of selecting a potential executive vice president and building a ticket could be a rather complex one.

First, though our By-Laws and elections policies allowed student body presidential candidates to formally declare a running mate, these potential E.V.P.'s were never listed on the ballot. Instead, our governing documents required any incoming student body president who campaigned with a running mate to present their declared partner as their first candidate for appointment during the annual transition meeting. In effect, this meant that the student body *did not* have the power to elect their executive vice president directly. Instead, the Senate from the prior administration had full discretionary authority to either accept or reject the proposed E.V.P appointment, procedurally rendering one-half of the proposed ticket moot. While it was highly unlikely for the Senate to turn down a candidate that had gone through the rigors of the campaign process, earning the approval of the student body, the lingering possibility of rejection reduced S.B.P.-E.V.P. tickets in our elections to a mere exercise in fan service for what some had already deemed a "popularity contest".

Such concerns bled into the second factor complicating this process, as one could not deny that a little bit of name recognition went a long way in these races. Like any community, we had our very own pool of informal "celebrities", comprised of the familiar faces that could be found frequently around campus or were commonly associated with a number of social groups. Though past E.V.P. candidates tended to come from within the rank and file of the S.G.A., many of them had still maintained additional connections and affiliations to major campus groups and organizations that typically branched off in a different direction from the associations of their S.B.P. counterparts. Although both members of the ticket would share a core following through their common S.G.A. experiences, they would each fill the gaps in their partner's social networks in order to create the broadest pool of potential voters that they could possibly assemble.

It was a reality that aspiring candidates simply had to face, as the process of forming student body presidential tickets had grown into a hardened tradition on our campus. Even so, it was not an aspect of the campaign that was necessarily dreaded or despised by candidates. Despite its inefficiencies, having two names attached to a campaign still provided a significant strategical advantage over running by yourself.

While the tactical significance of this decision did not escape me, it also did not determine my chief priorities in naming my desired E.V.P. Above all else, in selecting a running mate I wanted an individual that I could trust. The E.V.P. served as the right hand of the S.B.P., and having someone that I could turn to and confide in would greatly alleviate the stresses of the position. The close working relationship between the leaders of the 2011-2012 Administration had, in my mind, set the gold standard for

SBP-EVP match ups at the time. I needed both a dedicated manager as well as a confidant. I knew that it was a decision that I could not risk taking lightly. If persisting rumors proved to be true, our coming race would be an exceptionally close one.

Long before our peers prepared to cast their votes, S.G.A. onlookers would begin placing their bets as to who would likely rise up and throw their hats in the ring. I was just one among three potential candidates for the student body president's race that year. Like those who had preceded us, we had each made our marks on the collective consciousness of our peers through years of dedicated service of to the S.G.A., which were of such a profound intensity that one might even say our commitment bordered on fanatic devotion. There was no denying it; we were textbook student government insiders. In one way or another, we had each become prominent voices for the activities and values of the organization. And yet, each of us held records of service to separate and very distinct causes, having followed different paths throughout our S.G.A. careers.

Sitting at the top of the list of potential candidates was the president of our class. After rising above the other, nine initial contenders from the fall 2009 race to claim the office, he had held on to his title with each passing cycle to lead the Class of 2013 for the majority of his undergraduate career. As a member of the Senate, he brought a degree of refinement and eloquence to the Legislative Branch. Our class president was an exceptionally powerful public speaker and proved to be an even fiercer debater. Typically the one to play "Devil's Advocate" in our meetings, he carried himself with a profound air of purpose and never failed to back up his positions with a logical response conveyed with an artful poise. Not only

169

did he fearlessly extend an opposing view in our legislative sessions, but the Class of 2013 president had built his reputation upon his willingness to challenge the College Administration on issues where he believed the student body was getting the raw end of the deal. His platform would, undoubtedly, focus on this committed strong-suit of his, a powerful and unwavering advocacy for his fellow students. And yet, a well-established platform was not the only ground on which I found good reason to consider him a worthy adversary. Outside of the S.G.A., our class president was also a leader in one of the campus' two main fraternities, a significant voting block that already afforded him a formidable head start.

Second on the list was our Vice President of Club Affairs. Funny enough, the V.P. and I had already faced each other as political rivals earlier in our careers; we both sought the office of class vice president in the fall of 2009. After losing our bids to another candidate, we both joined the S.G.A. as members of the Junior Senate. While I returned to the Senate after winning a resident senator's seat in the spring of 2010, he decided to take another shot at joining the Class of 2013 Board. For the next year, he worked closely with our class president as our class treasurer but soon found this smaller cohort to be lacking in the greater excitement that one could find among the larger Executive and Legislative Branches. Jumping back into the fray of campus-wide politics, he ran for one of the uncontested resident senator positions in the infamous 2011 race. Before the 2010-2011 Administration had officially passed the gavel on to their successors, however, he decided to relinquish his seat in Senate to accept an appointment as the Vice President of Club Affairs for the coming term.

Over the years, he had proven himself to be just as fiercely devoted to student issues as he was loyal and kind. A robust personality had helped him to immediately mesh with any board that he joined, making him an ideal choice to serve as the main point-of-contact between our club presidents and the S.G.A. Indeed, his charming and easy-going nature, backed by a noted record of substantive achievements, made him a very strong candidate. He was the type of leader that any student could feel comfortable around, epitomizing the old desired image of a candidate that you could sit down and share a cold drink with while voicing your own ideas and concerns. Outside of the organization, the V.P. of Club Affairs was involved in intramurals and a number of other clubs, in addition to serving as a highly respected R.A. in a freshman residence area. I knew he would not have any trouble attracting others to his cause.

Then there was me. No matter how I cut it, I knew that I was looking at an uphill battle. These two were each tremendous leaders in their own rights, and I was thrilled to have kept pace with their efforts over the years to earn my place alongside them in the coming contest. We had each carved out our own, distinct swatches of the campus for ourselves and attracted dedicated followings among varying subsets of the student body. Working together, we would surely be unstoppable. And yet, fate had set us all on a crash course. Each of us had been aspiring to claim the title of student body president since we were freshmen. Though there was no ill will borne between us, we nonetheless stood as obstacles in each other's paths to attaining a desire that had defined our collegiate careers. This election promised not only to be a close race but a deeply emotional one.

That is why sudden whispers of a dropout caught us all off guard. By September of 2012, rumors began to suggest that the Vice President of Club Affairs would not be seeking the student body presidency after all. If this proved true, then it would be a game-changer for the coming contest. As a three-way race, it was difficult to call the match in favor of one man over the others. And yet, if he could now be pulled to one side of the contest as a running mate, the number of votes that would most assuredly accompany him could tip the scales of competition quite handily.

It just so happened that the V.P. and I had been assigned to a conference committee for the Association of College Unions International ("A.C.U.I.") later that fall. Together, we would be traveling to S.U.N.Y. Potsdam as a part of our college's delegation and, in this time away from our home campus, I saw the perfect opportunity to make my pitch. Coordinating with local teams from affiliated colleges, we made frequent trips to the S.U.N.Y. New Paltz campus, based in a community sitting just across the Hudson River, throughout September and early October. During these little excursions, I tried my best to verify the rampant rumors as discreetly as possible. After all, I did not want to risk verifying my intent to run too soon, inadvertently drawing out battle lines early on should he reject my offer. Moreover, I knew how much seeking the presidency had meant to him. I did not want to risk offending the V.P. by giving the impression that I was trying to talk him out of the race if it was in fact something that he still had his heart set upon.

Still, I knew that I was confronted by a very stern deadline. The words of advice from our past student body president echoed in the back of my head with each passing week. At the absolute latest, I knew that I had to have my materials finalized and ordered before the campus cleared out for Winter Break in December. This meant that I had to balance my attempts at discretion against a steadily approaching cut-off date. More importantly, the persistence of the rumors meant that I would not be the only one vying for his ear. Like blood in the water, the prospect of recruiting such an influential figure would surely bring a number of figures circling 'round.

I made my first attempt at obtaining the truth in late September, during one of our drives back to campus as we stopped for lunch just before the bridge. While we dug into our hamburgers after a long day of meetings, I asked him whether or not he had given any thought to continuing his S.G.A. work as a senior. Rather than take the bait, he simply shrugged it off as too far out to even think about at this point. I pressed the issue no further. A swing and a miss: strike one.

The pressure of the looming race had brought a number of my old, bad habits back into the mix; I let my timid nature get the best of me. After that initial side-step I left the matter alone for a while. I even went so far as to foolishly lull myself into complacency by hoping that his dismissive response would be the same should the other side come calling. So, we set our attention back to the task at hand, preparing for the conference coming up in the early weeks of November. All the while the two of us were being praised as a productive team, and I could not help but try to capitalize off of these comments by dropping casual hints and probing his responses for some sign of agreeability. And yet, each attempt proved as fruitless as the last. His intentions remained an absolute mystery to me, and I refused to delve any further. Strike two.

As November neared, I knew that I was backing myself into a tight corner. All that truly stood in the way of my asking him to be my running mate, outright, was fear. Here was an individual that I held in the highest of esteem and had honestly looked forward to running against in the election that coming spring. I saw him as a good friend, a fitting rival, and I feared *insulting* him in some way by suggesting that he should resign himself to the position of "Number 2". There was no doubt in my mind that he was suited to be the student body president himself and would make an exemplary E.V.P. if he decided to take on the role.

More than that, however, I feared his *rejection*. My own quest for this office stemmed from a need to prove myself on campus. It was a challenge that, in my eyes, he had already overcome. Once again, I found myself vying for the approval of an S.G.A. peer that I had come to admire. Rather than being driven by the hope of having him as a partner, I was stalled by the fear of being unworthy in his eyes. All the while, I was running out of time.

As my personal deadline for wrapping up campaign logistics closely coincided with our conference, I began to view S.U.N.Y. Potsdam as the site of my last stand. Ultimately, I thought that the V.P. of Club Affairs might appreciate a more theatrical approach to the matter, and hoped that such an injection of levity might otherwise ease any awkwardness in rejection or other misunderstandings. So, I planned to literally *propose* the idea of a potential partnership to him, with a candy ring and all.

Even as I lined all of my ducks neatly in a row, I still found it hard to pull the trigger. From our car ride up to the conference to the night of the formal dinner, I kept coming close to laying it all on the line before silently stowing away my courage and stuffing the candy ring back into my pocket. I told my self again and again that there would be a better time to raise the issue. In reality, I was still terrified by the thought of his potential rejection. Having allowed myself to kick the can so close to the impending deadline, I knew that it was quickly becoming a matter of "now or never". All I could do at that point was muster my remaining courage and leave the ball squarely in his court. Whether Potsdam would go down in our history as my Austerlitz or my Waterloo was entirely up to him.

Swallowing my pride and setting my fears aside, I reached into my coat pocket and fished out the candy ring. The night was clear, and the first hint of a winter chill had kept us moving at a brisk pace. Our delegation of five was making its way from S.U.N.Y. Potsdam's hockey arena to the main student center, and the two of us were drifting toward the back of the pack. As we chatted, I turned the subject once more to the upcoming election. He laughed yet again, shrugging off my response in his usual fashion, but I was finished with waiting. Dropping to one knee, I called out to him. He turned to see me kneeling with a ring pop held out in my extended arm, and I asked him to be my E.V.P.

Then came the dreaded pause, the nervous laugh. He realized that I was serious. His smile turned to a grave expression as he reached for the right words to fill the silence. He began his reply in almost a whisper, "I thought you already had a running mate."

"No."

That was all I could manage to stammer as I attempted to get back up to my feet. I suddenly felt as though the world had disappeared right from underneath me.

Lessons Learned

One of the things that I love most about my work with public organizations is the front row seat afforded by my roles in working with and exploring a wide array of personalities, opinions, and perspectives. Truly, no two people look out at the world and see *every* aspect in the same light. This can make for inspiring artwork and rich stories, but it can also be a nightmare for the public officials tasked with bringing this multitude of views together in concert to accomplish a collective task.

Compounding the difficulties in stringing each of these elements together to create a cohesive plan or policy is the reality that individual perspectives can slip through the cracks all too easily. As we came to find very quickly during our stay at the hotel, many students had simply resigned themselves to the perceived solitude of their stay, believing that there was no effective channel for converting their concerns into more impactful changes. They surrendered themselves to the belief that no one was listening, so they stopped talking.

Yet once such a channel had been extended to them, and counsel was afforded through a waiting ear on the other end, nothing could stop them from seizing upon the opportunity. The students who would later run for their area's governing board not only proved to be incredibly dedicated and innovative, but were simply *motivated* to make a difference. It was not simply the perceived apathy of their elected officials on the main campus, but their own lack of familiarity with the existing agencies and processes that had stifled their budding voices.

While our S.G.A. was not wholly innocent in the matter, the door to collaboration had not been entirely closed from the offset either. Had a more forceful push at integration come from the students at the hotel, it would have likely been met with open arms from their campus peers. And yet, such an attempt never arose, due largely to the fact that the intricacies in forming such a relationship were unknown to the parties sitting on both sides of the table at that time. My own involvement with the hotel had been prompted by a conversation with one of their R.A.'s, who had finally sought me out during one of my open office hours because they were not sure where else to turn and I was developing a reputation as someone who could help get things done. Still, no one quite had the answer for mending this divide. Up to that point, no one had asked. Thus, nothing was done.

Certainly, there is something to be said in all of this regarding the perils of hesitation. In waiting too long to engage the V.P. of Club Affairs in a serious dialog on the upcoming election, I missed my chance to bring him over to my team. While all aspiring leaders should take the time to weigh their options carefully and do their homework, one must also be sensible in determining the right moment to act. As one of the attorneys I worked for once noted, "attention to detail is great, but don't ever let it get in the way of delivering a project in a timely fashion. I'd rather have a quick effort, faithfully executed, than a perfect product delivered at the very last minute."

Not all scenarios will afford proper time for debate and discussion. Some issues will appear to the untrained eye as non-urgent or relatively minor in scope, only to erupt into more dire episodes or ensnaring quagmires. Great leaders recognize that it is often necessary to wrap up the discussion and just get to work, even if all of the pieces have yet to fall perfectly into place.

This requires a tremendous degree of awareness as to the present state of your organization, its needs, and the limits of its abilities. But most importantly, such a daunting task requires effective and routine communication. As no, one person can realistically direct their attention toward every level or angle of an organization around the clock, leaders utilize the skills of those around them to bolster and supplement their own abilities. When the chips fall and the die is cast, however, even members of the most established networks will find themselves turning to a single individual for direction. If the system is built upon healthy relationships and the leader has placed themselves as more of a nucleus, receiving and transmitting information in all directions rather than relying on a narrow hierarchy, then the organization will be better suited for overcoming and adapting to those challenges that do arise unexpectedly.

To cultivate such an ideal environment, leaders must find a way to overcome fear itself. It was the fear that accompanied being a new face in an established community that had initially left our transfer students feeling as though they had been set in the corner, and it was a fear of challenging the established social order that had kept so many of them lingering there. Likewise, the very same fear of rejection that I had tussled with throughout high school and my earlier days at college had resurfaced to impede my efforts at the offset of my greatest undertaking. To make our mark at the hotel, we set out to empower our residents to surmount their fears by altering their perspectives to pursue a greater priority. In fostering their own spirit of community independent of the larger campus identity, we gave

178

them something to invest in. By focusing on existing programs, as well as their own interests & strengths, they were able to rise above their initial concerns and initiate action. In my own journey, however, this was a lesson that I still struggled to embrace.

THE LEADERSHIP PROFILE: *Exercise Nine*

There is an old Cherokee legend about two wolves living in the heart of every person; one is evil and the other is good. It is a story that I shared during an event in my senior year, yielding a lesson that I have carried with me for the rest of my career. It started me thinking on the two constants in my life: ambition & anxiety. For every step forward that I have taken, my aspirations have always been matched by fear—of criticism, of the unknown, of failure, and so on. For as long as I can remember, there has always been this little voice in my head that stops me dead in my tracks whenever I set out to do something big or exciting. It tends to put up a good fight. And yet, I keep moving. I manage to keep climbing ahead of that voice because my desire to reach the summit of my imagination outweighs the doubt it tries to pile on top of me.

As the legend says, in the end, the wolf that wins is the one that we choose to feed. If there is both anger and love in your heart, it is not always your first instinct to set aside your rage and let your compassion seize the day. With time and practice, however, it does become easier. There was a time when that dreaded voice was enough to shut me out from every opportunity that I came across. Only in learning to feed the aspects of my personality that I wanted to live by, namely the ambition to make a name for myself, did I eventually find it easier to set my fears aside.

And yet, I believe there is more to the legend than training one wolf to simply beat out its sibling entirely. It is not a contest but a constant; the battle between these two forces can never truly be finished. Instead, the moral of the story, as I have come to see it, emphasizes balance. It is more important to understand the wolves inside of you and what it takes to settle them down, rather than seek to eliminate one altogether.

After all, my ambition has driven me to reach some terrific heights, but sometimes it pushes too far. And though my fear may stop me cold on occasion, those momentary pauses have also afforded opportunities for reflection. They have allowed me to set the matter aside and figure out whether or not I am still headed on the right path. Only in feeding both sides, for all the good and all the bad they each bring, can we truly grow. And so I wonder, what two wolves have you got inside of you?

Draw a circle somewhere at the heart of your profile and draw a line through its center, dividing it into two equal halves. Think about the two forces that are most constant in your life. They may be among the strengths and weaknesses that you have already listed or something else entirely. Look back on the example of a past failure that you jotted down before, think of your current role and daily activities, and pull out the common threads that appear in all of these scenarios. What drives you? What stalls you? Give a name to each of the wolves fighting inside your heart.

As you go on, be sure to reflect on the importance of these spirits in your life. In paying close attention to them, you will be more in tune with which one you are feeding at any given time. Though I tend to yield to my ambition, letting the excitement it fosters push me beyond my fears to reach new heights, there have undoubtedly been times when I have had to turn and feed the other wolf. Like a proper anchor, my apprehension has kept me from straying too far from my original goal or acting too impetuously without taking the time to weigh my options.

Once you have assigned a name to each side of the circle, erase a small portion of the dividing line from its center. Let this be a reminder that we are not meant to separate these forces completely, or let one reign over the other. These forces must be allowed to come together in an endless dance, one that helps to guide us in becoming who we are meant to be.

10 – THE ELECTION

"When can their glory fade?
O the wild charge they made!
All the world wondered."
-A. Lord Tennyson

When the dizziness had subsided and I was finally back on my feet, we stood there together in a moment of silence. Having signaled to the rest of our group to go on ahead, the Vice President of Club Affairs and I thought it best to clear the air.

He explained that the rumors were true. The College's policies prohibited the student body president from maintaining another full-time role on campus, and he could not afford to give up his position as a resident assistant. His hopes of seeking the presidency for himself had ended sometime over the preceding summer break. Adding to the saga, he shared that there had been yet another rumor winding its way through our student government that fall—one that had escaped my attention entirely. It suggested that my campaign was in far greater shape than it truly was. Under the impression that I had already compiled a full roster for my prospective administration, including an E.V.P., he accepted an offer from our class president's campaign team at the S.G.A.'s Halloween Haunted Trail event just a few weeks prior.

I do not quite recall when he finished recounting the story. His words were drowned out by a steady ringing in my ears, my blood rushing to my face and prickling against my skin under the steady chill of the November air. I felt cold, hollow and exposed as I tried my best to maintain my composure. His word had been given, the deal had been struck, and our three-man race had now become a battle of two against one. Strike three. Game over.

Just like that, the status of my campaign spiraled from "stable" to "critical". At long last, I knew just who I would be facing and the situation could not have been more dire. Hoping to pull myself out of this tailspin, I figured that there was still one more card left to be played. After returning home from the conference, I rallied together Team Johnson in an emergency session. After sharing the news on the V.P.'s decision, I introduced them to my runner-up.

I had pegged my friend from Toastmasters as a top E.V.P. choice early in my S.G.A. career. As one of the nine brave souls to run for class president in our first few weeks on campus, she quickly grew to be a bit of a powerhouse within the S.G.A., starting right along with us in the junior senate and rising up through her role as the previous Vice President of Club Affairs for the 2010-2011 Administration.

Her experience in working with club officers and various other campus organizations stood to be the best counter-play that I had left up my sleeve after losing the current V.P. to the other side. More importantly, she and I were close friends that had worked together on a number of large projects throughout our collegiate careers. I knew that I could confide in her, and I had dreamed of running on a ticket with her since our freshman year. And yet, there was a good reason as to why she had not been my initial choice for the position.

The controversy surrounding the 2011 election had soured her to the S.G.A. and led her to seek out a new path for her campus career through Toastmasters and various student life projects. These lingering memories left her with a strong disdain for the politics of the organization; it was not an experience that she was looking to repeat. Having found tremendous success, as well as a means of serving the community away from the S.G.A., I knew that she was perfectly happy right where she was. When I set out to plan my campaign, I initially resolved not to pull her away from the niche that she had worked so hard to carve out solely for my own selfish gain. But now, in desperation, I could only turn to her.

And her answer, as expected, was simple and sweet. I could not bring her around to rejoining the S.G.A., though she promised to support my candidacy in any other way that she could. We were both disappointed, to some extent, but also shared a sense of closure in the knowledge that it was all for the best. Recognizing the brutal fight that loomed ahead, and slightly envious of the peace that she had found outside of our ranks, I did not press the matter further. Instead, hers was but the first in a steady stream of rejections as I continued to work my way through a list of potential running mates to no avail. Out of ideas and nearly out of time, I turned back to Team Johnson for a miracle.

With the pressures of our various deadlines mounting upon us, my team of trusted counselors recommended a drastic course of action. As freshmen students had comprised the largest voting block in past S.G.A. elections, my team suggested tapping a current freshman student as my running mate. Though lacking in formal experience, a rising sophomore candidate would undoubtedly hold considerable influence over their peers, perhaps even outweighing the V.P. of Club Affair's own sway as a freshman R.A. Furthermore, participation in the coming race had significant benefits to offer a freshman candidate as well. If we were successful, then they would suddenly be holding one of the most powerful positions on our campus right at the onset of their collegiate career. Even if we failed, the race would provide them with considerable exposure and established name recognition for mounting future campaigns of their own.

There was also no shortage of potential candidates to choose from among the freshman class at that time. One student had already established herself as a proactive servant of the student body by taking over the resident senator position vacated by the V.P. of Club Affairs during the prior semester. My campaign team also eyed the president of the Class of 2015, who was off to a strong start of his own in championing the ideas of his peers to the greater campus community. Not only had he emerged victorious ahead of a traditionally large crowd in seeking that first presidential opportunity, but he and his board had broken the mold for class programming by developing unorthodox, though highly engaging, class activities.

Even so, I was not entirely sold on the prospect of recruiting a freshman to serve as my running mate. Having watched a number of my friends face the trials of a student body presidential contest in the past, I was not willing to subject a freshman to that kind of scrutiny for my own political gain. All too often, a defeat in the S.B.P. race was not something that candidates bounced back from. Win or lose, it typically marked the end of an S.G.A. career. Now that my two rivals were working together, the opposing campaign posed an extraordinary challenge, and there was no guarantee that even a play for the freshman vote would be enough to turn the tide in my favor. Despite the potential benefits of running in a race of this scale, my freshman running mate would have to forego seeking any

186

other S.G.A. position in order to campaign on my ticket. If we lost, it would more than likely spell the end of a bright career for a dedicated young member of the organization. That was not a risk that I was willing to ask them to take.

I was also not entirely ready to give up on the idea of somehow recruiting the V.P. of Club Affairs to be my E.V.P. He was undeniably suited for the job. Fearing my campaign team's focus had started to prioritize flash over substance, I became concerned that our scramble to pick someone—anyone—simply to plug the holes in our own campaign would ultimately rob the student body of their most qualified E.V.P. candidate.

So, I decided to run alone. I would face both of my opponents in an honorable fight and hope that my message would be the one to win the day. If, after facing these highly unfavorable odds head on, I could prove successful, then I would once again ask him to be my E.V.P. Without a running mate of my own, I would not be obliged to put anyone else up for appointment before the Senate. Even if he rejected me once again, I could rest assured that I had done all that was in my power to recruit the best available candidate. In the meantime, however, I would not be running entirely alone. At the very least, I could trust in my dedicated team to stand by my side until the very end, no matter the outcome.

Despite my sound conscience, this decision had done nothing to improve our situation. Running alone meant that I would be relying solely on my own resources, and Team Johnson was not prepared to mount a campaign large enough to overcome two, powerful opponents at one time. I did not have enough money to purchase custom printed t-shirts—I could barely afford enough color posters. In a three way race, at least, I had hoped that I could tread water long enough to hold my own as we each strove to stand out above each other. Now that my opponents would be working together and pooling their resources, I had to find a way to keep from being swept away into the background by a deflated budget.

Scraping together all that I had saved from my earnings as a cashier at a local market during breaks, I managed to come up with a total of fifteen campaign shirts. Far from professional quality, they were homemade customizations of generic, blue undershirts emblazoned with a hand-drawn, iron-on design that my cousin had made for me. To add to the overall underdog aesthetic, we stuck a piece of duct tape across the back of each shirt with "VOTE JOHNSON" scrawled out in permanent marker. They were few. They were crude. They were mine.

In fact, our shirts would quickly become something of a novelty during the campaign, as my friends were frequently asked why they were covered in duct tape, prompting a trained campaign pitch before their bemused onlookers. Ours was a shabby, tenacious, grassroots effort. As soon as my candidacy had been formally declared, we hit the ground running at full speed. We wasted no time in scattering flyers and folding signs throughout the campus. My slogans were visible on every table, in every common space, and upon every bulletin board from the main grounds right back to the hotel.

Each night, we ventured into a different residence area with fliers and candy, knocking on each and every door until we had nowhere left to turn. In our hurried pace, I did not realize just how quickly our campaign had managed to gain traction within our community. As we rounded out our first week of pounding the pavement, there was not a single poster or table tent from our opposition to be seen. I would later hear that a member of their campaign team had once confided that, if they did not get organized soon, they feared that I would be poised to steal the election right out from under them.

By the start of the second and final week of campaigning, however, they had prepared their response. After assembling nearly two-hundred bright pink shirts bearing their names and campaign slogan in baby blue font, there could be no doubt in anyone's mind that a fierce battle was underway. Their posters had the finished quality of a professional print, thanks to a skillful photoshoot conducted by a friend in the art program. Compared to my crude Photoshop compilations they were top grade, and it was not long before every common area bore the markings of our political battlefield. Our teams tore through the campus as we continued to campaign door to door and plaster any open space with a healthy layering of fliers and table toppers projecting our smiling faces.

In the heat of our battle, my spirits began to rise once again as unexpected allies flocked to my campaign. In addition to a few of our R.A.'s who quietly broke from their peers to endorse my campaign, the creative mind behind the student body's "Marist Memes" Facebook page offered to support us in any way that he could. Carefully traversing the prohibitive line between active and online campaigning, he created a slew of hardcopy posters for us. Though we could not tap directly into his growing digital audience on social media, we were thrilled to have his spirited support and artistic direction. Another welcome return was our third freshman roommate, the former Elections Commissioner. Having run a number of political campaigns of varying scales, he stepped in as an unofficial campaign manager to advise me in the heat of our contest. In a reunion befitting of a made-for-TV special, I found myself surrounded by the cheerful and devoted faces of a number of peers and allies from various chapters of my campus career.

This race was unlike anything that I had experienced before. Despite running campus-wide campaigns for the Senate twice in the past two years, the battle for the office of the student body president was a different beast entirely. Though there was no animosity borne between the three of us as candidates, smaller circles rooting for one campaign over the other had taken on our causes with potent passions. In addition to the positive support that I had experienced, the three of us also became the targets of some particularly nasty attacks. We would occasionally hear spiteful comments case in our direction and frequently found a number of our posters cruelly vandalized throughout the campus as the race wore on. In one instance, someone had run through a sophomore residence area tearing down and defacing each of our fliers, forcing me to set aside crucial campaign time to clear and replace these damaged articles.

In those moments where passions and tempers reached their boiling points, we came close to losing our composure and devolving into an all-out clash of wills. Following this incident, I received a call from the V.P. of Club Affairs one evening, asking if a member of my campaign was responsible for the damage, as my posters had apparently survived the onslaught. After assuring him that I would never issue such an order, he revealed that a friend of his, who lived in the impacted area, claimed to have witnessed a member of my team tearing down their fliers. He even provided a description: a male with dark hair and glasses in a "Johnson" campaign shirt. Confident in his source, he wanted a list of all of the people to whom I had given shirts.

A wave of relief rushed over me upon hearing his description. I knew that there was no way a person matching *that* description could have done it. After all, I had only fifteen shirts to hand out, and the majority of my team was comprised of female volunteers. Of the men in our group, only two of us wore glasses: our new roommate from the hotel and myself. Although he did match the remainder of their description down to the last detail, I was still sure of his innocence. As a transfer student, he was not regularly on campus and relied primarily on the shuttle for transportation. More importantly, his student I.D. would not allow him access to the residence area in question without being invited by someone inside, which made it all the more unlikely that he would go through the necessary trouble just to tear down a few fliers. Furthermore, when it came to our canvassing of campus residences, he had never even been assigned to area in question. I had.

I told the V.P. that I was certain that my team was not responsible. I admitted that I had been campaigning in the building the day prior, hanging replacement posters for a few of my own that had been torn down or damaged. I recounted that both sides appeared to have been targeted over the weekend and, in one instance, I *did* remove one of their posters from a stairwell because it had been viciously defaced. That was the only instance of a bespectacled male in a Team Johnson t-shirt taking down an opposing poster. I could guarantee it.

This was the closest our horns came to locking during the race. We each faced pressures in defending our dreams against the scrutiny, indifference, and even ire of the rest of the campus population. We had agreed from the offset to run civil campaigns and even met once in the middle of the contest to discuss the potential aftermath of the election. The three of us knew that we each wanted to stay involved with the S.G.A. in some capacity as seniors. More importantly, we each held a sincere desire to continue working together as a team under the new administration, no matter who wound up being in charge.

As our campaigns kicked off, we knew that one of the underclassman candidates seeking a seat in the Senate, whose members faced an unopposed race, would be interested in foregoing their elected office for a position on the Executive Board. Following the trend set by the V.P. of Club Affairs in the prior year, this would create an opening in the Legislative Branch subject to an appointment by the incoming S.B.P. As both sides now intended to appoint the same person as their E.V.P., the opening in the Senate could potentially be used to pull the losing student body presidential candidate back into the organization.

The prospect of having such a safety net did not entirely remove anxiety and uncertainty from the 2012 race. There were a number of technical complications, combined with good old-fashioned bad luck, that sent us reeling off course at times. Building off of his efforts to create a more collaborative relationship with the campus media and broaden the S.G.A.'s reach within the student community, the sitting student body president decided to change up the program for the 2012 student body presidential debate night. Instead of holding the event in a public forum, like its traditional venue in the student center, we would meet on the soundstage of the campus television network for a live, televised event. The debate would be broadcasted over the campus' cable network in an attempt to reach a larger segment of the student population, as well as flex the muscles of both of our organizations in coordinating a next-level campaign event.

On the evening of the debate, I went off to the campus TV station alone while the rest of Team Johnson gathered in the living room of a friend's house on campus to watch the main event. Having drawn up my line of questioning shortly after our phone call regarding the flier incident, my initial draft came across as more aggressive than I had intended it to be. After running it by our sitting student body president, seeking his counsel just moments before the broadcast was set to begin, he advised me to dial back on my emotions and reflect on my reasons for running in the first place. Before the cameras began rolling, I had to start over from scratch. After all, wounding the other side was not my objective.

My opponents and I had each set out to make a difference in our student government and on our campus, working diligently over the past three years to make our own impressions on a community that we loved. Though we certainly faced our share of disagreements throughout our terms, there was no need for animosity or rancor between us. After cooling off a bit, I took my seat at the table and looked forward to a spirited discussion, the culmination of our S.G.A. careers.

As two campus TV technicians prepared the system for its live broadcast, the class president and I took a moment to prepare. The V.P. of Club Affairs joined us in the studio along with the current student body president, executive vice president, and Elections Commissioner. Across from us sat two other figures, members of the campus media who would serve as our moderators. The president of the campus radio network and a talented writer whose blog, *Marist in Progress*, was exclusively covering the election were tasked with hosting the evening's debate. As the pre-show work continued, my opponent and I bantered back and forth, letting the weight of our contest slowly sink away. For a few moments we laughed and joked together, playfully maneuvering across the news desk that would serve as our shared podium throughout the program. It felt like we were freshmen again, facing the unknown perils of the political bog not as bitter rivals but as friends.

I would like to think that this spirit of comradery carried itself into our debate in some form. Though we each could not resist the temptation to jab at one another at least once or twice in the heat of the moment, the overall tone of the debate was largely positive. Unfortunately, it is hard to say for sure who came out on top in this match up. Due to technical difficulties, the program did not air as planned. Instead, the campus television network proceeded with their Plan B and hoped to broadcast the debate at a later time, prior to the election. Unfortunately, we learned sometime toward the tail end of the race that the data file storing the program had been corrupted; the debate footage was lost entirely. Though the student body would never witness the battle of spirits that took place that evening, I like to think that it left an impression on those present in the room.

Our debate would be the last of the official campaign events before the process began winding down and the polls prepared to open the following week. Losing the ability to share the debate footage meant that our campaign had lost a critical opportunity to speak directly to the student body. For a financially strapped operation that relied on this kind of exposure, it dealt us a serious blow. Unable to keep up with the sea of pink shirts that flooded the campus, I relied on door-to-door campaigning as my primary means of directly engaging potential voters in those final hours. Gathering Team Johnson in our hotel room once more, we laid out our plans for the last leg of the race. Under the election reform bill passed by the 2011-2012 Administration, active campaigning would no longer cease on the evening before polls opened. Instead, candidates were now permitted to continue their efforts right up until the last vote was cast.

This made our campaigning excursions feel even more like they were part of an endurance race. From a strategic standpoint, we had to carefully plan our door-to-door visits so that we remained relevant in the eyes of the campus community without becoming a full-blown nuisance. If we loaded our efforts too heavily toward the start of the voting period, we would prompt a strong initial push but leave plenty of room for our opponents to catch up and close the gap over the next two days. Alternatively, if we waited until the last minute we risked missing the opportunity to reach students before they cast their votes.

Furthermore, although active campaigning was now permitted during the week of voting, there were still a few lingering policies that had to be carefully navigated in order to avoid a disqualification. Online campaigning was still strictly prohibited, though the online voting system used by the S.G.A. did allow for some wiggle room. Candidates and their followers were allowed to share a link to the voting system via their own social media accounts, so long as it was a vague, generalized posting that could not be construed as an endorsement. For example, posting a general "get out and vote" message on my personal page with a link to the polls was perfectly ok, but including any reference to my candidacy or the causes that I promoted along with the link could be grounds for immediate disqualification. Even posting a photo of myself wearing one of my own campaign t-shirts, with no further comment, could be grounds for expulsion from the race.

Our S.G.A. policies also prohibited campaigning of all forms in or around the S.G.A. office and all designated polling stations. While one of my campaign members could run around campus with a laptop and say, "Hey, can you take a minute and vote for my friend?" they had to stop endorsing me as a specific candidate within a certain radius outlying these designated neutral zones. Preparing to narrowly traverse this line as gracefully as we could, my team and I set out our plan for the home stretch.

When the polls opened on Monday morning, everyone on Team Johnson was wearing their duct tape strewn shirts. One of my Core Four companions had also baked a sizeable batch of little blue cupcakes with "Vote Johnson" flags and was not afraid to trade a pastry for a vote as she carried her laptop in tow. Others tried to collect as many of their friends as possible to follow them to a nearby polling station once their classes had ended. We were tenacious. We were coordinated. And yet, I could not shake the fear that the odds we faced were truly insurmountable.

After all, you could not go to a basketball game on campus without seeing a wall of pink shirts in the student section, and I found the faces of my opponents beaming at me from their campaign posters around every corner that I turned. My resolve soon faced another, crushing blow when the opposing campaign received an endorsement from a rising campus celebrity and mutual friend. An aspiring musician with outstanding school spirit, he had included their team shirt in the closing moments of his music video for his hit single, an ode to our campus called "I Love Marist". The scene depicted its star performer removing the campaign shirt of our current administration to reveal the pink campaign shirt of my opponents before jumping into the Hudson River, a symbolic moment representing the transition between administrations.

In those days, I learned that it is incredibly difficult not to take these little losses personally. Having invested so much time, sweat, and energy into my campaign, I could hardly separate criticisms against it from attacks against myself. As people you have worked and fought alongside for so long begin lining up to endorse your opposition, it becomes all the more difficult to see it as a matter of "they really like them" over "they really don't like me." A similar thought nagged at me while I was watching that video. As I closed my laptop, I tried my best to unwind the knot that had settled in my stomach. Would the outcome of the race really be that clear? Did I actually stand a chance at all?

While it all seems rather childish with the clarity of hindsight, these are the thoughts that grab at you through the haze of a campaign. Foregoing food, foregoing sleep, my days had all been spent in pursuit of this singular ambition. Rationality does not necessarily flourish under such conditions.

As the contest wore on, I continually found myself in need of a retreat. Living in the hotel, away from campus, certainly provided some distance from the usual gossip. But to truly put my mind at ease, I felt that I needed the comfort of a familiar space. So, towards the end of the campaign, I spent most of my downtime on campus safely tucked away in the room that had been my sanctuary for the past three years, our S.G.A. office.

♦

On the second day of voting, just as my team was taking a quick break before making our final rounds through the freshman dormitories that evening, everything was unexpectedly turned on its head. I had decided to spend the afternoon after the last of my classes settled into my usual seat in the office, quietly retreating into the steady stream of projects that lit up my laptop screen and had otherwise been neglected during the race. Suddenly, an S.G.A. friend appeared at the door and motioned for me to join them in the hallway. Their face was drained of all color as they glanced around nervously and shared the news: a rumor had broken out around campus; it claimed the student body presidential race was currently separated by only one vote.

My mind did not pause to consider the veracity of the statement; its focus was singular. My heart lodged itself in my throat as I clutched my old flip phone and stumbled to string together a quick text message: "We're close. Don't stop now." Catching our second wind, Team Johnson canvassed the campus with freshly baked cupcakes, candy, and every last ounce of energy that we could muster. All the while, a single thought kept racing through my mind, "One vote. *One vote.* By G-d we've got them trailed by just *one vote!*"

By the time we finished, the sun had already set and the brisk chill of evening blanketed the grounds. As I collapsed back into my seat in the S.G.A. office, I was embraced by a rather pleasant numbness. My heart was no longer racing under the excitement of holding so closely to the coattails of my opponents. Instead, it had been quelled by a sense of fulfillment. We had exhausted ourselves in this final push, and I could rest assured knowing that there was nothing more that we could possibly have done. Struck by a tinge of joy in knowing that this race was so close to being finished, I sent out one last note to my campaign team, a message of thanks.

◆

Before I close this particular chapter, something more must be said about the people that comprised Team Johnson. As my closest friends on campus, I leaned on them very heavily. I pushed them to extreme lengths during the race and was very fortunate to have them follow along. Despite their own deadlines and obligations, they devoted countless hours to the fulfillment of my dream and patiently put up with my on-the-brink-of-a-mental-breakdown style of leadership throughout the waning hours of the race. Their dedication and support helped me to realize that great efforts are not achieved by the strength of one individual alone but the combined energies of a devoted group.

Coordinating Team Johnson helped me to establish a management philosophy that I would apply to a number of teams and boards throughout my career. Above all else, I led by the principled belief that a leader should never ask of another person something that they are not personally willing to do themselves. I led my campaign from the trenches, right alongside my team at every turn. So long as they remained fighting valiantly beside me, I could feel invincible in the face of overwhelming odds. I was confident that we had done our best and that I could not have possibly asked of my team anything more than we had already given. Leaving our hearts on the battlefield, all that remained was left in the hands of the student body.

◆

On the night the election results were to be announced, Team Johnson met one last time at the hotel. Collectively gathering our wits, we came together at our home base and prepared to bring this episode to a close in the same fashion as we had first set it off, together. The S.G.A. was hosting an elections party in the Cabaret, introducing the new administration before a live audience. We would be making our grand entrance as a team, then huddle together and brace for the news. Offering one last toast, one last hug, and one last cheer, we readied ourselves for whatever was to come next.

As we split up into different cars for our drive to campus, I broke off from the convoy for a quick detour. Parking across the street from the main grounds, I strolled up the hill to the chapel for a quiet moment of reflection. Standing before the statute of St. Marcellin Champagnat, founder of the Marist Brothers and progenitor of their profound legacy, I offered a solitary prayer. There, in the cold of that February night, I thought back to my earliest moments on campus; my entire career flashed before my eyes. All that I had done, every project undertaken and cause championed, was executed in the hope that I could grow beyond that timid little boy who wanted nothing more than to make a positive impression. Clasping the outstretched hand of the metallic Saint, I found in his stare a feeling of acceptance. As I returned to my waiting team, I finally began to feel at peace.

For just one more evening, we sat at odds with the individuals that comprised the opposing team, clustered together in our own little cohorts. The Cabaret had been decked out for the occasion with patriotic flair and the campaign videos strewn together by both teams played in a loop via a projector in the background. While some wore campaign shirts, other members of our team had dressed up for the occasion in suits and dresses of their own. After running together non-stop throughout the preceding weeks and months, assembling and enacting our campaign strategies with haste, those last thirty minutes before the final announcement seemed to drag on for an eternity. Even so, it was an eternity well spent. With nowhere left to run, and no more lines to pitch, we were finally free to enjoy each other's company without a looming agenda or deadline. Raising our glasses together, we toasted to the honor of a race well won.

◆

Scanning the jovial audience before her, the executive vice president for the 2011-2012 Administration approached the mic. "We're going to get started in a few minutes," she announced excitedly, instructing the eager congregation to hold tight for just a short while longer. Off to her side, the student body president glanced up from his notecards to find my opponents and me flitting through the crowd, playing the parts of good politicians. As he caught each of our eyes, he quietly motioned for us to join him out in the hall.

As the sounds of pre-celebratory chatter faded behind us, the reality of the scene began to sink in. With the E.V.P. trailing in his stride, the S.B.P. closed the door behind us. We stood in the silence of that hallway for a tense moment, each trying to peek down at the card in his hand for some sign of the imminent call. Sensing our impatience, he cleared his throat for our attention and followed this signal with a comforting laugh. Regardless of what happened next, he told us, he wanted to let us know that he was proud of us all.

As his own election experience had not fostered the happiest of his memories, the S.B.P. was keenly aware of the emotional weight that had been thrust upon us. More importantly, with the bulk of his term resigned to a period of convalescence in the wake of the 2011 races, he appreciated how deeply we understood the importance of pulling of a group "win" with a smooth election cycle. He was grateful that neither side lost sight of the bigger picture, maintaining a civil and respectful competition right up to the ringing of the closing bell. Before we could truly mark the end of this journey, however, there was still one thing left to do.

Nodding to my opponents with a solemn sense of comradery, we returned to our respective groups for the big announcement. A sudden hush fell over the crowd as we drifted back into place, their eyes attentively darting from the three of us, scanning our faces for any indication of triumph or defeat, before turning back to the S.B.P. and E.V.P. as they skirted the walls of the Cabaret to take their place behind the mic. As the audio from the looping videos was cut from the background, the static hum of the audio system rang through the air before yielding to a deep silence.

The S.B.P. began by welcoming the event's attendees, reflecting on the significance of our communal investment in this important process. Although he did not raise the specter directly, his words highlighted the noted differences in our student body from the year prior. Whereas the former cycle had been marked by division and animosity, this evening's celebration brought champions of opposing causes together in a spirit of honorable competition, swapping campaign war stories from neighboring tables with neither scornful glare nor bitter remark. He applauded both teams for running honorable races, close races.

He triumphantly shared that this year's voter participation had eclipsed all prior averages on our campus, just surpassing our Election Commissioner's goal at 36%. In the end, he revealed, a mere 5% of voters would separate victory and defeat.

We were all on the edge of our seats by this point, hanging on to his every word as a few of our individual team members tried to do the math in their heads. "That means we had about 1,600 voters!" One whispered excitedly. "Yeah, and that means only 80 of them turned the tide."

My mind immediately cut back to the second day of voting and my hurried meeting in the hallway. "One vote," my friend and informant had told me, "you guys are only separated by one vote." Now I believed it. As I relived those tumultuous final hours, the true ferocity of our competition was illuminated in a startling clarity. I was so downcast in my disappointment over not having resources comparable to our opponents' that I had completely overlooked the results of our vigor. Our grassroots renegades had run neck-to-neck with the titans I had built up in my mind.

As the student body president concluded his remarks and was handed the official result tabulation from the E.V.P., a member of my core team reached out from my hand. Scenes from the preceding years flashed through my mind as the internal narrative that I had spun for myself finally aligned with reality. The moment had arrived. For one sweet instant, anything truly seemed possible. I could close my eyes and hear my name echoing over the loud speaker.

And it played out perfectly, just as I had imagined, except for one detail. The name they called was not my own. Falling back into my seat as my opponents rose to take their victory lap, I was embraced by an unusual numbness. My teammate's hand slipped from my own as they drifted sideways with a sort of shellshock. As we watched the class president make his first speech as the S.B.P.-elect, I felt neither rage nor sorrow. I was embraced by an indescribable calm.

In my mind, the three years preceding this episode had been building to a single pursuit that, in one moment, came crashing down upon me. I had built my concept of self, almost entirely, around this dream of becoming student body president. Somehow, I had managed to convince myself that, to become a respectable individual, I had to first establish my worth in the eyes of the community. I confused votes with respect, believing that the student body's approval of my ability to represent them as the face of our school would be the greatest determination of my value.

It was this narrow line of thought, not the outcome of the election, which proved to be my greatest folly. Sitting in the Cabaret, surrounded by my friends—some of whom seemed more crushed by the results than I was at the time—I felt as though a terrific weight had suddenly been lifted from my shoulders. As my opponents took their victory lap around the room, I made a mental inventory of all the little blessings that came flooding back to me in that moment.

Over the course of the three years that preceded this contest, I had dedicated myself to a cause that I believed in. Through the principled approach I adopted, I built a professional reputation that I could be proud of; I became an active part in a community that I loved; I found a team of amazing, dedicated friends who were willing to go above and beyond for me when I could offer them nothing in return; and, to my great relief, it had not been a blowout. A mere sliver of the total votes cast had determined the outcome of our race. Our team had shared its message with the community and the narrow margin of our loss told me that we had been heard loud and clear. It did not feel like such a tremendous defeat after all.

The very first mistake I made in my undergraduate career was tying my definition of success to a particular office. I had confused the student body presidency with what I really wanted to achieve, a greater sense of confidence and self-fulfillment. In running my race the way I wanted, in accordance with the principles that I had developed over the course of my career, I had finally reached a point in my life where I was willing to bare it all before the campus and say "This is who I am, this is what I believe in, and I want to serve *you*." I had even found a group of people who not only believed in that message but loved and respected the person who sought to share it.

I had accomplished all that I set out to do and then some. After shaking hands with my opponents, my peers, I returned to my friends as they stepped out into the night, closing that chapter of my life once and for all.

Lessons Learned

This was the "moment of truth" in my collegiate career. After working my way to this point with a specific goal in mind, I finally had the opportunity to put my resolve to the test. Speaking candidly, there were certainly moments where I considered abandoning my plan of seeking the student body presidency for a safer route to re-election. When I realized that I would be running against two, well-established candidates as a ticket, rather than as individuals, sticking to my seat on the Senate became a very tempting option. Nonetheless, having seen how the campus responded to an uncontested race in the prior cycle, and recognizing that I would never be able to forgive myself for passing up my one shot at becoming the S.B.P., I charged head on into a fight that part of me never really expected to win.

Sometimes we have to lead our own, noble charge against the odds to reach the next stage in our careers or pursuits. There will not always be a clear and simple path forward. In your life, you will undoubtedly face moments where the sky appears to be clear for miles and miles and the thought of complacency seems to be its own, sweet reward. Settled comfortably in our position, the path to reaching another, greater opportunity may only come at the cost of abandoning the *status quo*. In these instances, it may be all the more appealing to just sit tight and forego the trouble of a challenge. For leaders, however, this is not a decision that we undertake lightly.

As the head of a team or organization, our role involves elements of both advocacy and stewardship. In suspending our own personal beliefs regarding the viability of an initiative, we are tasked with taking on the responsibility of representing our product, project, or program with unwavering zeal. Sometimes this requires us to forego the comfort of our present situation and delve into the waters of uncertainty in order to bring about the end which best suits our cause.

To overcome my fear in the face of seemingly insurmountable opposition, I had to learn to be an advocate for myself and my team. Seeing all of the time and effort that my friends were willing to put into my campaign helped me to realize that I was fighting for more than just a job title; I was fighting for everything that I claimed to stand for, everything that had caused them to believe in me. I learned to look beyond my own, personal fears to distinguish "Michael Johnson, the individual" from "Michael Johnson, the student body presidential candidate". This has proven to be an invaluable skill in politics, as I have, on occasion, been challenged personally for the stances that I have taken on particular issues. In these cases, separating out my own interests and feelings from the merits of a policy or initiative has helped me to focus on the central issue and disregard the lowly jabs that were directed at me out of anger or spite.

After all, for the sake of maintaining our own sanity, we must all find some way to cope with the occasional gibe. Leaders ultimately place themselves on a platform for scrutiny and ridicule when they step up to guide their peers, a reality that is inescapable in public and private organizations alike. Whatever coping method you decide upon in the end, I would strongly advise you against allowing the prospect of these types of comments and attacks to deter you from seeking a leadership role altogether. In exploring opportunities to lead, the preeminent thought in your mind must be this: "Am I willing and able to provide a service?" If you answer in the affirmative, believing that you have something to bring to the table that will ultimately benefit your constituents, then you have met my sole criteria for leadership eligibility. Regardless of background, political view, expertise, or scope of vision, all that one truly needs to become a leader is the willingness to give himself or herself up in service for the greater benefit of an organization, community, cause, or simply another individual.

I wholly recognize that a fair share of the credit for the impact that I have made on our campus is due to the incredible team of people that I have had standing beside me throughout my career. Having organized Team Johnson on a foundation of trust and mutual respect, I entered the race with more than just an extra set of hands to circulate fliers. The ideas and insights that they were able to extend from their vantage points within the campus community helped me to regain my traction after suffering what would have otherwise been a knockout blow.

Furthermore, although many of the individuals that comprised Team Johnson had no prior involvement or interest in student government before the race, they soon found themselves engrossed in the politics and drama that colored our organization. Quite simply, we were able to create a shared culture from a singular goal that came to define yet another facet of our friendship. From an administrative standpoint, it also created the bedrock upon which I was able to build my campaign and motivate my team to extend such an incredible effort. Despite being underfunded and relatively understaffed, we were able to go toe-to-toe with our sizeable opponents right up until the closing moments of the race.

If there is one, final note to be shared with aspiring leaders in light of this episode, let it be this: a leader must possess a profound sense of dignity and grace that, at times, exceeds their individual capacity for composure. In separating my self-view between public and private personas, treating the former like a corporate brand, I came to understand that my conduct reflected back on others apart from myself. As a representative of the S.G.A., my demeanor could be interpreted as a reflection of my class, the S.G.A. as a whole, and even the College itself. It is a responsibility that I have always undertaken with the utmost seriousness.

Nevertheless, as I stood in the Cabaret that evening, I found myself resisting every childish impulse to simply break down and withdraw from the cheering crowd completely. For all of the expectations piled upon us, leaders will sometimes find themselves bracing against an overwhelming weight that seems almost impossible to bear. In these moments, we are faced with the temptation to either lash out or steal ourselves away completely. Great leaders, however, are those who can summon the courage to face these challenges with a smile. Even a wild charge head-on toward defeat can be a thrill, if you have the right people by your side to share it with.

THE LEADERSHIP PROFILE: *Exercise Ten*

The narrow margin that separated our race, a mere 5% of the overall vote, is due largely to the efforts of the people that I had around me. There is no way that I could have met that mark on my own. Therefore, a portion of our own, individual profiles must be dedicated to others— specifically, to those who we can count on to be in our corner when we need them the most.

Take a moment to sketch out a space for these influential people in your life on your profile. Fill it with a list of the individuals that comprise your dream campaign team. That is, if you were to step out in the public eye to champion some idea tomorrow—whether it involved advocating for a cause that is important to you or defending a project that you hope to one day launch—who can you trust to stand in your corner? Whether it is a friend or a neighbor that you know you can rely on, an educator who has mentored you in the past, or an associate you have worked with for some time, we all have networks of varying sizes that can be utilized to move the ball forward.

What ultimately separates these individuals from the potential partners you listed in Exercise Four, however, is the more intimate role that they play in developing your leadership journey. Whereas the prior list represents potential professional allies, the current exercise asks you to call to mind those individuals who have come to play such an integral role in your story that their impact goes well beyond traditional networking to include a social-psychological component. The Core Four and Team Johnson were, for me, more than just a campaign team. They were a

211

surrogate family, the closest friends that I had at the time. I knew that I could count on them for anything and everything all at once, a peace of mind that served as a guiding light in the more harrowing moments of the election cycle. Truly, even an uphill climb can feel like a walk in the park if you know that the right people have got your back.

That is why we will set this particular space aside for the cast of supporting actors in your life story. Find a place that sets them apart from other players and emphasizes the important role that they fill in both realms of your journey: the personal and the professional alike.

It is also worth noting that such praises are an honor, not an obligation. Inevitably, I have drifted out of touch over the course of my career with some of my team members. In time, priorities change and these things will simply happen. A friendship, for better or worse, is not a life sentence. I caution you to be wary of this as we ascribe these names to our profiles, simply to acknowledge that the loss or absence of a friend will not jeopardize your pursuits. Just because they are no longer such a frequent part of your life does not mean that their role in your story, let alone their impact upon it, is in any way diminished.

11 – THE LEGACY

"Long is the way and hard,
that out of Hell leads up to light."
– John Milton, *Paradise Lost*

Losing the election did not mean that my S.G.A. story had come to an end. Though some had suggested that I take the opportunity to bow out and retire, like so many who had come before, I knew that this was not the right choice for me. After all, I loved my work with the S.G.A. and believed that the largely civil campaigns run by both sides throughout the race had, hopefully, left the door open to continued collaboration. After all, bringing the losing side back into the student government was something that we had readily discussed throughout the election. So long as I felt that I could still be of use, I would not close the door to any possible opportunities to continue working with the new administration.

That is why I did not hesitate to submit an application for service under the new team. Though it seemed highly likely that I would be able to rejoin the S.G.A. in some capacity, I still recognized that there was no guarantee. In relinquishing my seat in the Senate to seek the student body presidency, I now found myself faced with a rather narrow list of prospects.

Of course, my best hope would be to return to the Senate itself under a different arrangement. As rumors had previously suggested, one of the newly elected resident senators would be resigning from their office in order to seek an appointment to the Executive Board in the coming transition. As we had already witnessed a similar exchange take place one year prior, I knew that this opening in the Legislative Branch would be

213

subject to a presidential appointment. Though my opponents and I had toyed with the idea of using a potential opening in the Senate to pull back the runner-up in our own contest, we had not yet set anything in stone.

After all, the practice of swapping out and refilling Senate seats was neither common nor encouraged. The S.G.A. did not want individuals flooding the Senate race to simply secure a position within an administration before jumping ship to chase a more favorable spot on the Executive Board. Such a loophole held potentially devastating repercussions for the organization, as the mere illusion of foul play could irreparably damage the S.G.A.'s standing on campus, which was already on the mend from "rather tenuous" to "fairly respectable". Furthermore, routinely relying on the Executive Branch to staff the Senate could put a serious strain on the impartiality and independence of the Legislative Branch. As such, the resident senator position was not on the list of offices provided on our typical application form. With that in mind, I did not select any of the afforded options and left this space blank on my submission in the hopes of keeping the door open to reclaiming my old seat, without eliminating any other possibilities.

Even if my plan to rejoin the Senate should fail, and the incoming student body president decided either not to accept the resignation of the ambitious resident senator or go along with my own gambit, it was still possible that my application might be considered for another position on the Executive Board. With each new administration, there were a host of vice president and director-level positions within the S.G.A. that were left open to the discretion of the incoming S.B.P.

The reason I did not set my sights so heartily on one of these existing options was that, despite the apparent plethora of offerings, finding a truly open seat on the Executive Board seemed rather unlikely. This branch existed as a micro-bureaucracy; it was a proving ground were talent was cultivated from lower boards and committees to groom leadership for future administrations. Although the office of the student body president and every seat within the Legislature would be shuffled around with each election cycle according to the will of the electorate, the boards and councils that branched out from the Executive Board continued to operate soundly in the background of our campus' governmental structure.

Having developed a keen expertise when it came to addressing their designated issue or program, these incumbents were rarely challenged or forced out without good reason. As a result, the S.G.A. adhered to an informal recommendation process, wherein each individual board was responsible for selecting its own leadership for consideration and approval by the incoming S.B.P. While some boards would simply allow their most senior member to make the call, others—like the Student Programming Council—relied on more democratic methods. When a sitting director or vice president did eventually graduate or move on to other projects, there was usually an underclassman protégé already waiting in the wings to assume control.

Some would argue that this traditional approach to the appointment process made it difficult for new talent to infiltrate the S.G.A. hierarchy. Others might even take one step further to lambast the practice as proof of our cliquish nature. While this did, undoubtedly, restrict the number of top-tier opportunities open to newcomers, I would have to argue that it was a necessary evil. Even the most established directors were subject to review and removal by the Senate during the annual confirmation hearings, and had to make a case for their assignment to another term at the helm of their respective boards. Situated just below these individuals, there were usually a number of entry-level opportunities for newcomers to learn more about the S.G.A., an individual board, or a particular policy area before seeking greater opportunities within the organization down the line. Although this may not have always been the most glamourous starting point for an S.G.A. career, it was certainly the most effective.

It was neither politics nor individual loyalties that allowed so many individuals to hang on to their positions year after year, it was simply experience. Having a knowledgeable candidate on hand was a blessing, affording a sense of administrative stability to an organization that faced the possibility of a drastic roster change with each new election cycle. As incoming administrations raced to make their individual marks on the history of our community and cross off a few items from their to-do lists before November signaled the mid-way point in their terms, our established hierarchy of administrative leadership and corresponding procedures encapsulated within each sub-board and council prevented these units from facing delays in the typical transition shuffle. Instead, our traditions helped them to carry on the momentum from the prior year and keep the ball progressing at a steady pace.

Of course, this also meant that the odds of my breaking into the ranks of the Executive Board at this point in my career were rather minimal. For each of the positions that I might have filled, there were already teams of candidates who had paid their dues in the hopes of ascending to claim the same, lingering slot as their own. Even if I did stand a chance at trumping their claims with my own seniority in the organization, I would not want to steal away the fruits of their dedicated labors and cut short the ambitions of one of my peers for the sake of buoying my own wounded record. So, I maintained an optimistic outlook and continued to set my hopes on the possibility of an open Senate seat. Not only did it seem to be my best shot but the best fit overall.

When the time came to sit down with my former opponents for a formal interview, I learned that they had other plans entirely. In keeping true to their word, they had indeed picked out a place for me in their administration. Rather than shuffle me back into the Senate to fill the recent vacancy or slide me into one of the existing Executive slots, they had come up with an even more interesting third option. Having recognized the continued need on our campus for the work of the Civility Campaign, as well is its own need for stable management, they intended to give it a permanent home under the auspices of the Executive Branch. As I had been involved with its inception and the early coordination of its program structure, they asked me to take the helm as the first Director of Community Relations for the S.G.A.

As I had explained before, the Civility Campaign was really in its infancy at this point in time. Our scattered experiences with developing programs designed to both proactively foster a spirit of community and respond to unanticipated acts of anonymous hostility and broader tragedy had left us facing a bit of a conundrum when it came to developing a solid mission for the Campaign. Since our sophomore year, the Campaign had experienced difficulties in balancing the various approaches undertaken by its individual coordinators toward meeting its dual responsibilities. As it routinely passed hands through the Senate, each new program chair brought with them a new vision or outlook for the campaign, rapidly reorienting its focus from month to month.

This shifting leadership structure prevented it from laying roots in a particular cause or policy area, let alone cultivate a fundamental sense of ownership within our community. This was due, in part, to the fact that the focus of the Campaign would shift drastically in its earlier days between national and local organizations across a wide spectrum of issues. Without a trained focus or a narrower breadth, it was difficult to make a lasting impact. Without a proper foundation to branch off from, the Campaign could not flourish into an entity of its own. As our collegiate careers were drawing to a close, my peers and I began to fear that the Civility Campaign would not be able to carry on much longer after losing the dedicated support of those who had experienced the events that prompted its formation firsthand.

In giving the Campaign a permanent home on the Executive Board, the new 2012-2013 Administration not only hoped to provide it with a stable leadership structure but refine its mission in an effort to establish it as a unique program that could thrive independently for years to come. Just as I did not want my Safety & Security Committee to become nothing more than a soapbox for an existing office, the S.G.A. did not want to see the Civility Campaign become an expressway for charitable causes that had little or no connection to our own community. In developing an identity of its own, the Civility Campaign would select projects and programs that tapped into a common focus more directly linked to our campus, expanding its overall impact and increasing its chances for growing into a sustainable S.G.A. legacy.

My experience as one of the original committee members for the Campaign and the chair of some of its earliest programs put me in a unique position to guide the administration in ensuring that the Civility Campaign outlasted our terms. Crafting such a legacy would not only require us to draft formal policies and practices but recruit local partners to help carry the torch. My S.G.A. experience was coming full circle; I once again found myself relying on old talents in community service to adapt to a new position and its related challenges.

In carrying the Campaign forward, I decided to maintain its present approach of forming monthly programs with specific causes or themes. Rather than take on broader, national causes, however, we would instead focus on local issues and highlight our campus-based service organizations. In rooting our efforts closer to home, I hoped that the Campaign would have a more direct impact on our student body. After all, our most successful programs in the history of the Campaign had been those that struck a chord with our community over a shared concern or vision. Not since the first candlelight vigil had we seen a comparable response from our peers outside of the S.G.A. In my eyes, the Campaign did not need to necessarily develop a message or platform of its own in order to begin crafting its identity; it functioned best when it allowed our students to showcase their own ideas and solutions.

In highlighting programs and organizations on our campus that were already dedicated to making a difference in our community, I hoped to accomplish two things. First, the Civility Campaign would serve as an amplifier for local grassroots efforts and programs, rather than competition. After all, our community was very civic minded. Between a Relay for Life for the American Cancer Society in the spring and an overnight fundraiser for St. Jude Children's Research Hospital in the fall, our students were targeted by a number of fundraising efforts throughout the year. If the Civility Campaign continued to echo larger national campaigns, it not only risked being overshadowed by these more established programs—our students had begun to tune out any new voices asking for donations as a result of this charitable overcrowding—but it would also fail in making the personal, communal connections that were vital to its survival. Secondly, by collaborating with existing clubs and organizations, I hoped that the Civility Campaign would become a truly communal effort, as opposed to yet another S.G.A. pet-project.

Fortunately, through my involvement around campus, I had developed relationships with a number of budding student organizations and spirited leaders over the years. In my S.G.A. career, I had formed a sizeable network of young professionals who were always ready and willing to lend their support to one of my projects.

Still, despite sounding like a win-win for all of the parties involved, I knew that there would still be a bit of salesmanship involved in recruiting my first partners to sign on with my plan. While these groups were undoubtedly dedicated, teaming up with the S.G.A. to host a single event was far different from jointly taking on the responsibilities of managing a major campaign. Each organization faced its own demands for fundraising and membership recruitment, which led to an understandable weariness in committing to a project of such an ambitious scale—particularly one that had demonstrated difficulties in finding its footing over the past few years. In order to lead the charge, I decided that it was best to start by focusing on recruiting one, strong partner. If I could succeed in bringing at least one influential name onto the Campaign, then others might steadily rally alongside us in time.

I had the perfect group in mind. H<3rt1 ("Heart-One") was an organization founded by one of our alumni with the mission of raising awareness of dating violence and domestic abuse on college campuses. As a relatively new club, I had presided as Senate Speaker for its formal adoption. Their founder's passionate approach to the topic quickly rallied support, and it did not take long for them to assemble a thorough and professional presentation for Senate for approval. From that point on, H<3rt1 blossomed rapidly as their efforts expanded beyond campus meetings to include partnerships with local battered women's shelters in the area. While H<3rt1 continued to coordinate programs and activities that raised awareness, collected supplies, and recruited volunteers, their founder made rounds across other college campuses to establish additional chapters. She later went on to play a key part in shaping the national dialog on policies and public responses to sexual assaults on college campuses. Following her graduation, leadership of the original chapter passed on to a spirited young woman from my class with a powerful passion for service initiatives.

Having worked with both the new club president and her predecessor in hosting shared programs through the Campaign in years prior, I approached her with my new vision. Not only would H<3rt1's tremendous success bolster the credibility of the Campaign but its history as a home-grown organization from our own campus would extend that crucial, local appeal that we needed in order to establish ourselves as a reflection of our community. Fortunately, the new president shared my hopes for the Campaign and enthusiastically supported our new focus. They became our first partner in transforming the Civility Campaign into a lasting campus legacy.

One of our first programs together was an all-day Dance-A-Thon that brought yet another campus partner to the table, the College's Dance Ensemble. Renting out an all-purpose room on the third floor of our student center, H<3rt1 invited local organizations dedicated to addressing domestic violence and related issues to fill tables and booths that lined the walls while the Dance Ensemble's members led attendees in a number of dances and other physical activities. As music played in the background, a monitor at the front of the room displayed informational videos and slides on H<3rt1's inception and continued mission.

Aside from the wonderful turnout that it produced, the Dance-A-Thon fulfilled our vision as an ideal model for future Campaign activities. Under this new outlook, the ultimate role of the Civility Campaign was to act as a "missing link" in bringing together campus organizations to serve a common mission. In weighing the talents and shortcomings of various organizations, and grouping together those that held a similar focus, we would serve as a catalyst in bringing them together to play off of their respective strengths and weaknesses to create a greater impact.

While the Dance Ensemble got to showcase their skills and recruit new members, funds collected during the Dance-A-Thon went to support H<3rt1's programs and partnering charities. The Civility Campaign helped both of these organizations in providing additional resources and administrative assistance in securing the venue and related supplies. The experience proved that we could be successful in our new focus, bringing existing organizations together to amplify their combined impact, rather than simply injecting new causes into an already crowded arena. More importantly, we picked up the Dance Ensemble as another routine partner in Campaign activities. They have continued to work with H<3rt1 in the following years to make the fall Dance-A-Thon an annual tradition.

I owe a great deal of gratitude to the leaders of H<3rt1 for all of their support in not only helping the Campaign find its footing but also encouraging me to get a hold of my own bearings in defining this new role. Indeed, their president and I became regular participants in meetings with campus administrators to plan a series of events that not only raised awareness for causes related to domestic violence and sexual assaults but also tied in my connections from Safety & Security to foster supplemental policy discussions as well. As the Campaign continued to grow upon this new foundation, I lobbied my friends at the helm of the 2012-2013 Administration to consider changing my title from "Director of Community Relations"—which people tended to associate more with a public relations or marketing role—to the "Director of Community Outreach". This adjustment, I felt, best communicated the true purpose of the role: engaging local partners and organizations to foster collaboration and capitalize on their existing strengths in an effort to garner a greater outcome for our community.

By focusing on campus organizations and expanding outward to the neighboring community, we could produce a more targeted impression on our student body and external neighbors. As more grassroots organizations began turning to us for our resources and guidance, we started to recruit additional partners in carrying on the banner of the Civility Campaign for years to come. While the Campaign took on a more proactive role in promoting and pairing up established organizations, I was sure to maintain a responsive component to the entity as well. While Hurricane Irene had afforded the S.G.A. its first, real test in responding to large-scale disasters just one year prior, the newly reformed Civility Campaign would soon be faced with its greatest challenge yet.

◆

Superstorm Sandy swept through the North East region of the United States in October of 2012. Having weathered our fair share of storms on campus in years prior, no one was anticipating the level of destruction wrought by this, particular squall. As we braced ourselves nonetheless, my housemates and I planned on bunkering down at home to let the storm pass with a movie and a quiet board game. Without access to local news channels over our campus' cable network, our view of the storm was momentarily limited to what passed just outside of our window. Though torrential rain was descending upon us in sheets, there did not appear to be any, immediate threat.

In fact, spirits remained so jovial that our little neighborhood made a game out of the monsoon. As the lights to our courtyard flickered under the strained output of a back-up generator, some residents raced out into the storm in an attempt to circle the quad and return to their doorsteps before the steady glow of the surrounding lampposts was fully restored. Watching our peers race desperately through the rain, or otherwise cheer each other on from our doorsteps, helped to draw our minds away from the potential for peril. We could not imagine just how devastating this storm could truly be.

When morning broke the next day, there were no immediate signs of horrific damage or wanton destruction; the Poughkeepsie area had been hit relatively lightly by the storm. In looking back at the damage uncovered in the wake of Hurricane Irene just one year prior—which included rumors of collapsed academic buildings, the flooding of a handful of campus parking lots and residence areas, and a small landslide that had obstructed the tunnel that connected our campus to the riverside—many of us believed that we had gotten off easy this time around. It would not be long, however, before worried calls from home brought news of Sandy's true power, shattering our momentary sense of relief.

The days that immediately followed brought startling clarity to the grave reality of the situation. Sandy's devastation was widespread, but had come down most heavily on a number of areas that our students called home along the coast. With some communities completely wiped away by the torrent, many of our students were left wondering whether or not they even had a home to go back to over the upcoming holiday break. Our campus community rallied together around those in need without a moment's hesitation; there was a collective and immediate desire to get out and do *something*. As the newly minted Director of Community Outreach, my inbox quickly filled with Emails from students who wanted to know what they could do to play a part in our developing relief efforts.

The Civility Campaign became the central point for coordinating the College's response to Superstorm Sandy. Rather than have a dozen or so different efforts competing against one another to raise funds and supplies for various communities impacted by the storm, the College Administration backed the S.G.A. in channeling all initiatives and related programs through our office. In working with our administrators and other student leaders, including our Campus Ministry, we kicked off our response with a campus-wide supply drive, filling a row of donation bins—several repurposed industrial dumpsters—in the lobby of our athletic facility in less than a week. And yet, though we continued to collect money, food, clothing, and other necessary goods with great success, there was still a yearning to do even more permeating throughout our student body.

One afternoon, as I sat in the S.G.A. office sorting through the most recent pile of donations that had been dropped off by one of our clubs, I turned to see a familiar face at the door. As I greeted the Director of College Activities, he smiled back warmly and told me that he an idea that he wanted to run by me. As it so happened, he was currently in a meeting with two students who each sought to organize relief projects of their own. Having brought the two of them together to see if they might be able to work collaboratively in some capacity, he recalled the recent success that we had enjoyed in undertaking a similar approach through the Civility Campaign. He asked me to take a crack at helping these two devise a plan to coordinate their efforts, rather than split off on two separate ventures.

That is how I came to I find myself sitting across from the president of the College's Habitat for Humanity chapter and the student leader of our Public Praxis Program. As I began to tell them about the supply drives and

226

other programs that we were presently running, I saw that none of it was really capturing their attention. As it turned out, they were not interested in coordinating another drive or fundraiser; their intentions were far more specific. Our Habitat for Humanity and Public Praxis organizations each wanted to plan field trips to rebuild communities severely impacted by the storm.

This request, as you might imagine, raised some eyebrows. After all, the storm had a severe effect on the distribution of gasoline throughout New York State; transporting a group of students from Poughkeepsie to a distant worksite and back would prove to be far more challenging than coordinating your typical field trip. More importantly, construction projects in times of crisis were far different from the usual builds that our general, inexperienced volunteers were used to. While the members of our Habitat for Humanity chapter had at least some knowledge of the type of work involved in a project of this scope, recruiting additional volunteers meant tapping into a pool of students who had no background in construction work. This created more than just a simple risk for someone in our own group getting hurt; relying on unskilled volunteers could potentially put us in a position that risked hindering ongoing relief efforts, rather than help them. That is, without the luxury of additional time to train and equip volunteers, sending too many inexperienced hands down to a major worksite could prove to be more of a burden than a blessing. On top of it all, we still had to answer some rather basic questions regarding logistics and liabilities before seeking approval for our trip.

Nevertheless, the passion and tenacity of the two club leaders behind the idea was undeniable. Relying on both of their expertise, I started to believe that we had a rather solid chance at making this plan work. Having participated in a number of build projects throughout the country, the president of our Habitat for Humanity chapter had identified an opportunity for volunteers of all skill levels to participate in relief efforts on Long Island. His team would lead the charge in recruiting more experienced volunteers to tackle construction related projects while Public Praxis recruited additional laborers to assist with general clean up activities. As the Director of College Activities had anticipated, combining their resources and experiences helped to fill in many of the gaps that made the effort appear so daunting at first glance. Once they had set aside the prospect of splitting off on two separate ventures and directed their efforts toward a single site, all of the remaining pieces began to fall into place. As word of our planned trip started to spread throughout the student body, the added wave of communal support only helped to propel these efforts closer to formal approval.

Soon enough, we entered the home stretch on the route to implementation, a series of meetings that involved the two club leaders; members of the campus faculty and administration, including representatives from the offices of College Activities, Student Life, and the Office of the College President; and myself. Although we appeared to be making significant strides forward in these meetings, I sensed that there was still a hesitancy to give the program the green light.

Coming back from class one day, I poked my head into the Office of College Activities to see if I could get a better sense of our status from its Director. At this point in time, the impending renovation of our student center had forced them to relocate their office to a smaller auxiliary room within the building. As a temporary worksite, untouched boxes packed with supplies and mementos from their old space remained piled up next to their desks. An entire barricade had separated the Director's desk from the main entrance, creating a makeshift foyer amidst the clutter.

As the usual place for students to turn when they were in need of a solution to just about any problem on our campus, these towering collections of treasured memories mixed with the warm charms of its inhabitants to further the Office's connection to a fictional idol. It was our very on "Room of Requirement", seemingly pulled from the pages of a *Harry Potter* book and complete with its own bespectacled, warm-hearted Director. Between the move, the storm, and this proposal, I knew that even this gentle soul, a personification of patience, had a great deal weighing down on him already. Still, we risked losing precious time as the end of the current semester crept closer and closer. I feared the project would lose its momentum entirely if our discussion stalled into the New Year.

Sitting beside his desk, I asked him rather casually for his thoughts on the proposal. The Director of College Activities was one of my favorite conversational partners, though perhaps the one with whom I shared the least in terms of actual dialog. The majority of his thoughts we expressed with the subtle lift of an eyebrow or the twitch of a smile, his glittering eyes scanning the faces around him like the pages of an open book left sprawling in broad daylight. He could always tell when one of our members was on the tip of a wit's end and met our youthful brand of anxiety with a refined compassion befitting of the brotherhood that he so deeply honored, our Marist founders.

229

On warm sunny days, he would burst through the S.G.A. office's doors and say something to the effect of "Children, come; join me." As he made his way to the towering window at the back of the room only to catch himself and say, "No, you are not children any longer." Playfully delighting in the slight disappointment we felt in being reminded of our waning adolescence, his eyes would sparkle warmly as they turned back to the picturesque scene vividly transpiring just behind us. "Ladies, gentlemen, would you look at that?" Indeed, we could not draw our eyes away. Such was his nature, to bring us back down from the height of our ambitions and the brink of disillusionment to embrace the now, to see the beauty that sat immediately before us and *appreciate* it for what it was.

I knew that I could speak with him openly on any subject. And so, we bantered back and forth for a while about the planning meetings, the dedication of the student leaders steering the coordination of our plan, and the overall success of the other relief efforts going on around campus. After a while, he noted that there were still some concerns from within the College Administration regarding safety. While enthusiasm and spirit were all well and good, we could not really comprehend what it was, exactly, that we would be rushing into until we had already dropped a team of fifty or so students right in the heart of it. Hearing his piece, I could certainly understand and respect our administrators' concerns, but also felt that letting this proposal subside unfulfilled would have been devastating for all those involved in its planning, students and administrators alike. That is when I decided to make a bit of a career gambit. I promised the Director that, if he could find a way to get us down there, then I would make sure everyone made it back safely, soundly, and without incident.

If he had any grave concerns about my offer, he did not let them show. As one of the greatest mentors and role models our S.G.A. had, our moral compass in human form, I knew that our Director of College Activities was just as committed to seeing our idea take flight as we were. More importantly, I believe he recognized that we, as seniors, were rapidly approaching a point where we would have to take that leap of faith and learn to soar under the tremendous weight of responsibility that these types of moments in life tend to impose upon us or risk slipping back into a place of silent complacency. If we could pull off a project of this scale, then it would signal to our community that our student groups were, indeed, capable of implementing and accomplishing tasks far beyond our typically anticipated capacity. In stringing together our planned trip, we were looking well beyond the traditional scope of student projects to define a goal that was entirely our own, and a part of me hoped that our efforts could serve as a beacon for a more valuable lesson: no task should be deemed impossible simply because no one has ever attempted it before.

Picking up the phone, the Director made a series of calls that would finalize our plans for the trip to Long Island once and for all. Not only did the Office of College Activities secure a bus to bring our team down to the worksite and back, but the College Administration also rounded up plenty of gloves and goggles, as well as a crop of individual lunches for all of our participants. Providing us with everything they could rally together to aid us in our mission, they joined us in taking that crucial leap forward. The project's success now rested squarely in our hands.

◆

I clung to my clipboard nervously as our rag-tag band of volunteers boarded the bus. Lunches were stocked safely in the compartment below us, directions had been printed and confirmed, and supplies were being distributed to our volunteers as they checked in, eagerly anticipating the work that awaited them. Everything appeared to be running smoothly. As we set out, however, it became clear that the rest of our day would not unfold quite as we had planned. Detours and other traffic complications arising from the aftermath of the storm had not been reflected in our pre-planned route and led to unanticipated delays. This made us late for our initial registration time and prevented our rendezvous with a team of alumni volunteers that had liaised with the leaders of our Habitat Chapter.

When we did finally arrive, we were quickly swept up in the frenzy of the environment. A nearby pickup truck of volunteers was getting ready to ship out to a demolition site as we rolled in and called out for additional hands when they saw us trailing off of the bus. After sitting for so long on the ride down, our volunteers were eager get to work. A sizeable portion of our group quickly began to break away from rest of the team to join them. But before they could all pile into the back of the truck, my managerial instincts quickly kicked into gear. I passed on my phone number to an appointed group leader with strict instructions to keep me informed of their movements. Watching them break away so hurriedly served as a sobering reminder as to just how difficult it would be to keep a close watch on all of our roughly 50 volunteers. As my eyes followed their vehicle as it sailed away to join a growing convoy of military and construction vehicles, I began to wonder whether or not I had bitten of more than I could chew.

Much to the delight of my fraying nerves, there was not a lot of time to be afforded to internal reflection at that point. The presidents of our Habitat for Humanity chapter and Public Praxis program, along with our one faculty liaison (the Adviser of our Habitat for Humanity chapter), joined me as we sought out the brains behind the operation at this site. Making our way through the sand filled streets of the Breezy Point community, we had our first chance to really look around and assess the damage for ourselves. What remained of many of these coastal homes protruded from the sand like lingering monuments to memories long since passed. Piles of wood and other debris that had been collected from the sea's edge were now neatly stacked alongside those homes that were fortunate enough to weather the storm largely intact. Indeed, most of the neat little houses dotting the shoreline seemed to be in rather fair condition; I couldn't help but think that they looked largely out of place amidst the surrounding desolation.

Many of the street signs and sidewalks had been buried under a rogue wave of sand that had broken free from the dunes to flood the roadways and fill in just about everything else. Traffic lights now hung darkly over those routes that had been quickly uncovered to permit the passage of roving military convoys and the occasional pickup truck that ferried volunteers from one end of the inlet to the other. As its residents and the influx of volunteers steadily worked their way back to normalcy, it seemed as though an air of calm had settled over Breezy Point, NY.

As we approached noontime, however, the streets quickly buzzed with life. They were filled by a wave of eager volunteers toting shovels, brooms, and garbage bags as they made their way downtown, replacing the silence with a sense of mirth as they scurried from place to place. While many of our more skilled Habitat volunteers were now being shuttled on their way to a small grouping of houses that had been flagged for demolition in the back of another pickup truck, the rest of our group pushed ahead through the bustling clusters of volunteers toward the site's makeshift base of operations. In a small church that had survived the brunt of the storm, we were introduced to the man in charge, the CEO of Habitat for Humanity Westchester.

With a clear passion for his work, his personality shined with an electric wit that left little room for pause or awkward silence, cutting right to the point with a sense of compassion that had attracted volunteers from throughout the tristate area and beyond to follow his lead in restoring the Breezy Point community. Exuding a sincere warmth, and embodying a "lead from the trenches" style of management with tremendous zeal, it was easy enough to see why so many people were willing to rally together around him. During our time onsite, he never shied away from throwing on a pair of gloves and jumping in to lend a hand as we darted from worksite to worksite. At lunchtime, he could be found posted readily behind a grill, not stopping to take a break himself until all of his volunteers had been tended to.

After a quick round of introductions, we followed him through the hollowed out hallways of the church for the grand tour. The main room of the building now served as a holding site for donations that had been shipped into the area, its pews overflowing with assorted goods or otherwise pushed against the walls and out of the way of the sprawling mountain of supplies. Just behind the altar, the administrative hallways had been cleared to serve as a makeshift dormitory for long-distance volunteers that had signed on to work throughout the winter. As their base of operations, it was also the central meeting point for Habitat's team members, local authorities, and other service organizations seeking to provide aid. As time went on, and relief efforts persisted through the winter and early spring, the structure continued to serve a variety of roles as the volunteers faced new challenges brought about by time and Mother Nature alike.

The more he showed us, the more eagerly we anticipated our work. Fortunately, he wasted no time in dividing us up; there was plenty for everyone to do. While the remaining volunteers from our Habitat for Humanity chapter had been assigned to a more detailed work crew, the president of our Public Praxis group and I were tasked with leading our remaining volunteers in an effort to literally sweep the streets clean. We were directed to a small team of Habitat volunteers in charge of the roving work crews that dominated the roadways. With brooms and trash bags in hand, we made our way down the main stretch, clearing off sidewalks and side streets in the hopes of instilling a feeling of normalcy for each of the sections that we passed through.

Every now and then, we would stop alongside a convoy of trucks to help load or unload supplies at makeshift distribution sites. Mostly, our assignment steered us deeper into the winding streets and cul-de-sacs of the Breezy Point community in silent contemplation, broomsticks in hand. It was through this vantage point that we got a much closer look at the remnants left behind by the storm, occasionally unearthing valued trinkets and other, scattered mementos stolen away in its wake. Collecting these precious treasures, which included family photos, historical documents, and even a portfolio of beautiful oil paintings, we assembled a small pile of goods to turn over to the Habitat team for their growing trove of lost memories.

Our spirits were continually lifted throughout the day by the indescribable kindness of Breezy Point's residents. These were people who, despite losing almost everything they had, still came out into the streets carrying whatever they could cook up to thank us for our help. We were moved beyond words by their resilience and compassion. Seeing people so committed to their spirit of community that they would not let such horrific circumstances stop them from carrying on their traditions of gratitude and reciprocity is something that I will never forget. Indeed, the resilience of their unwavering spirits reverberated throughout our congregation, carrying with it an air of hope.

All too suddenly, however, any sense of warmth that lingered from their inspiring kindness quickly abated as we neared the coastline. Towards the end of the afternoon, our work had brought us to the segment of the Breezy Point community most severely impacted by the storm. The wall of battered, yet standing, houses that had dotted our path throughout most of the morning had parted to reveal a wide expanse of shoreline. Amid a barren wasteland of twisted wooden frames and scattered shingles, a single American flag fluttered above the debris. During the peak hours of the storm, a fire had run rampant through this quiet corner of the community.

236

All first responders could do was stand back and watch it burn. Having left hardly anything behind, the somber scene brought us all back to face the stark reality of our task.

Despite the sudden chill that cut through us, I was able to breathe a sigh of relief when a familiar troupe of faces rounded the corner at the far end of the expanse. Our Habitat team had finished with their assignments and was making its way back to the church when our paths unexpectedly crossed. We were now missing just one other cohort.

As we rallied our Habitat and remaining volunteers together, I called the group leader from our initial breakaway team and learned that they were not too far behind us. Picking up our things, and waiting to begin the steady hike back to home base, a few of our students knelt down in a nearby garden to reassemble a seashell arrangement in the shape of an American flag. Whether they had delved into a demolition project that sent them tearing through the woodwork of someone's childhood home or joined us in uncovering the scattered tokens of another life, all of our volunteers wore familiar looks of somber reverence that reflected the profound impact that our trip had left on each of us.

Rising above and beyond the simple rush of gratification one feels in making a donation, our rebuild effort helped to reaffirm a core pillar of our campus community, the importance of service to others. In seeing the people of Breezy Point come together to so courageously take back their homes from the grip of Mother Nature and eclipse the scars left by the storm, our volunteers witnessed the kind of resilience and compassion that can only be found through unity in the face of tragedy. *That* was the reward that made our excursion so worthwhile, despite the risks and worries that had dogged its inception.

After a quick headcount confirmed that all of our volunteers were present and accounted for, we boarded the bus for our return trip home. This would be the first of two trips to Breezy Point that term; our delegation reunited in the spring of 2013 to rendezvous once more with the Westchester chapter. I am proud to say that these trips had their desired impact on our student body as well, affirming our ability to collectively organize in order to make a difference in communities well beyond our home in Poughkeepsie. More importantly, we proved that it was possible to carve out a new path toward attaining our goals where none had previously existed.

The Breezy Point trips would serve as the capstone in my experience as the first Director of Community Outreach for the S.G.A. Having sat on the initial committee that formed the Campaign, I was honored to be the one to carry it into its next—and apparently lasting—iteration. Today, the Civility Campaign is alive and well on the Marist campus. Through the leadership of at least four other Directors, the Campaign has become a valued voice in discussions on sexual assault and Title IX, as well as matters relating to race, gender, and broader civic engagement. Above all else, the position remains focused on fostering a spirit of community, not only for our campus but throughout the City and Town of Poughkeepsie. Despite the small role that I played in its earliest stages, I never could have imagined that the legacy of the 2010-2011 Administration would become such a tremendous part of my own campus story, but I am so incredibly grateful that it did.

Lessons Learned

Competition is a constant in any industry, but it is becoming a point of particular concern for public and non-profit organizations. Human beings are largely civic minded and often feel compelled to make a positive impact on their communities. This altruistic drive, coupled with entrepreneurial initiative, has led to the development of a wide array of service organizations that strive to address specific issues among myriad societal concerns on a daily basis. At a local level, I have seen how this growth can also put a strain on existing organizations and social structures. With major, annual fundraisers on our campus including the St. Jude Committee's annual letter writing campaign, Relay for Life, and a blood drive coordinated jointly by Greek Life organizations—in addition to a number of other first-time initiatives for emerging causes—our community was being tapped left and right for contributions in one form or another.

In using the Civility Campaign to bring together like-minded individuals and organizations in an effort to pool their resources toward a common goal, we not only helped them to broaden their collective impact but scale back on the relentless financial demand levied against our student body. Sweeping aside the clutter of solicitations, students were able to engage with these groups directly to learn more about their missions and develop lasting relationships. By teaming up with similar organizations to play off of each other's strengths and weaknesses, we were able to break the typical, competitive mold to lay out the terms for our own win-win scenarios.

More often than not, the best solution to a glaring issue is staring us right in the face. Although there is no doubting the value of an entrepreneurial spirit, in seeking out entirely new grounds to sew our own ideas and visions we might overlook the potential to steadily build upon existing components. On occasion, leaders may recognize that crafting a new venture from scratch is not the best course of action. Rather than re-invent the wheel, truly innovative individuals will assess the potential in existing components and construct a "missing link" that binds together these various pieces in furtherance of a single goal or shared focus.

This proved to be the secret ingredient that helped our incarnation of the Civility Campaign to find its footing. In leading the program, I knew that the last thing our campus needed was *another* service organization. Instead, I believed that my new office could be used to create a lasting network that empowered our existing clubs and service groups to communicate and collaborate with one another more affectively. The Civility Campaign became the guiding arm through which local service initiatives could come together and see what their peers were bringing to the table before wading into action.

Fully assessing the hidden potential ascribed to such opportunities requires leaders to maintain a mission-driven perspective. At times, this may require taking the back seat, allowing another organization or cause run the show in order to produce the greatest product or turnout for your underlying cause. Once again, leaders must be able to sidestep their own egos and recognize that their way of doing things is not always the best. Sharing the spotlight, or foregoing it entirely, will occasionally afford us the opportunity to seize a far greater prize.

Indeed, this humble approach to leadership helped me to keep certain doors and bridges open and intact throughout my career. Though it was not always easy to swallow my pride and rejoin an administration that I had found myself competing against only a few months prior, I ultimately recognized that we were all working toward the same goal. Even if we had not always necessarily been on the same team, we acknowledged that we were all members of a much larger community.

This shared vision helped me to return to a project that I deeply cared for and led to one of my most impactful years with the S.G.A. At no point did I ever feel ostracized or outcast from the 2012-2013 Administration; my former opponents each had tremendous capacities for collaboration that helped us to pick right back up where we had left off before the race. I am grateful to them both for their willingness to welcome me back into S.G.A. with open arms. As this example shows, respect can be a powerful force in turning even our most impassioned rivals into valuable allies.

THE LEADERSHIP PROFILE: *Exercise Eleven*

If tomorrow brought an unexpected change that forced you to start over at square one, how would you begin to piece everything back together? If you suddenly found yourself free from all of the general obligations, debts, and commitments that fill your life, as well as the activities and responsibilities that helped to provide you with a sense of direction, what would you do first? Though I should hope that none of you encounter such a drastic change in your lives unprepared, it can be just a little thrilling to wonder where in the world we might find ourselves if we were freed from all of the little strings tying us to our current roles.

If you were suddenly flung out into the job market, knowing all that you know now, what is it that you would look for? Financial stability? Job security? The chance to do something you love or something that you felt was important or meaningful? Would you be willing to travel far away or would you prefer to stay close to family and friends? These questions help us to shed light on what drives us. More so than a regular paycheck, some people truly love their jobs because of the people they are with, the work they do, or the opportunities they create. It is a different experience for everyone.

That is why understanding what matters most to *you* is so important. We are not always going to want to get the same things out of life as our friends and family, so following in the footsteps of others might often divert us from the path that we are truly destined to tread. We nonetheless find ourselves clinging to such anchors at times in our lives because the sense of stability they provide creates a powerfully alluring incentive to hold on to. This familiarity can obscure our original vision and impose additional barriers to summoning up the courage to face down the risks associated with major life changes and the attainment of a grand vision. Breaking free from such restraints often requires a leap of faith.

Jot down a few of the items or ideas that matter most to you. Though the path you take toward attaining this defining goal is bound to shift and change with time, these key concepts will serve as trail markers that continually guide you in the right direction, no matter how dark the clouds appear to be just beyond the horizon.

12 – The Reverie

"Give me but one firm spot on which to stand,
and I will move the Earth."
– Archimedes

As I entered my senior year, my to-do list began to wind itself down considerably—especially now that our work at the hotel was completed. Spending one year onsite had helped us to assemble a better picture of the quality of life for our students there, as well as develop an appreciation for the rift that had formed between its residents and the greater campus community. By this point, the shuttle system was operating regularly, our residence life staff continued to build upon their standard programming, and a trusted friend and S.G.A. peer would be taking over as a new resident assistant. Everything seemed to be well on its way toward closing the cultural gap and bridging these two segments of our community. I knew I could trust that this subset of the student body was now in good hands as they continued to move forward.

Thus, my friends and I decided to return to on-campus housing for our senior year. Teaming up with my roommates from the hotel, we set our sights on one of the College's premier residence areas, the Fulton Townhouses. This space consisted of housing units for eight people that included a kitchen and common area on the ground floor, with two levels of bedrooms and shared baths stacked on top. The buildings were then organized into neat little cul-de-sacs around shared courtyards and other communal amenities. Seated just across the road from the main campus, and connected via a newly constructed underpass, these townhouses formed a quiet little community all their own on the hills that rose away from the river and the grey stone silhouette of the larger campus.

Fortune or fate—depending on your perspective—once again intervened when we were approached by a friend from campus who had a plan to join a pair of mutual friends in the lower section of the Fulton townhouses. Content with the spot that they had selected, we agreed to pool our priority points in the hopes of joining his house. The terms were simple enough and the company was good; it seemed that we could not strike a better bargain if we tried.

As it turns out, we had hit the jackpot. We thought we were simply securing top-tier housing but, in fact, this arrangement proved to be the first step toward expanding the Core Four into a close-knit social network that has remained an active source of support in all of my adventures to this day. My days in Lower Fulton 15D were some of the best in my life. Although I may not have succeeded in making the widespread communal impact that I had envisioned when I first launched my campaign, I managed to find all that I could wish for and more in the company of this astounding group of individuals. After spending the first three quarters of my undergraduate career deeply entrenched in student politics, senior year provided ample opportunities to step back and settle into a well-deserved sense of retirement.

Even though I planned to cull back some of my actives around campus, this did not mean that I had given up on my efforts to make a mark on the College. Indeed, my senior year represented a very crucial stage in attaining my goal of creating a personal legacy, and stepping back plaid a large part in those plans. While my first three years were spent laying a

245

foundation and developing a mission to guide my aims, our final year would require a bit of personal separation from my projects to ensure that those who would follow in my footsteps were prepared to run the show on their own. In their longevity, I would have my legacy.

As someone who had always felt the need to watch over his projects like a hawk, I did not expect this to be a simple task. And yet, faced with the moment at last, I suddenly found myself oddly at ease, letting go of my compulsive attachments and settling into a quiet life with my friends in Lower Fulton 15D. We all seemed to be operating on the same wavelength. From designating house themes to testing our abilities in weekly trivia nights at the local Applebee's, we enjoyed each other's company tremendously. Our community in Lower Fulton permeated with the balanced charm of a Floridian retirement community, mixing the steady calm of "senioritis" with the regimented routine of those few, lingering commitments that we each still had left on our plates.

In addition to my new role as the Director of Community Outreach for the S.G.A., I was also completing my second and final internship for the criminal justice program. My peers in the program and I had also begun splitting up into working groups for our senior capstone course, an intensive research project and presentation that would require extensive coordination. These more weighty demands would take the place of the various, flitting projects that had filled my undergraduate term. But rather than focus on their arrival, my attention was transfixed elsewhere. Spellbound by the quiet and easy-going life that I had suddenly found with my friends in 15D, I did not notice my cluttered schedule precipitously coalescing into a monstrous blob of deadlines and other, miscellaneous appointments.

Despite striking a rather tenuous balance between my remaining board meetings, classes, and internship hours, I continued to add to the list blindly. It started innocently enough, when a young S.G.A. member announced an ambitious new project and I agreed to enter the campus' first "Mr. Marist" competition, a pageant of school spirit that I simply could not resist being a part of. This move was followed by a steady stream of smaller odds and ends that ranged from early preparations for our impending "alumnihood" with members of our class board to other, general club leadership meetings. Even as my roster of new commitments continued to build precariously, I also accepted an invitation from a friend to fill in as the school mascot at an upcoming basketball game.

As it turns out, I was not prepared to embrace my "retirement" after all. My desire to roll back my involvement had instead created a social vacuum in my life that showed no sign of tapering out. Moreover, I had grown so accustomed to saying "yes" in seeking to fill theses gaps in my time that I began to question whether or not I remembered how to put my foot down when I finally reached my limit—if I could even discern such boundaries at all. Sadly, this inability to draw the line meant that I would ultimately have to re-learn the hard way. And just when I thought that I had mastered the trick to keeping all of these balls in the air, a sudden tremor threatened to bring my expanding juggling routine crashing down around me.

As a crucial week that included a major deadline for the Mr. Marist competition and my date to step into the furry shoes of our mascot rounded the corner, I found myself visited by an unexpected guest, the flu. All too quickly, I went from being well ahead of the game to stuck playing catch up. As my fever began to steadily subside from what I perceived to be its peak, I dragged my exhausted body around campus from one critical appointment to the next, cancelling or postponing anything that could be stretched to the following weeks. Against my better judgment, this did not include my upcoming mascot duty. Not wanting to let down my friend, and left with little time to find a replacement, I swallowed my medicine and prayed the mask would be enough to conceal my condition.

I regretted this decision almost immediately. Balancing the oversized head of our mascot atop my own, I felt the steady shivers of a feverish bone chill creep through me after stepping into those big, furry trousers. Despite feeling relatively well that morning, having prepared for the endeavor with a hearty nap, the warmth of the costume quickly brought my waning fever back to its peak. Relying solely on school spirit—and, perhaps, a touch of delirium—to maintain my composure, I began making my rounds through the crowded arena. I stumbled forward, a living bobble-head, as I struggled to keep the perpetually smiling face of our mascot securely set upon my shoulders.

Though it seemed to take a lifetime just to make it to halftime, I managed to perform my duties without incident. I would, nevertheless, have to make routine trips through the players' entryways to remove my helmet and catch a quick gulp of cool, fresh air or down every bit of water that I could find in order to keep my energy from faltering. Far from the public eye, I was gradually crumbling into a complete and total mess.

Fortunately, as I stepped back into the arena for round two, I miraculously regained control of my faculties long enough to power through the rest of my performance. Make no mistake, I had my close calls.

At one point, members of the band mistook me for their regular companion and pulled me up to the top of the student bleachers for their traditional mid-game dance routine. A stranger to the custom, and dangerously loosing my balance under the watchful eye of the jumbo-screen camera, I thought it best to bow out with a fist-bump and a wave to the audience before retreating to the safety of the ground level.

Once safely on the sidelines, I did manage to make at least one positive impression for the day. An adorable little fan dressed in bright red and white cheerleading garb had been trailing me for most of the game; she was a dedicated fan of the Fox. At the end of the match, her family called me over to take a picture, and her beaming smile eventually wound up on the College's Facebook page with me right by her side.

My moments in the Fox's shoes afforded me plenty of time for reflection. They helped me to appreciate that I could not cram every desired experience into the waning moments of my collegiate career. No matter how much I disliked facing the music, my time as an undergraduate was nearing its end. For better or worse, that meant packing it in, to some degree, as I prepared to say farewell to those organizations and individuals that had played the most influential roles in my narrative as an undergraduate. In addition to the S.G.A., I had continued to play an active part in Toastmasters and the Emerging Leaders Program in my waning days as a senior. Both boards had grown into two of my closest social networks over the years, and I tended to view our regular meetings more as family gatherings than business endeavors.

Although, when it came to finding a true home away from my family in New Jersey, nothing could compete with the spirit of comradery that we had fostered in 15D. Having branched out from the Core Four, this small social circle brought together a group of individuals so alike in mindset that we quickly became inseparable. When we returned home each evening from classes and other activities, we would settle into our living room together for board games, movies, or other crafts and competitions. On weekends, we would prompt each other to seek out new adventures in the Poughkeepsie community, exploring parks and recreational areas throughout the county that we had otherwise never considered or sought out on our own. Even the looming shadow of graduation would not wear upon the bond that we had formed, as our 15D family has continued to reunite throughout the years following our time in college.

◆

Of course, my own family also played a tremendous role throughout my collegiate career. Supportive of my every endeavor, they poured their hearts into my student body presidential campaign just as much as I did. In addition to finalizing the now famous fifteen shirts that represented my campaign, my mother affixed witty slogans to individual pieces of candy for us to distribute in our attempts to woo voters. Even from afar, my parents found ways to fill those quiet moments that chased me during my loneliest hours on campus and helped me to see my new community as a home away from the one that I had known all my life. That is why I was particularly thrilled to have them join me for the final "Family Weekend" of my college career. After all of the twists and turns this story had taken, I was grateful that they could share in the closing of one, very important chapter.

As in past years, I spent that morning as a volunteer, driving golf carts for the Office of Student Affairs to shuttle arriving families to and from various points on their schedules. Weaving through the campus, I carried them from activity to activity while I waited for my own parents to arrive. The hours passed quickly as I retraced my underclassman steps with the electric zip of the golf cart's glide. When we finally reunited on the main green, I brought them along for one last tour across the grounds.

It was through their eyes that I saw just how drastically things had changed in the time since they first dropped me off nearly four years prior. With the addition of an elaborate main gate, including towering stone faces depicting a pair of regal foxes; the renovation of central academic buildings to match our widespread architectural motif; and the erection of a brand new, $35 million center for information technology, mathematics, and business courses, the College had grown rapidly over a considerably short period of time.

To an outsider, it was almost unrecognizable. Entire roadways and parking lots had been removed or re-routed to accommodate the colossal new addition at the heart of the grounds and the grey stone façade that defined our newest fixture had now become a major theme in campus construction. Many of the older buildings that had not been wholly replaced were given new life behind matching touchups. Even the pedestrian traffic around campus flowed more steadily, as a newly excavated underpass reached below the neighboring highway to bridge the campus to its upper-classman residence areas and art studio. Though the grounds had evolved to give off a more mature, regal air typically attributed to Ivy League institutions, its heart resonated with a warm sense of familiarity.

The expressions that greeted us throughout our tour belonged to the same bright faces that welcomed us to the community in 2009. Our steady procession of reunions with old counselors, advisers, and professors tinted our last lap together around the campus with a fine mix of emotions. Despite fondly reveling in the bitter-sweetness of this final visit, there was still one last stop to make before we called it a night. As we made our way through the main lobby of the new technology building, our paths were crossed by an all too familiar, yet unexpected face.

I watched as the College President rounded the corner of the grand stairwell, striding toward the building's entrance with a great sense of purpose. Not wanting to delay him from whatever event he was bound for, I extended a simple nod in his direction. Without hesitation, he averted his course and made his way over to us. With a smile on his face, he stretched out his hand and took mine in a sincere shake before pausing to re-introduce himself to my family and compliment me on my work for the College over the past four years.

Up until that moment, I had pretty much forgotten the initial promise that I had made to myself at the start of my collegiate journey. Over time, my desire to be someone worthy of catching the College President's eye had warped itself into the singular ambition of becoming the student body president, causing me to lose sight of it entirely somewhere along the way. To find myself standing there, literally living out my dream in the presence of my family, left me utterly speechless. "Thank you, sir" was all that I could manage to mutter as he turned once more to resume his

252

original course. It made me realize just how far I had strayed from my initial goal, confusing true respect with some fleeting title or award. More importantly, the gesture affirmed that all of my little efforts throughout my years as a student leader had indeed left their mark. In the end, it was not an election that had earned that handshake; it was the kindness, devotion, and sincerity that had underscored each endeavor leading up to it that formed the basis for my legacy

.

♦

Our last few days in 15D that preceded graduation were filled with plenty of goodbyes and a lot of "lasts". Our lives were changing, and our beloved campus was changing with us. By May of 2013, the student center was preparing for a major renovation, with parts of the building already cleared out and ready for summer construction to begin. One warm afternoon I happened to pass by the campus' main theater, located on the top floor of the student center—just down the hall from our S.G.A. office— as the work crews hauled out a heap of old audience chairs. Stepping into the cavernous auditorium, I stared down at the floors, scraped clean as the last of the metal frames was pulled from the ground and hauled out to a dumpster in the back.

Closing my eyes, my mind filled with the melodies of distant numbers and the roaring applause of triumphant productions long passed, still floating in the ethereal air that hung over the space. I could only imagine the impact this sight might have on one of our dedicated student performers who had taken to calling it "home".

Over the past four years, we had each settled into our very own corners of this shared world, forging in the quiet halls of our "Harvard on the Hudson" a sanctuary all to ourselves. Many of those old scenes, untouched by time, exist now only in memory.

Our S.G.A. office followed suit shortly thereafter. As our current space was scheduled to be cleared out and repurposed into an auxiliary room for general use, the next S.G.A. office would be set up in a newly constructed wing of the building. The posters of past projects and events, along with the campaign T-shirts of our prior student body presidents— every memory of the teams that led the way before us—had been processed, packed, and neatly tucked away by the incoming 2013-2014 Administration.

My final moments within our hollowed out temple were spent in my usual corner, sitting beside the towering windows that overlooked the Hudson. The weather did not fit the somber occasion. Sunlight flowing from the clear, blue sky brought a touch of warmth to the breeze that passed through our window as it carried in the sounds of the river below. My feet propped up against the sill, I rocked back and forth in the student body president's chair. It was once rumored within S.G.A. circles that anyone who sat in this particular chair prematurely was cursed to lose their race for the presidency. Quietly laughing off such superstitions, I leaned back to enjoy the view. I had no more races to run.

Our journey had reached its end. As the rest of the campus cleared out once final exams had closed, the Class of 2013 settled in to its "Senior Week". In the days preceding our commencement ceremonies, there would be no class work, no club meetings, just the opportunity to enjoy the company of our communal family for a brief moment before parting to discover what awaited us beyond these grounds. Finding ourselves graced with more time but very limited financial resources to further capitalize on this newfound freedom, the residents of Lower Fulton 15D coordinated their own Senior Week activities.

We took the time afforded by the break to enjoy the company of those members of the campus community that had a profound impact on our group. We spent the occasional evenings reminiscing with the security officer who regularly patrolled our area and always took the time to check in on us throughout the year, a friendly face who had watched over many of us since we were freshmen. On another evening, we held a house dinner for a member of the Marist Brothers and Board of Trustees who was always willing to lend an ear and offer guidance, a man who would become the Monsignor Darcy to my Amory Blaine as I struggled to weave a more coherent picture out of the various narratives that would dovetail from my Marist story. We did all that we could to make our final moments on this campus count, racing the clock in an attempt to reach out to everyone who had impacted our time at the College.

And yet, despite my uneasiness in leaving all that I had built behind me, there was one aspect of graduation that I found myself eagerly awaiting. There would come a moment when they called my name to cross the stage and receive my diploma from the College President. Traditionally, the calling of a student's name would be met with an eruption of cheers from the audience, and the young egoist in me always wondered if my name would muster a sizeable applause.

The prospective scene played out in my mind as I wound my way through the intricate web of sidewalks that spread throughout the grounds on the seat of my bicycle, one last ride on our final night. As the sun set against the edge of the Hudson, I made my usual pass through the cluster of freshman buildings, gliding up through the towering trees that cast their shade over the Donnelly science building and the quiet hermitage that nestled beside it to frame a replica of Michelangelo's Pietà with their natural beauty. Picking up my pace, I sped through the winds that poured over the rolling hills of the main green as I crossed beneath the colossal shadow of the Cannavino library, reigning over the heart of our grounds. From there I rolled down the steep arm of the campus' main road, through the tunnel that carried the railways along the river's edge, and down to the shoreline of that majestic waterway. As I leaned over my handlebars to watch the sunlight dance across its surface, my excitement bristled with anticipation for what lied ahead.

Our commencement day, like many of the moments that shaped my collegiate career, naturally, did not unfold quite as I had envisioned. After carefully watching the forecast, our administrators decided it would be safe to proceed with an outdoor ceremony. At the last minute, however, storm conditions worsened and members of the Class of 2013 found themselves huddled together in the nearby academic buildings as we waited for the procession to begin.

This, of course, made it somewhat difficult for many of us to focus on the ceremony. In addition to the butterflies that typically swell in the pits of our stomachs around graduation time, our class fought against the rain and the cold to reach that moment when all eyes would be upon us for one, last time. When it was finally my turn to cross the stage, everything around me fell silent. In one fluid motion, I watched the student preceding me exit and disappear into the crowds below as I approached the center of the platform on autopilot. I did not turn to the crowd or even stop to listen for any sign of their reaction. This was it, the true end to my undergraduate career. Reaching out one last time, I closed this chapter of my life with a final handshake from the College President.

Lessons Learned

In speaking with underclassmen looking to carve out their own chapters in our campus' history, my go-to piece of advice has always been to follow your passions in finding your niche. In starting with something that you love, you are more likely to form a network with individuals that share your interests. These interactions will allow you to further establish the framework for bridging personal connections stemming from a common goal. From that point on, maintaining an open mind will empower you to rise above peer influences and challenging endeavors to continually expand the scope of your personal and professional grids. It all starts by identifying a point that feels true to your concept of self. Let it be the firm spot from which you begin to move the world around you.

For me, 15D became the embodiment of this ideal network. Arising from my most fundamental connections, the Core Four, it blossomed from a series of interactions that were among the most impactful of my career. Even to this day, its members remain among my closest friends. Many of them, however, came into my life purely by happenstance, stemming from various associations and opportunities arising from my campus activities and the connections of other friends. Thanks largely in part to their continued support and encouragement, I have come a long way from being the shy little kid who first started out on this adventure.

Unfortunately, it is also the case that not all of our connections will withstand the test of time. I have fallen out of touch with a number of people that I was extremely close to at the beginning of my career. Time and distance simply take their toll, and it is difficult to foresee whether one's role will be short-lived or long-standing in the narrative of your life. Nonetheless, their impact is eternal. It is through these interpersonal connections that we leave our most lasting marks in the memories of others, and neither time nor space can truly erase these lingering imprints. Although I may not be the best in keeping in touch with these old allies and close friends, I like to think that we maintain a powerful bond. In many instances, we are able to pick right back up wherever we left off when we were last together. Despite our distance, it would be foolhardy to dismiss them from my narrative altogether.

In pursuing my initial goal—to become someone worthy of the College President's recognition—I also made a tremendous mistake in narrowly defining my objective. Early on, I confused my sense of purpose with a particular office. As a result, I grew to define the terms of my success or failure by my ability to win a single race and become the student body president.

This ambitious goal really had very little to do with the kind of growth that I sought to inspire within myself. Only after my race had ended, and the battle was presumed to be lost, did I come to realize that I had, in actuality, grown beyond my timid roots to become the type of person that I wanted to be. Aside from our Family Weekend encounter with the College President, I would also shake his hand when he presented me with the Hermitage Award for community service during the College's baccalaureate award ceremony, as well as one last time upon crossing the stage for graduation. I may not have been the student body president but, in looking back on it all, I believe that what I took away from the experience vastly outweighs the promise once held by that particular office.

By the time commencement rolled around, I had established a strong working relationship at nearly every level of the College's administration. In four years, I had grown from being a sullen loner content with hanging out in the background to an active and well-respected member of the campus community. That timid soul emerged as a personage, a spirit that presides over its grounds to this day.

Not long ago, I was deeply touched to hear from a recent S.G.A. alumnus that my career had been one of the inspirations behind their own student body presidential campaign. Knowing that my presence continues to linger on our campus, motivating students to seek out new opportunities and play a greater role in their community, goes well beyond anything that I could have ever asked for. The greatest legacy that we can strive to impart is in laying the foundation for our ideals and pursuits to outlive our own time. It is a feat accomplished by passing down our trust in their stewardship on to the waiting hands of a new generation of leaders.

In summing up the wisdom of my experience, I have found that it simply was not worth devoting too much time or energy to worrying about one aspect of my life falling into place over the others. The narrative is far too rich to be defined by one outcome alone. It derives is most enthralling qualities from the contributions of those we share it with, the impressions that we receive and impart in bringing our stories to intertwine with those of others around us. The more involved you become, the more vibrant your story will be. If you can start by staying true to something that means a whole lot to you, then everything else will come together in the end.

THE LEADERSHIP PROFILE: *Exercise Twelve*

Our next exercise may require some additional research. Now that you have taken the time to spell out what is important to you—setting out a goal to pursue and laying out the core principles and values that will help to steer you toward it—and identified the skills that will both help and hinder you along the way, take some time to research organizations whose missions and visions align with your goals. They do not have to be private corporations. Indeed, I would say that it is preferable that you begin looking at civic and non-profit organizations that share at least one, small aspect of your vision.

Most importantly, make sure that these selections reflect something that you enjoy or are otherwise passionate about. These organizations represent pools of like-minded (or "like-hearted") individuals that may form a likely base for expanding your own, personal network. For the established leader, these groups are connectors that can bind your own mission or organization to a wider audience. If, however, you find yourself faced with the kind of dire situation that we explored in Exercise Eleven, then they may also serve as the building blocks for pursuing a new idea from scratch.

Make a small list of potential organizations that align to your overall vision somewhere in your profile. Challenge yourself to go out and visit a couple of them. If a group does not already exist that addresses one of your core missions or concerns, or you have found an existing organization but it does not have a chapter in your area, then I would also challenge you to go one step further and consider becoming a charter member. Look into what it would take to start a new club or introduce a chapter of an existing organization in your hometown or workplace. You never know, creating such an opportunity where none currently exists might even draw a pool of talented individuals that share your views and interests right to you.

13 – THE REBIRTH

"History will be kind to me,
for I intend to write it."
– Winston Churchill

The days immediately following my departure from college passed in a blur. Despite my best efforts, I did not have a full-time job lined up after graduation. So, I spent most of my time in the ensuing days organizing, reorganizing, and reviewing the various application packages that I still had left floating out in the ether.

Having relied almost entirely on web-based application systems during my time as an undergraduate, I had only just begun to extend my efforts to physical mailings and in-person drop-offs. At one point, I even felt so daring that I mailed an introductory package directly to the Global Chief of Human Resources at Royal Caribbean International, a company that I have admired for a long time. The move did get me in touch with a hiring representative, but nothing ever materialized beyond a very pleasant Email exchange. Undeterred, I went right back to the drawing board.

As time wore on and the post-graduation adrenaline began to fade, my transition from collegiate life to the "real world" started to feel like a precipitous fall back toward rock bottom. None of my applications were returning any hits, with many of the public organizations that I had reached out to denying me so much as a "Thanks, but no thanks." I could stomach a flat out rejection, but this trend of being absolutely ignored left me feeling as though I was spinning my wheels without a proper sense of direction. Having only just left a community where I felt connected, respected, and simply *needed*, it was absolutely devastating. As I later described it to one of my friends, it felt as though I had gone from being on top of the world to the bottom of the totem pole in nothing flat.

Fortunately, I was wise enough to realize that this was not an entirely new experience. Much like my freshman year at college, I had been suddenly thrust into an unfamiliar environment and expected to pull together various, uncertain pieces into a concrete plan of action. Once again, I sought to break new ground with a familiar tool, fostering involvement through community service. Expanding upon my prior experiences with the S.G.A. and other service organizations, having been a member of the Key Club in my high school days, our local Kiwanis Club was the first organization that I joined out of college. As time went on and I continued to develop strong working relationships with my fellow Kiwanians, I was eventually introduced to other local boards and service opportunities. It was from one of my fellow Kiwanis officers that I learned of an opening on the Township's Drug Awareness Council, a great outlet for the energies that I had previously devoted to campus safety and my criminal justice studies.

This volunteerism may have helped me to form a solid foundation in my post-college life but it did not pay the bills. For most of the summer following graduation, I continued to work in the retail world, part-time. I had returned to the food market that employed me throughout my undergraduate career. In this role, I filled various odd hours throughout the week that allowed me to devote the rest of my time to my civic pursuits. Eventually, I tacked on yet another position, joining the asset protection department at another local retailer—I told myself that at least this job was more in line with my criminal justice background than my other role as a market/gas station cashier. Unfortunately, this new company did not have any full-time openings, so I kept both positions—bouncing between the store and the market while finding the time for community projects somewhere in between.

Indeed, each of these positions—and the flexibility afforded in my part-time schedules—had helped me to build a somewhat sturdy foundation for weathering the steady changes that were pouring into my post-graduate life. Even as I fought to maintain this newfound sense of stability, I knew that I could not get too comfortable. After all, there was no pathway to a future career in either of these positions. While they certainly helped me to focus my energies toward doing something constructive, giving me the financial freedom to pursue civic alternatives, I recognized that my involvement merely presented a short-term solution to a long-term issue. My nerves began to get the best of me as the summer drew to a close and I still appeared to be no closer to finding a full-time job than the day I first left college.

Then, August of 2013 ushered in a series of events that would change the course of my life drastically. Sitting at the dinner table with my family one evening, my phone began to ring with a call from an unknown, blocked number. My interest piqued, I flipped back the cover of my phone and expected the rehearsed speech of a telemarketer. Instead, the voice that greeted me on the other end belonged to a representative from a District Attorney's office for a borough in New York City.

Good things truly did come to those who wait! A wave of shock and elation swept through me as the sweet promise of hope began to color my outlook in brighter hues. While all other doors up to this point had remained tightly shut, this opportunity presented a crack in the ominous wall before me, through which a sliver of light shone down to captivate my imagination and reinvigorate me entirely. I felt motivated to jump right back into the fray and not submit to the plight of my recent defeats. After hanging up the phone, I began to excitedly piece together the prior steps that had led up to this call.

In our closing weeks on campus, the criminal justice department had circulated a link to an opening with a prominent District Attorney's office. In the rush preceding and following commencement, I had forgotten about this submission entirely. Now, there I was, staring down at the phone in my hand as though the planets had finally aligned at my very fingertips. I could feel it in my bones; this was going to be the end of my search.

This job hunting period had also put me through a bit of a biographical phase. No longer having to keep pace with a scattered class schedule, I used some of my newfound downtime to read up on historical figures and glean what I could from the struggles and triumphs of those who had already managed to leave their mark on the pages of history. There was something reassuring about seeing how others would stumble and fall for so long before they finally reached a point of stability in their lives. As I relayed to one of my friends later on, it helped me to adopt a certain perspective, an appreciation that even the heaviest of blows can be weathered if you allow yourself to believe that your life story is destined for a grander finish. The problem with biographies when compared to reality, however, is that it only takes the turning of a few pages to see that fateful wish fulfilled. The journey of life, for better or worse, does not always unfold as neatly as those accounts polished with the deceptive gloss of hindsight.

I embraced this chance as the turning point in my story. My luck had even hit a bit of an upswing following that fateful call. In the weeks that preceded my interview with the District Attorney's office, I began receiving additional invitations to interview with other, notable firms in the New York City area. It seemed as though my ships were finally coming into port, the tides were turning in my favor at long last. With one final push, I expected to see all of my hard work finally pay off.

Throughout this procession of high-stakes interviews, I found myself instantly thrown back into "campaign mode". I was suddenly acutely aware of the way I carried myself, as though I was being monitored 24/7 by a team of unseen forces. It did not take long for the anticipation of finally landing a full-time job to begin wearing down upon me, as the strain of the interview process was just one more thing to pile atop a continually mounting workload. Racing back and forth between my two part-time jobs had become daunting as I struggled to keep myself from simply going through the motions. Now that the opportunity for an escape from the retail world had presented itself, I was even more determined not to let it pass me by.

It was this desperate longing to see my ambitions fulfilled that sent a sudden flutter through my heart when my cellphone began beeping unexpectedly one day as I ended my security shift and prepared to clock in at the market. I glanced down to see the name of a major firm flash across my caller I.D. and flipped back the cover as quickly as I could. Raising the speaker to my ear, I waited and then nodded along politely as I suffered their rejection with all the quiet dignity I could muster. "One down," I thought to myself, "this has to mean that something bigger is coming."

After all, I have always been a firm believer that everything in life happens for a reason. And while my faith proved strong enough to shake off this lone defeat, my resolve would soon be tested even further. It was not all too long after receiving that first call that I found a "Dear John" letter from the District Attorney's office waiting for me in my mailbox at home. After a long and productive month, it seemed as though I was sinking steadily back toward square one. Even the sudden flurry of interview invitations had come to a grinding halt.

That evening, with the District Attorney's letter of rejection by my side, I made one final play to hold on to the momentum that I had built. Attaching a copy of my resume to an Email, I sent a note out to an attorney contact and asked him to provide any feedback that he could. After my recent double dose of defeat, I was primarily looking for a sign of encouragement. I knew that he would be able to point me in the right direction.

♦

Having entered my life rather unexpectedly, I met this attorney when I suddenly found myself sitting as a key witness in one of his cases in November of 2012. Following a controversy regarding the eligibility of local college students to register to vote—after they had provided their campus mailboxes when prompted for their collegiate mailing addresses on their voter registration forms—one of my former roommates leapt into

268

action by securing *pro bono* representation for a class action lawsuit. Having been a supportive figure in my past S.G.A. endeavors, and seeing as I was one of those students who had attempted to register to vote in the area, this friend asked if I might represent our student body once more as the named plaintiff from our campus. As it is not all that often that a pre-law student finds themselves in such a situation, I agreed to lend my name to the case and take in the experience as an educational opportunity.

Little did I realize just what lied ahead of me. Though I was initially one among a team of students who would be representing their respective campuses at a hearing before a Federal Judge, Sandy's sweeping wrath had confounded their travel plans; I was the only one to make it down to the courthouse on the day of the hearing. This mean that, when the time to present our testimony came, I was the sole voice for the students of our region.

When summoned to take the stand before the Court, I presented my views and weathered a rather biting cross-examination—at one point, opposing counsel asked me how I would list my residence if I had ordered a *keg* for a house party. It was a fun question for a devoted teetotaler. Nonetheless, I relied on a tempered patience forged through years of S.G.A. and retail customer service experience to overcome the gibe in a calm, deliberate manner. Apparently, I conducted myself well. The judge ultimately ruled in our favor, allowing college students in our area to seamlessly cast their votes on Election Day without pause or question.

When it came time to say goodbye at the end of the proceedings, this attorney pulled me aside and extended his praises for my commitment and impassioned testimony. Impressed by my work ethic, he passed along his contact information with the offer to answer any questions that I might have about the legal field after graduation.

I did not typically like to seize upon these types of offers for help from people that I have worked with. I was always embarrassed to reach out and follow-up on these moments of generosity out of the fear that I might somehow lessen or distort our prior relationship. Even so, after watching all of my most promising leads dry up and wilt away in just a matter of days, I felt that it was time to set aside my sense of stubborn pride and open myself to the assistance of others. I knew that he had been sincere in his offer to keep an eye out for me after graduation, but I never could have expected (or asked) for what came next.

◆

The next day, my inbox greeted me with four new messages. Three were invitations for interviews with law firms in New York and New Jersey, and the fourth was a note from my contact. He said that he could not find anything wrong with my resume, so he forwarded it along to a few of his friends that were looking for help. This was an act of generosity that not only renewed my optimistic outlook but also inspired a deep sense of humility. While I was certainly fortunate to have someone like him in my corner at this time, I never would have caught my second wind if I was not willing to admit that I was no longer able to make any headway all on my own. Knowing when and how to reach out for help is a vital component in leadership. No individual can be expected to move mountains on their own. Leaders not only find ways to recruit others into their ranks but cultivate networks that allow them to draw in external assistance to further their cause.

Whether it is through friends, family, or our professional networks, there are always lingering opportunities waiting for us to claim them. Still, we must first have the courage to seek them out. I *hated* the idea of reaching out to others for leads, mistakenly condemning such efforts as a concession that I was unable to succeed on my own merit. It was not until I finally entered my first full-time role that I learned that I had been going about the process the wrong way this whole time. Networking was a necessity, not a liability. In one, particular example, I discovered that one firm relied primarily on external agencies to provide prospective employees as temporary assignments, rather than simply cast a net through the open market. Indeed, they would view the temporary assignment as a sort of casting call. If the person performed well, they might be invited to stay. With little need to turn to a broader, more uncertain pool of fresh new candidates, it has become all the more necessary to get your foot in the door by tapping in to existing networks.

That is precisely how I found myself sitting in the conference room of a Manhattan law office, the second stop on my tour of the three sites that had reached out to me in response to my contact's message. I had already met with an attorney operating a small, private-practice firm in the area of family law back in New Jersey the day before. She had put an offer on the table, and I was waiting to see how the next two rounds of interviews might play out before making any commitments. As the only one out of my three interviewers based in the city, I was particularly interested in hearing what the Manhattan office had to offer. Leaving the interview with high hopes, and the expectation of an answer in one way or the other over the next few days, I tried to keep my hopes from swelling once again.

This wait, however, proved to be far more agonizing than my prior rounds earlier that summer. The thought of the offer from the smaller firm continued to hang in my mind. It seemed like the safest bet. Their team was just settling into a new space, and the role that they had initially posed to me would be that of a paralegal/office manager. As their office grew and their support staff expanded, I might one day find myself managing a team of my very own. The office in Manhattan, on the other hand, was looking to fill an entry-level paralegal position in the area of corporate litigation. Although it was slightly beyond my field of study, they would undoubtedly afford me the opportunity to learn more about this area of the law from an established, highly revered firm in one of the most iconic cities in the world. Taking the offer in New Jersey would get me out of my current retail rut, but a potential offer from that New York office could be life-changing. I held out for the latter to get back to me as long as I could.

But as the anticipated deadline for their decision drew closer, I found it harder and harder to hold tight to my resolve. While the clock hand ticked steadily toward closing hours on the final day, I feared that I was awaiting yet another "Dear John" notice. Setting my hopes for a career in the city aside, I recognized that my primary goal was to simply get out of the retail environment and start building office experience. I called the attorney in New Jersey to accept her offer.

Met with the perky voice of her assistant instead, I ended my first call unsuccessfully. Even after calling back a short while later, I made little progress in reaching the hiring attorney and heard nothing back from their offices in the interim. Yet, having seen how thinly spread they were on the day of my interview, I did not initially think much of it. If she was in court or tied up on another project, then I would have an opportunity to get in touch with her later on. With my final attempt for the day, however, I once again ran into the same, polite response—she was away from her desk, and would have to get in touch with me later. By the time my retail security shift for the day had reached its end, and standard office hours were set to follow shortly thereafter, I began to fear that I had missed out on both of my leading opportunities.

That evening, our asset protection team went out for a group dinner. Despite their lively company, I could not keep my eyes off of my phone, praying for the electronic buzz of divine intervention. The meeting with the New York law office had been so promising and the New Jersey attorney seemed eager for me to accept the offer when I was seated in her office. How could both of them fall through on me at once? *Bzzzt!* Just as the servers set our main course before us, I was pulled from my sullen stupor by the sudden ping of my cell phone. I had one new Email, a job offer from the Manhattan office.

♦

I was hired as a full-time, entry-level paralegal for a corporate litigation firm in September of 2013, where I was welcomed with open arms and quickly brought up to speed by the other members of the support staff. They taught me the basics of corporate office life and even helped me to polish up my document drafting skills as I adjusted the outlook of my internal narrative from *Law & Order* to *Suits*. At the very least, my new office did afford me one fun tidbit to hang my criminal justice hat on. Our leading partner, after all, was the grandson of Thomas E. Dewey, the former New York Governor and legendary prosecutor best known for putting Charles "Lucky" Luciano behind bars. That was certainly a good enough start for me.

In joining their spirited crew, I was not only presented with the opportunities to delve right into complex cases as a member of a legal support team but also expand upon my work in the areas of leadership and service. My office has been incredibly supportive of my volunteer work in my home community, and I count myself truly fortunate that I was never able to complete my calls to that New Jersey attorney. Everything happens for a reason, after all.

Despite the daily commute to New York City and back, I have still maintained an active role on the Montville Township Drug Awareness Council and Kiwanis Club. These efforts, over time, helped me to develop a reputation within my home community similar to the one that I had carved out in college. By returning to my niche, I found all that I needed to rebuild my empire. This tried-and-true approach has even helped to open new and unexpected doors throughout my life's journey. In the summer of 2014, when a local politician declared that he would not be seeking re-election to his seat on the Board of Education, a few of my new colleagues reached out to suggest that I might be suited to fill the vacancy that he was leaving behind. I filed my papers just before summer turned to fall and was sworn-in to a three-year term with the Montville Township Board of Education in January of 2015.

Lessons Learned

All good things come in their due time to those who wait. The triumphs and tragedies from one period of our lives merely set the tone for the remaining chapters of our grand adventure; they alone do not determine its ending. The calculated brevity of biographies can be deceptive in neatly displaying the conquests of those who have come before us. They offer a sort of instant gratification in seamlessly directing our attention from their past failures to the accomplishments and accolades for which they are so well known. The dire gloom of those prior years of disappointment and stagnation are easily swept away in a handful of pages and the gloss of hindsight.

Even this book is a mere shadow of my overall college experience, lacking the smaller—yet no less impactful—moments that have since escaped the grasp of my memory. Included among them are the contributions of countless individuals, far too numerous to list in detail. Nevertheless, I cannot pause enough to express my collective gratitude for their involvement, as every encounter to date has played a tremendous part in transforming this narrative of a shy kid from the suburbs of New Jersey into a story worth sharing in a book of his very own. Though we may, at times, feel like nothing more than a side character in someone else's tale, we must always remember that we are the authors of our life story; only we hold the power to decide how these pages will be filled.

By this point, I am sure that you have picked up on a familiar pattern—my endeavors have rarely unfolded according to the plans that I laid out beforehand. Admittedly, I am no gifted strategist, nor could I ever claim to be a perfect director. If I may be considered a leader, it is only because I had the gall to seize upon the opportunities that presented themselves to me. More so than simply being in the right place at the right time, I have been able to string together a series of events and projects to reveal new possibilities. As I once learned as a student in our Emerging Leaders Program, a leader does not necessarily create opportunity from nothing but takes stock of pre-existing potential and fills in the missing links to connect the dots between vision and reality. My life story, to this point at least, has been an exercise in connecting these imaginary dots, overcoming external and self-imposed boundaries to uncover a potential that I held all along.

From my freshman year at Marist College to the pursuit of a full-time job after graduation, each of the successes that I attained have all stemmed from a willingness to work beyond the boundaries of my comfort zone in the pursuit of something greater. It has not simply been a series of gambits and calculated risks. Instead, it is the product of self-reflection and a sense of general awareness. Adaptation has proven to be one of my most valuable skillsets in rolling with the punches that life has thrown my way to stand up taller than ever before. More importantly, I owe the sense of confidence that I have been able to portray over the years to a powerful sense of purpose. In convincing myself that I could achieve something greater, I was able to wear my self-assurance as a mask to safeguard against lingering fears and propel myself forward in times of self-doubt.

Throughout the process, I have also been blessed to have a number of role models to look up to. From the student body presidents and S.G.A. members that I served with, to the members of the College Administration, and particularly my family & closest friends, surrounding myself with a diverse cast of characters and opinions has proven to be a tremendously rewarding experience. Yet, such admiration must be dispersed in moderation. Idolizing other leaders is like playing with paper dolls; they are great to look at, and they open doors to worlds of fantastic possibilities, but there is not a great deal of substance behind them.

There is not one absolute path to success. What has worked for stars of the silver screen, politics, athletics, and other venues of global acclaim will not always translate well into the parameters of your own life. More importantly, not all of the theories and guidebooks for developing leadership skills will truly mesh with your own style of leadership. It is, in my view, an innate skillset possessed by all individuals that can only be drawn out with persistence and willpower. It is a process of discovery unique to each individual. Nonetheless, we might still find comfort in the knowledge that others have traversed and stumbled upon such common grounds in their own pursuits.

It is in this same spirit that I came together with my old Toastmasters ally and fellow Marist alumni, Brittany M. MacLeod, to co-found a digital platform for young leaders to share their stories. Our website (www.MSLstories.com), the main forum of our blog series, brings together the experiences, advice, and personal views of young dreamers from around the globe under our emerging banner, *"Memoirs of a Student Leader"*. After taking the time to retrace my steps in assembling this book and sharing my findings with this old friend, we came to appreciate just how impactful a few shared stories had been on the development of our own professional networks and career paths. It was the impetus that sparked our desire to share our stories with the world. We have since come to describe our intended audience as "students in the school of life", and stress that these tales do not belong to former student government participants alone. Thus far, we have collected and shared the experiences of entrepreneurs, philanthropists, artists, athletes, travelers, and more. Indeed, everyone has a story to share.

Discovering the *right* narrative to follow can be a life-changing experience; a good story can enthrall us, inspire us, and change us. Glean from these examples what you will, but trust in your gut when it comes to deciding which paths best suit your ambitions. Start by developing a personal mission, then lay out a sketch of what it is that you hope to achieve in school, at work, or even life in general. From there, identify your greatest strengths and weaknesses. Push yourself constantly and strive to improve in those areas that need the most care while maintaining your proficiency in those through which you presently excel.

Carve out your niche in an area that you are truly passionate about and let your interests guide you toward individuals and opportunities that share this common thread. As you continue to move along in life, never shut yourself out to new and unknown opportunities. These unexpected blessings may broaden your horizons beyond anything that you could have possibly imagined.

Our life stories rarely match up with our initial concept; our fondest memories are often born from the unanticipated contributions of those who come to play a part in them. Leaders are, in this sense, master story-tellers. They know how to roll with these surprises to make something wholly unique and truly fantastic. They see their place in a bigger picture and help others to understand their importance by building a shared narrative. At the end of the day, leadership is not simply a matter of having a story worth telling, but discovering the voice to share your experiences in a way that helps others to do the same. No matter how insignificant you might feel, we all possess the same unbound potential, fueled by the blazing spark of the human spirit to stumble forth with primal yearn and take our place among the stars.

THE LEADERSHIP PROFILE: *Exercise Thirteen*

At this point, you should have a pretty solid outline for your Leadership Profile. Admittedly, at first glance it may look like a bit of a hodgepodge. After all, I rarely specified just *where* those boxes, circles, and lists should be placed in relation to your mission, let alone to one another. As I also did not specify their precise size, I imagine your notes have led to what might appear to be a rather abstract compilation of thoughts and ideas—a total mess.

Congratulations. It is *your* abstract compilation of thoughts and ideas—your mess. The size and scope attributed to each of these concepts has been determined by the weight or importance that you have subconsciously assigned to them. How much space did you dedicate to your past failures? How much did you set aside for new ideas and opportunities? How prominent do those two internal wolves stand out among the rest of these attributes?

Just as there is not one clean-cut model of leadership, I do not expect that the exercises throughout this book will produce a single, perfect leadership profile. While some may come out neater than others, they will all have their flaws and even a great deal of lingering vagueness. The Leadership Profile is not meant to be a final product, but the initial traces of a beginner's framework.

Although our *Memoirs of a Student Leader* digital offshoot is still relatively new, there are a few patterns that we have delighted in seeing. In recruiting new authors to contribute guest posts, we simply ask them to write a brief piece on a topic that they are passionate about or an impactful experience that has shaped their career. What we get back, however, is far from uniform. Without requesting any particular structure or offering any further guidance, the pieces that we have shared range from expanded lists and essays to personal letters and even a mock press release. Our minds have a distinct approach to processing information; it is a system through which we eventually assemble the vast stimuli pouring in from the outside world to define our very sense of reality. A key part of leading others in processing this data is to first develop a familiarity with how your own gears are spinning. There is a method to your own madness. Understand it. Trust it.

To explore its depths, start drawing lines between each of the concepts that construct your Leadership Profile as you look back on them in periods of self-reflection. In time, I hope that you will begin to see some similarities between certain categories. You will see that the factors contributing to your past failures appear on your list of skills that need to be strengthened. You will see that your "good" wolf can also be used to broadly describe many of the items on your list of strong suits. From these imperfect pieces, you will begin to assemble the truest picture of *you*.

EPILOGUE: LIFE BEYOND THE CLASSROOM

Having completed our initial lecture, there are still three lessons that I wish to impart before our time together comes to an end. In this epilogue, please enjoy two final stories on the power of crafting a personal legacy or brand, along with a wrap-up of this text's core concepts.

I

THE JELLYBEAN LEGACY

Not long ago, an old friend from college posted a simple photo of a jellybean jar sitting on an empty table to social media. The guessing games began almost immediately, with the perceived messages behind the image ranging from Mother's Day gifts to Reaganomics. To a handful of alumni, however, its meaning was as clear as crystal.

Having carried that same jar with me to nearly every S.G.A. meeting of my career, it holds a special place within the memories of certain members of our community. Originally a means of breaking the ice in my game night programs, the jellybean jar eventually became a regular fixture in our office. Each Wednesday, our conversations mingled with more than just the occasional tapping of a gavel, as the distinct sound of glass sliding across a wooden surface signaled the jellybean jar's movements from one end of the table to the other.

For longstanding members, it served as a communal nucleus, drawing forth collegial conversation and momentarily luring our thoughts away from our debates. For newcomers and outsiders alike it was a warm welcome, offering a delightful means of striking up a conversation before transitioning to their requests or inquiries. Indeed, folks from all walks and circles of life could find common ground around the beans.

As President Reagan once famously noted, "you can tell a lot about a fellow's character by the way he eats jellybeans." The 40th President of the United States, known for his love of the colorful little treats, not only found them useful in his efforts to quit smoking but employed them in crafting a more open and collaborative work environment as well. When, in my freshman year, I suddenly found myself faced with the opportunity to serve as a member of the Junior Senate, I turned to his leadership for guidance. As a more interactive means of breaking bread, I adopted President Reagan's signature treats in my own pursuit to break down social barriers and inject myself into a larger community.

Providing more than just an extra sugar bump to power through our discussions, the jellybean jar quickly became our version of the stereotypical office water cooler. As some S.G.A. members meticulously lined out their selections on the table before them, and others dove in to withdraw a random assortment (sometimes swallowed in a single gulp), the process provided us with a momentary retreat from the heat of debate and a fundamental stepping-stone toward strengthening interpersonal connections. Agreements as to what flavors people liked, as well as those they absolutely despised, helped to lay the foundation in exploring other commonalities. It was a simple, comforting point of conversation that helped outsiders to ease into the traditions and culture of the larger organization.

Much like the beans themselves, we all had our own, unique "flavors" to bring to the mix. Some were sour, others were sweet, and while

283

many folks could be described by more traditional essences, there were still others who were more difficult to peg to one category over another. Rather than clash, however, we blended into a rather nice medley by identifying opportunities to contrast and supplement one another. Indeed, great leaders learn to strengthen weaknesses in a team by pairing up complimentary actors. For example, you might group an individual with an inherently qualitative outlook with a partner more inclined towards quantitative analysis. Working together, their unique viewpoints will help to offset their individual shortcomings while broadening their overall outlook.

Attaining balance within an organization necessitates identifying areas of weakness and turning them into opportunities for growth. Recognizing these low points helps us to uncover the potential for collaboration that can, in turn, lead to monumental changes. Just as one might pair complimentary flavors to create a more delectable mix, organizational leaders undertake a similar mission in pairing together team members of varying backgrounds and expertise in the pursuit of a common goal.

Indeed, as very few people will enjoy a jellybean mixture comprised solely of licorice pieces, exploring opportunities for diversity within an organization can be absolutely vital for its success. A proper distribution of flavors helps to ensure that the mixture is more palatable to a wider audience and, particularly in the case of public organizations, strengthens the overall image of the body as a reflection of its clients or constituents. Early in my career, I took to the easier route of staffing my committees with close friends and colleagues. While it was simpler to coordinate, and certainly more comfortable to communicate with, people

284

that I knew very well, our board lacked a certain depth in the variety of opinions comprising its ranks, thus restricting its potential. As word of our meetings began to spread, and the interest of non-S.G.A. players was piqued, our little committee began to attract a broader audience. It was then that I began to appreciate just how truly impactful different, and even opposing, viewpoints could be to a governing board.

And yet, there is still a much deeper lesson buried beneath the beans. Seeing my old jar restored to its proper place within the S.G.A. office served as an endearing reminder that my legacy, in at least some small form, continues to outlast me on a campus that has been so incredibly impactful upon my own career. It is a testament to the tremendous effect that we can have on one another.

From classmates to co-workers, we have the potential to drastically influence the perceptions of others through our actions, words, and attitudes. More so than a specific title or accomplishment, it is the impression left by the way we have made others feel that outlasts us when we are gone. From mastering the principles of human resources and basic management wisdom, to the fostering of a larger spirit of community, no concept is more essential. Leading from the heart recognizes that reaching individuals at a personal level taps into a well of deeper motivation and commitment, which serves to drive and sustain your shared vision. Not only will such an individualized approach help to spur commitment in the short-term but—as the story of the jellybean jar illustrates—it also holds the potential to promote long-term commitment by strengthening ties to organizational traditions.

Quite simply, and to borrow from the tagline of an old S.G.A. administration, "Actions speak louder than words." In time, the symbols we take to wearing as shields within the public arena develop their own perceived personalities and meanings from the actions of their creators. Our brands are defined in terms beyond mere words; they are compilations of appearance, performance, and character. In combining these ingredients, good will built through sincere efforts can outweigh the most aptly selected terminology. Indeed, this impact represents the same sentimentality that drives people to spend a little more on one brand over another, because it reminds them of their childhood, bears the endorsement of a beloved public figure, or evokes some deeper emotion that resonates with us on a more personal level. Such a power can make even a simple jellybean jar seem so tremendously endearing.

Weaving through the aspects listed on your leadership profile is far more than a solitary exercise. It requires us, at times, to surround ourselves with projections of our peers and envision the larger role that we have to play in the networks around us. Understanding the motivations that drive and direct these other players, to a certain extent, is necessary in anticipating their reactions to our own outputs. In placing ourselves in their shoes to better glimpse their worldview, we can more readily weave ourselves into the mix, assessing what traits and actions are required to balance the blend and create a more lasting impression.

I struggled through my four years as an undergraduate in an effort to make a difference. In the end, however, my legacy does not only live on through the projects that I started or the titles I held; it is carried on by the people that I have influenced along the way. The secret that has made this jellybean jar so very special is hidden in one simple rule:

"Strive not to make your presence known, but your absence felt."
– ANONYMOUS

II

CRAFTING A PERSONAL BRAND OUT OF THE SHADOWS OF THE PAST

In following that sweet example, I feel that I should expand upon one more crucial concept that has been invaluable to me in shaping my post-graduate career. I have always been fascinated by the art of brand messaging and—perhaps, consequently—a fierce champion of brand loyalty. When I began my first job as a cashier for a local restaurant, I took to wearing our embroidered polos with pride outside of work. In fact, this became a point of conversation during my interview for the Junior Senate in my freshman year, as I laid out my hopes of uniting our sense of school spirit through our own S.G.A. brand. As time went on, and I transitioned from working as a cashier in that little café to a food market/gas station in a nearby town, my fervent championing of brand messaging did not cease. In my sophomore and junior years, I brought many of my new company's core values to the S.G.A. Senate, and could always find a way to steer my discussion with club and other leadership boards to the principles of customer service.

Marist College quickly came to play an equally important role in my life, as my very sense of identity was eventually rooted in my new role as a "Red Fox". Indeed, my wardrobe was not all that began to bleed bright red after my admission. From the pens and pad folios that I carried to the choice of décor throughout my living spaces, Marist had a profound influence. Like my former employers before them, I had begun to cling to the imagery of our college community so readily that the lines between fascination and identity began to blur precariously.

As a shy kid who never quite felt like he belonged, the promise of being a part of a larger community hung before me as a sorely tempting prize. I turned to those logos as a collective shield, trying to convince myself before all others that I belonged, that I was a part of the team. I buried my own fears behind a veil of school spirit. My greatest fear, above all else, was fading away into obscurity. Racing to leave my mark on our campus, I found a calming sense of security behind the Fox. Like Clark Kent shedding his pedestrian attire to reveal the bold crest of Superman, I felt invulnerable with our mascot emblazoned across my chest. A trusted anchor, it rooted me to a much larger community and the belonging I so desperately sought.

What spurred my transformation from onlooker to leader, and set the Marist brand apart from the others that I have adopted over the years, was the substance behind the imagery. Although my prior employers had inspired a commitment to customer service and empathetic communication, the message of our college and its founders resonated with me more soundly, fostering a much sturdier ethos. Built upon the three pillars of academic excellence, a spirit of community, and a commitment to service, and coupled with the principled belief in "doing good quietly"—as passed on to us by the Marist Brothers—the *Red Fox* grew to embody a much deeper dogma that influenced more than just my sense of style and penchant for spouting quirky leadership slogans. These principles molded my character throughout my term as an undergraduate, much like the persistent cradling of earth that presses coal into diamond.

As a member of the Student Government Association, I took care to ensure that my actions were a proper reflection of the needs and interests of my constituents. While wearing the image of the Marist Red Fox, I truly began to feel as though I was walking outside of my own skin, operating as a part of a much larger organism. This disciplined attention to detail, coupled with a newfound sense of purpose, spurred a great deal of self-reflection in curbing old habits and fostering new ones. Over time, this perspective helped me to overcome personal shortcomings while honing those traits and skills that had gone wanting up to this point. I had first turned to this logo as a means of fostering that sense of stability and acceptance that I so desperately desired, and the confidence it inspired helped me to grow into my own. Rather than devolving into a crutch, however, the symbolism of Marist College collected around me like a cocoon. Red Fox pride would inspire a far more meaningful and lasting transformation.

My attention to personal branding was not only reflected in my fashion decisions and mannerisms but through my approach to social media as well. As an emerging medium, websites like Twitter and Facebook offered untapped potential for engaging new audiences and sharing our organizational vision. As our S.G.A. policies at the time had not yet caught up to the trend, digital communications remained a widely underutilized resource in our earlier administrations. Sure, we would post general alerts about upcoming events and activities on our S.G.A. pages, but none of us truly understood how to best capitalize off these messages to establish and sustain meaningful interactions. More importantly, we seemed to be largely ineffective in forming a unified sense of *identity* through social media.

This became one of the issues that I sought to address when we first established the Safety & Security Committee. In cultivating a campus-wide dialog on campus safety policies, I knew that I had to portray the heart behind the organization as well. I created a Facebook page for the Safety & Security Committee and, later on, the Civility Campaign. As a digital marketing novice, however, I found it difficult to juggle three distinct, albeit similar, identities at one time. I soon defaulted to my personal account in sharing information for both causes. As a result, I inadvertently wound up absorbing these two entities into my own, personal brand. I became a recognizable face for both projects, giving each of them more personalized marque in return.

What had started out as a coping mechanism—the mask of a lonely kid—quickly blossomed into a huge learning opportunity. Rather than continue to lean on the symbols of others' principles and accomplishments, I began to adopt their successful strategies for marketing and promotion to form my own, personal brand. My work through the S.G.A. and my word shared in collaborating with other campus leaders became my product.

As politicians and leaders, we have to learn to package ourselves in a certain way to reach large audiences and share our visions with teams and constituents that may not be so closely linked to our desired goal. This is, quite naturally, far easier said than done. Learning to speak in front of an audience is but one piece of the puzzle. A crucial element in crafting a more substantive impact is developing the platform through which your own message can be shared. It is one thing to turn yourself into a microphone for artificial or external messages but another prospect entirely to take that next, great leap in sharing *your* views and offering them up for public dissection (not to mention standing by to defend them against the inevitable criticisms). Overcoming our fears to communicate a more organic, personalized message with a larger audience first requires us to win over our harshest critics: ourselves.

Indeed, I had largely spent the first part of my collegiate career running from my own sense of self. I was awkward and shy, and I could not easily count myself among my already minimal fan base. Retreating behind borrowed logos and other trinkets from established professional brands was partly a defensive exercise, indulging in fantasy in order to avoid facing the reality of my own shortcomings.

Pretending that I was a part of something bigger helped me to forget everything that I hated about myself as an individual and embrace the illusion of all that I hoped to, one day, become. Through my work with the Student Government Association, I learned to fight for those causes that I cared about, to speak out for others who had not yet found their voice, and I eventually grew to stand beside these convictions without fear. In time, learning to stand up for these other groups and concepts helped me to face my own demons. As a result, I began crafting my personal brand out of the principles and ideals that I chose to embody. In time, I learned to work through my perceived weaknesses to develop a message of my own design.

Soon, my name became synonymous with campus safety and community service projects, with the principles of customer service, with responsivity, civility, and more. My fascination with brand messaging had helped me to create a persona that was indistinguishable from the core concepts that I chose to promote. It allowed me to develop these committees into something far more valuable than a sales pitch for campus policies; my approach helped me to forge a new reputation. It was this semblance of a personal brand that helped me to set myself apart from my peers across the country to earn a seat at the table for the national summit on campus safety. It also formed the fundamental layer of trust that proved essential in overcoming reflexive doubts to advance my more ambitious projects, like the plans for our Sandy relief excursions. Akin to establishing corporate stock, the good will built behind my personal brand helped to drive some of my greatest projects beyond the planning stages and into the pages of history.

Looking back on these accomplishments in my senior year made leaving our campus all the more difficult. Although I had made significant strides in pushing off from my crutch of marching under borrowed banners, the new persona that I had crafted was still largely tied to my work as an undergraduate. In leaving this impactful community to return to my hometown, I once again relied on service projects as a means of adjusting to a major life change. While I could have easily turned to the Kiwanis logo or even our local high school's mascot, the Mustang, upon joining the Board of Education, I decided that it was time to piece together a logo of my own. Paying tribute to the campus that proved to be instrumental in my underlying transformation, I chose a favorite fox lapel pin of mine as the basis for this new design. With a bit of creativity, and the assistance of a web design application, I altered the familiar image into something entirely new, a fox of my very own.

Though far from perfect, and perhaps even a little "sinister" looking, this image has quickly occupied a very special place in my heart. The more I look at it, the more it grows on me. The familiar visage of the fox, obscured in shadows, holds its own symbolism of a fading mark, an imprint slowly vanishing from a once vibrant surface. And yet, it also bears a striking sternness that conveys an underlying resolve, the determination to push on despite all that has weighed upon it.

More importantly, it brings life to the character that I have dedicated a brief career to shaping. Stemming from the efforts and experiences of a shy kid who wanted nothing more than to leave a mark, here it finally sits in bold clarity. After years of championing the missions and visions of others, my career has built itself to a point where I can stand before a large audience and say, "this is who I am, this is what I stand for, and I am here to serve *you*." This logo is simply the formal embodiment of that accomplishment, an expression of my professional identity.

At the risk of sounding narcissistic, I must stress the importance of learning to be *on your own team*, first-and-foremost. We all have something valuable to bring to the table, and risk sacrificing our special talents when we allow fear to stifle these ideas and perspectives that are ours alone to share. I stumbled through this learning process by leaping from organization to organization and symbol to symbol in attempting to piece together what was truly important to me. Fearing conflict and derision, I came to rely on the logos of others as veils to obscure my own allegiances and opinions. In forging a brand of my own, I have learned to stand proudly beside the projects and causes that I care about, rather than simply hide behind the convictions of others. Indeed, I have become far more productive since I stopped worrying about pulling my punches or diluting the messages that I hope to share.

Today, my fox serves as the icon for one of my favorite projects. Working alongside a fellow Marist alumnus, my old Toastmasters partner in crime, we have launched a website for young leaders to share their stories. MSLstorics.com, the homepage for our *Memoirs of a Student Leader* experience, welcomes readers as students in the "school of life" and guides them through the testimonials of their peers to uncover common threads and reflect on shared experiences. Our project recognizes that stories, like the many I have shared with you throughout this book, hold deeper truths that can guide us in discovering what is most important to us. Life is all about perspectives, and in bringing so many of them together, it is our hope that these shared stories can change the world.

I also make a point of sharing my fox with the people that have shaped my journey. Most recently, I bid farewell to those Red Foxes whose journeys had only just begun when my own campus story was coming to an end. The Marist College graduating class of 2016 was not only the last to received their diplomas from our outgoing College President, but the same group of freshmen students who carried on the projects and programs that my class had left behind. In borrowing from a practice employed by an old high school principle in my hometown, I began distributing the same pewter fox pins that inspired my logo's design to undergraduates, alumni, and administrators that had influenced my own collegiate career. From our College President and the student body presidents that led by example, right down to the freshmen students that have carried these lessons on over the years, I share my fox in the hope that others will be inspired to find their own message and grow to one day walk proudly beneath a banner of their own design. Beyond all else, the greatest discovery that awaits us in life is that internal rendezvous that finally brings us face to face with the voice that pierces the quietest corners of our minds, our earliest ally and sincerest critic, the self.

> "He stretched out his arms to the crystalline, radiant sky
> 'I know myself,' he cried, 'but that is all!'"
> -F. SCOTT FITZGERALD, *This Side of Paradise*

III

IN CLOSING

"He found something that he wanted, had always
wanted and always would want—not to be admired, as
he had feared; not to be loved, as he had made himself
believe; but to be necessary to people,
to be indispensable..."
– F. Scott Fitzgerald, *This Side of Paradise*

Today, my schedule remains just as colorful and crammed as it was during my days as an undergraduate. Outside of work, I am still actively involved in my hometown community as President of the Montville Kiwanis Club, an elected member of the Board of Education, and an appointed member of the Drug Awareness Council—Municipal Alliance. Though I do not get to visit quite as often as I would like, I have still managed to keep my eye on the budding careers Marist's student leaders, watching the development of some truly stellar administrations and their initiatives with absolute delight. The Civility Campaign continues to have a dedicated home under the Executive Board (now officially renamed the "President's Cabinet"), which has even come to adopt the old Safety & Security Committee under the office of a student "Vice President of Safety & Security".

The S.G.A.'s elections process also appears to be flourishing under new policies that allow for online campaigning, passed under the 2012-2013 Administration. Indeed, in watching a recent election cycle unfold, the creation of Youtube videos and other digital materials appears to have offset the need for costly t-shirts and other, physical campaign materials. Despite

297

some bugs in the process, the widespread use of social media has helped to remove some of the financial barriers that once discouraged individuals from mounting an extensive campaign. These are wonderfully welcome additions, as levels of engagement among the student body in the elections process appear to be on the rise.

Apart from these occasional whispers—and the latest postings of *The Marist Circle* in its new, digital format—I do get to venture back to Poughkeepsie at least once a year when my friend and former roommate, the 2010-2011 Elections Commissioner, and I make our presentation "From the Classroom to the Boardroom" for the Emerging Leaders Program. After sharing stories collected from our years in the S.G.A., we engage students in an activity that has participants develop their own platforms for desired projects and programs on campus, which are then shared with current members of the Student Government Association. To borrow from an old saying, I suppose you can take the boy out of student government, but you just cannot take student government out of the boy.

Even now, I find myself looking forward to the closing of one chapter and the beginning of another, relying on the principles that have steered me thus far to make the most of my journey. After three years of service, I have shared my decision not to seek re-election to the Board of Education with the Montville community. My term will expire at the end of 2017. And as I look back on this time spent with a district that has played such a large role in my journey to become who I am, I find myself particularly pleased with the final project that will represent my legacy within this community. After months of planning and deliberation, I will be working with our district's Communications Officer and a branding committee consisting of district administrators, faculty, students and community members to unveil a new district brand, our very first, at the onset of the new school year. In helping our school system to establish an identity of its own, from drafting its mission and vision to being an active voice in the formation of its logo and motto, this one-time wallflower will help to give it a voice for generations to come. Life certainly has a rather fantastic sense of humor.

◆

For those that have taken the time in following along with this story to jot down their own notes and draw out little diagrams where instructed, I will leave you with this final task. Just as we instruct our students, imagine that you are an advisor to a budding political campaign. Pretend, for a moment, that you hold the ear of someone who wishes to make a difference in your social circle, your office, or your community. What issues or ideas would you present to them? What priorities or opportunities for change would you point out? How would you guide them in outlining their own Leadership Profile?

Gather these notes together with everything that you have laid out thus far and give them a good, long read. Connect the dots between the visions that you have described and the issues that you have identified. When viewed together, they will begin to set out a roadmap to opportunity, which can be sewn together with the common threads that link your visions, your strengths, your weaknesses, and your goals.

More importantly, if you stop to think about it, I would be willing to wager that you also know one or two people that could help you set these plans into motion. Just as we share the notes of our attendees with attentive S.G.A. leaders, there are surely volunteers within your own community who are ready and willing to take on a new project or challenge. Having spent a considerable amount of time on that side of the table, I can assure you that there are folks like that out there, waiting to listen. Thus, the difficult part is not always in finding people to share our ideas with, but the *voice* to communicate them. While our presentation helps to close the loop by showing students just how readily their ideas will be seized upon, I admit this is somewhat of a cliffhanger for you, dear readers. From here on out, the fate of your "happily ever after" is set squarely in your hands.

Though neatly tucked away in the preceding pages, this adventure has not always been free of conflict. In chasing down your dreams, you will inevitably encounter naysayers, critics, challengers, and other antagonists. What is important to remember, however, is that these conflicts do not (always) arise from personal vendettas, but merely differences in perspective.

We all see the world in varying shades and hues; my interpretation of a given issue or situation is no less valid than your own—or anyone else's for that matter. All too often, we lose sight of this reality. Our modern political discourse is dominated by a pervasive "*Us v. Them*" mentality that ostracizes anyone who dares to bridge the gap. In the coming years, we will not only need innovators and entrepreneurs to continue to discover bold new directions for our society to explore, we are going to need bridge builders.

There is, indeed, a deeper wisdom to be gained in appreciating the power and perils of perception. As someone who played a large and active role in our campus community, graduating without a job lined up beforehand left me in quite a slump. As I sat idly in my old part-time jobs, I found it hard to see the light at the end of the tunnel. It was only after I returned to my freshman approach, carving out time for service projects and hobbies that excited me and cultivated a sense of fulfillment, that I was able to look past the monotony of my current situation. I had to remember that Rome was not built in a day, just as surely as I will not be the C.E.O. of Royal Caribbean Cruises Ltd. tomorrow—as nice as that might be. Instead, as with any endeavor, patience and perseverance are vital assets. In chasing down your goals, be sure to set aside ample time to enjoy the present, reflect upon your trajectory, and ensure that the destination that you are pursuing still represents the place or position that you would truly like to reach in the end.

◆

The Churchill quote that opens Chapter 13, *"History will be kind to me, for I intend to write it"*, is one of my favorites. If there is one thing I have learned in studying the social and behavioral sciences, it is that nothing in this life is guaranteed to us. Yet, despite all the hurdles and pitfalls that we perceive to cordon off our path to success, the human capacities for ingenuity and tenacity are truly astonishing. Though we may tend to see ourselves as minor characters wondering aimlessly in the background of some great, big production, it is important to take a step back

301

and remember that *you* are the star of your autobiography. In guiding you through the process of crafting your own Leadership Profile, it is my hope that these activities have helped you to identify a sense of direction in compiling the tools necessary to make your own mark on the pages of history. More importantly, I hope that you will take the time to stop and share what you have learned to guide others along the way.

It is through this process of working with others, imparting something of ourselves in their stories, that we expand our own sagas. This intermingling of experiences sets forth the road to all possibilities in writing and re-writing your own role in the grandest act in the history of all mankind. The only limitations in seizing upon these opportunities, if such restraints truly exist at all, are born from our imagination.

My "ah-ha" moment came in recognizing the terrifying degree of authority that I had afforded to others in managing my own life. Things did not begin to change until I accepted that the power to fulfill all that I wished to accomplish was set squarely at my feet from the onset. The adventures that filled these pages, and the opportunities sought by anyone trying to find their place in the world, are the products of a single action: mustering the courage to take that first step. I share them in the hope that they will awaken something in you, the will to get out there and do something grand. This is, after all, your life story; only you can choose how the remaining pages will be filled.

I greatly look forward to hearing your tale.

ABOUT THE AUTHOR

Michael D. Johnson attended Marist College, graduating summa cum laude in 2013 with a BS in criminal justice and a certificate in paralegal studies. He also received a master's degree from Marist in 2017 after studying public administration. *From the Classroom to the Boardroom* began as a presentation for the Emerging Leaders Program at Marist, which Johnson gives annually with a former classmate. The pair was recognized for their work by the National Society of Leadership and Success in 2015.

In the fall of 2014, Johnson was elected to the Montville Township Board of Education. He is an appointed member of the Montville Township Drug Awareness Council and the President of the Montville Kiwanis Club. Johnson is also the cofounder of the website *Memoirs of a Student Leader*, which highlights the personal stories of young leaders from all over the world. He works in Manhattan as a paralegal for the law firm of Dewey Pegno & Kramarsky LLP.